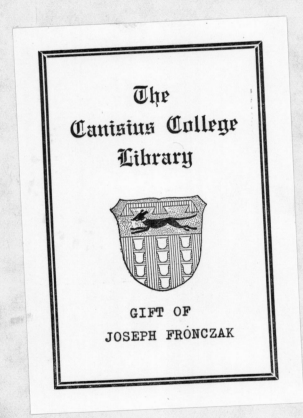

ARCHITECTURAL DRAWING

Faith Hospital, St. Louis, Mo.; Joseph D. Murphy, Architect.
Renderings to show effect of sunlight in January and in July.

ARCHITECTURAL DRAWING

Perspective, Light and Shadow, Rendering

by SHERLEY W. MORGAN, A.B., B.ARCH., F.A.I.A., *Professor of Architecture and Director of the School of Architecture, Princeton University*

Illustrations executed by WILLIAM FEAY SHELLMAN, JR., B.S.ARCH., M.F.A., *Assistant Professor of Architecture, Princeton University*

McGraw-Hill Book Company, Inc.   New York · Toronto · London   1950

ACKNOWLEDGMENTS

Grateful acknowledgment is hereby made of the cooperation of the following distinguished architectural draftsmen in the preparation of this book. The examples of their work which appear among the illustrations give visual proof of the power of expression which can be achieved through architectural drawing based on sound principles:

CHESLEY BONESTELL

WALKER O. CAIN

FRANCIS A. COMSTOCK

HUGH FERRIS

VINCENT FURNO

HENRY A. JANDL

CHARLES Z. KLAUDER

SCHELL LEWIS

BERNARD M. McMAHON

JOSEPH D. MURPHY

CHESTER B. PRICE

MIES VAN DER ROHE

WILLIAM F. SHELLMAN, JR.

Thanks are also due to MRS. AGNES MOONEY, who never lost interest in typing the manuscript, no matter how many times revised.

CONTENTS

INTRODUCTION

THE SCIENCE and art of representational drawing have been the subject of many publications. The New York Public Library catalogues several hundred titles on perspective alone. Some of these treatises are primarily geometrical; others are largely concerned with aesthetic effects. Some take the point of view of the painter; others that of the mathematician. Almost none has been addressed to the architectural student whose needs embrace both a sound scientific means of exact drawing and an appreciation of the artistic possibilities of his medium.

He must be able to put his ideas of space and form on paper quickly, easily, and accurately. In the process of studying his designs, he must express them visually for his own decisions as to how they may best be developed and perfected. Then he must present them pictorially so that they may be understood, appreciated, and approved by others. Finally, he must precise them so exactly that the structures which he has imagined may be erected in actual materials. Occasionally he may be called on to record graphically an existing architectural monument which was the work of others.

For all these purposes he must first learn the science of orthographic projection through the study of descriptive geometry. It is assumed in this text that he has mastered at least the fundamentals of theoretical graphics including the problems of points, lines, and planes. Along with this knowledge he is expected to have acquired reasonable skill in the use of standard drafting instruments and equipment. Assuming this background, the following pages attempt to show him how to analyze and solve the questions which will confront him when he seeks to make drawings for the purposes mentioned in the preceding paragraph.

The material contained herein has been organized primarily for classroom use, and for later quick reference. It cannot be learned without practice, any more than one can learn to play an athletic game well, merely by reading "how to do it." The problems at the end of each chapter must be solved individually by each student who wishes to acquire real skill. Those who work out the exercises with reasonable diligence will find that they have acquired a valuable technique which will enable them to solve any problem in architectural representation.

Although the text is not intended for study without guidance, it is believed that it may be so used, especially in conjunction with other works developed specifically for that purpose.[1] In such cases a warning is essential. Do not skip ahead, particularly in learning perspective. Until one is absolutely sure of his basic principles and of his procedure, the possibilities for mistakes are endless. Even experienced draftsmen may become confused. Within the past few years at least two books have been published containing perspectives made by projecting onto a plane not perpendicular to the central visual ray! You too may fall into some such error unless you are absolutely certain of your fundamentals. Learn by heart the ten rules of Chap. 10 before you try any experiments.

In order to simplify reference from written discussion to explanatory drawing, the pages of text are arranged to correspond to the illustrations, and both are identified by the chapter number, so that they may be easily located. It is hoped that this will avoid unnecessary turning of pages and will save time in using cross references from text to illustrations.

If we wish to make drawings that will be optically consistent and geometrically correct, we must take into account the fundamental assumptions of all graphic representation before deciding on the best procedure. Three-dimensional objects are shown on paper either by lines or by areas of light and dark whose boundaries are usually first determined by lines (either remaining visible or used merely for construction).

[1] An excellent short text for the student working alone is Lubschez, Ben Jehudah, "Perspective," 4th ed., New York, D. Van Nostrand Company, Inc., 1926.

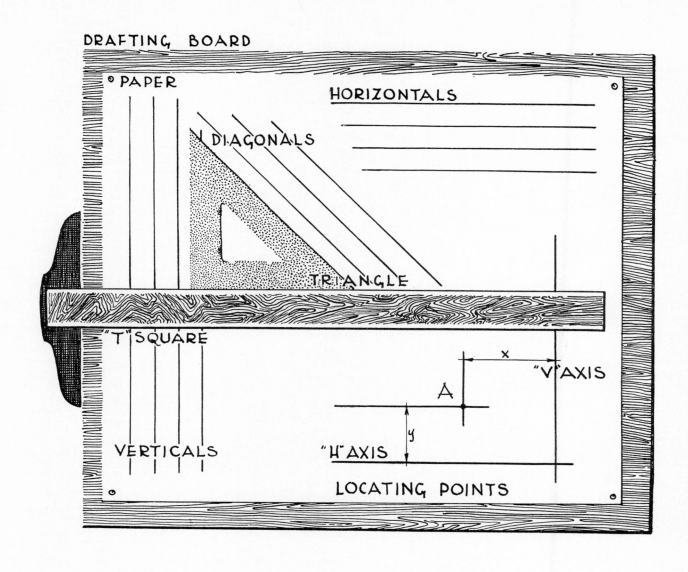

DRAFTING BOARD

PAPER

HORIZONTALS

DIAGONALS

TRIANGLE

"T" SQUARE

"V" AXIS

A

x

y

"H" AXIS

VERTICALS

LOCATING POINTS

BAD

GOOD

INTERSECTIONS

Lines are found by drawing through established points. Points are fixed by measurement from axes which locate them in reference to the intersection of two coordinates. Such construction lines theoretically have no width, but there is a limit to the fineness of the line which can be made with any instrument guided by the human hand and eye. Hence all intersections are actually areas rather than mathematical points having only position. They can be most accurately marked if the coordinates are at right angles to each other, and the process of measurement is quickest and surest if mechanical means are easily available for drawing parallels to the axes.

Our time-tested drafting equipment is designed to give us these advantages. With a T square we can readily draw as many horizontals as necessary to determine the lateral position of all points, while a triangle enables us to be equally facile in providing verticals for our second series of measurements. Our guide lines cut each other at 90° and give us the best possible intersections. All construction lines are under mechanical control, and thus errors due to human inaccuracy of hand and eye are reduced to a minimum and are constantly checked. Parallels are automatically so drawn, rather than being dependent on our ability to make precise measurements and to join exactly the points determined.

For the same reason we must seek methods in perspective drawing that give sharp intersections to determine points and which are under general control rather than dependent on a separate construction for every point. On this basis, two methods for making a graphic solution of any problem in *linear perspective* have been selected as best meeting our requirements. After explaining the principles involved, these are developed in detail in Chaps. 4 and 5. Each important step is shown in a separate figure so that there will be no confusion as to the sequence in which the solution is developed. It is hoped that this will make obvious the process by which a perspective drawing is worked out.

As a further help in knowing "what to do next," a written analysis of each step involved is included for each method. Many years of experience with beginners has shown that most of their difficulties arise because they are uncertain of the order in which steps should be taken. A finished drawing often requires such an apparently complex mass of construction lines that it seems impossible to grasp the logical simplicity by which it was built up.

The pictorial power gained by being able to draw correct perspectives is so great that it is well worth the effort involved. Once the basic principles are clearly understood, the graphic processes are relatively simple and can easily be mastered. In Chap. 10 they are reduced to ten fundamental propositions for ready reference, but these should be learned as part of the experience of making perspectives. No one should attempt to learn them by mere repetition. We appreciate the reason for principles only as we find in practice that we need them.

The more perspectives we make, the more we shall appreciate the importance of the rules. We shall absorb them almost unconsciously if we "learn by doing." Perspective can be so baffling to the individual—as it was for centuries to the whole human race—that each step must be thoroughly mastered before going on to the next. This can be accomplished only by solving each problem for ourselves—over and over again if necessary—until it is completely understood. Only practice will make perfect, and only when we are sure of our grasp of *linear perspective* can we go on to the free expression of our ideas in tone and color through *aerial perspective*.

A

B

Chapter 1

USES AND LIMITATIONS OF PERSPECTIVE

MAN HAS realized since prehistoric times that the actual shapes of objects in the external world around him are quite different from the forms that his eyes report to his mind. A friend or enemy as large as ourselves looks like a mere pygmy when he is far away. We know that the spear in his hand is longer than our arm; but if he levels it directly at us, we can see only a point. His circular shield seems to become an ellipse when he lays it down to greet us; if we look at it edgewise it seems a thin rectangle. Only the experience of our whole lifetime enables us to recognize the true object, and its relation to other forms, from the varying impressions that the eye receives.

This apparent discrepancy between what we see and what we know poses a very difficult problem, as soon as the desire arises to make a record of things or events. What is to be carved on a smooth rock, or scratched on a bone, or drawn on a skin? Shall it be the actual things, or the way they looked? There were many bison in the herd which we now wish to represent on the cave wall. Shall we put them all in, even though some were behind others and farther away? If we leave some out, which ones, and why? Shall all be the same size? Not only primitive man but every youngster today is puzzled by such questions as soon as he begins to make pictures in order to explain his ideas to others. The Cro-Magnon artists produced extremely naturalistic effects by decorating their caves with the animals that they knew, represented as they saw them in life (Illus. 1-1-A). Other early peoples took a different approach, and reported the facts by a system of conventions.

If an Egyptian artist wished to show you pictorially a bowl containing flowers, he made two drawings of it: one looking down from above, showing you its roundness and contents; the other a side view showing its height and profile. He made his human figures obey the *law of frontality*—each part of the body was depicted in its broadest aspect so as to emphasize its important qualities, even though this produced an almost impossible posture. No attempt was made to show distance by size—instead relative height indicated social rank. The result was a very accurate system of recording facts, but a completely unreal reproduction of the way things appear. Rigid adherence for centuries to such conventions made Egyptian wall painting and bas-relief more like writing than drawing, and denied their graphic art all three-dimensional effect (Illus. 1-1-B).

So little Greek painting has survived that we know it chiefly from vases and from literary descriptions, but apparently the Greeks never fully solved this artistic problem (as they did most others). Except perhaps in the handling of color and stage settings,[1] they never learned how to produce the appearance of depth on a two-dimensional surface. The Romans made some limited attempts to do so, as in the frescoes of Pompeii, but these show only objects parallel to the picture. Otherwise all artists down to the time of the Renaissance were baffled.

Then it was finally realized that the answer lay in considering the wall (or papyrus or canvas) on which the drawing was to be made as a transparent screen between the observer and the object to be presented.[2]

---

[1] In the introduction to Book VII of Vitruvius we find that: "Agatharcus, at the time when Aeschylus taught at Athens the rules of tragic poetry, was the first who contrived scenery, upon which subject he left a treatise. This led Democritus and Anaxagoras, who wrote thereon, to explain how the points of sight and distance ought to guide the lines, as in nature, to a centre; so that by means of pictorial deception the real appearances of buildings appear on the scenes which, painted on a flat vertical surface, seem nevertheless, to advance and recede." (Lubschez, Ben Jehudah, "Perspective," 4th ed., New York, D. Van Nostrand Company, Inc., 1926.)

[2] The Greek philosopher Anaxagoras understood this basic principle as early as the fifth century B.C., but no general application of it was made until the sixteenth century A.D. Vitruvius quotes Anaxagoras as stating, ". . . in drawing, the lines ought to be made to correspond, according to a natural proportion, to the figure which would be traced out on an imaginary intervening plane by a pencil of rays proceeding from the eye, as a fixed point of sight, to the several points of the object viewed." (Lubschez, *op. cit.*, pp. 113–114.)

"St. Jerome" by Albrecht Dürer.

ILLUSTRATION 1-2

If we take a definite *station point* from which to look at an object and hold up a piece of glass between us and it, we can trace out on this interposed *picture plane* a pattern which will correspond exactly with the apparent shapes of objects in the three-dimensional space beyond (see Illus. 2-3-A). The geometrical relations between objects in space and their projections on the intervening glass can be worked out accurately for any given point of view. Thus simply, the basis for a scientific solution of the difficulty was established. The name *perspective* (seeing through) was chosen as descriptive of the process which had eluded mankind for thousands of years.

After the picture plane has been established there still remains the basic geometrical problem of how to determine accurately the amount of change which a given dimension will suffer because of its distance from the eye. Alberti first found a simple construction for this purpose by means of a model,[1] and published his solution in 1435. It was later regularized by Leonardo into the "costruzione legittima" which was used for centuries by Italian painters. In 1505 Jean Pélérin (Viator) published in France an even more useful formula (see Chap. 9, Sec. 2).

Dürer studied both these works but did not completely understand them, as is proved by the slight errors in his own construction which appeared in 1525 in his famous "Unterweysung der Messung." The peculiar charm of his woodcuts is doubtless due in part to the slightly inaccurate basis of his perspective. His drawings are correct enough not to shock us, and yet we feel in them a subtle unreality due to their lack of exact correspondence with the world as we have learned to know it through our eyes (Illus 1–2).

All the great artists of the Renaissance threw themselves enthusiastically into the development of the new science. Its main principles were soon established, but much confusion remained until Dr. Brook Taylor, the English mathematician and successor of Newton, published his "Linear Perspective"[2] early in the eighteenth century.

The great importance of Taylor's book lay in its establishment of an absolute two-way correspondence between the varying **appearance** of an object and its true unvarying **dimensions**. Until the theory of perspective had been scientifically established there was no method known to man by which a drawing could be made, from which the object portrayed could be accurately reproduced. Designs for buildings, fortifications, machines, etc., had always previously been mere diagrams. Now the woodcut and lithograph made possible the exact reproduction in unlimited numbers of the exact representations produced by *linear perspective*.

By the end of the eighteenth century Monge[3] had developed the theory of perspective projection into the simpler system of orthographic projection, and the tools were ready for the great industrial developments of the Age of Invention. At last a "technique of invention" was available. Ideas could be recorded and disseminated exactly. It is no exaggeration to say that the studies of the old perspectivists were among the most essential of the preliminary discoveries on which the modern world is founded.[4]

Dr. Taylor established a logical reconciliation of apparently contradictory phenomena. The rules he laid down were equally applicable to drawing from nature or from the imagination. Unfortunately, his propositions were too scientific and mathematical for most of his contemporaries. The painters to whom his book was addressed had difficulty in applying his principles to their practical problems. Many of the former misconceptions were carried on by commentators, although concealed beneath a welter of special terminology. Students were confused into trying to remember formulas and exceptions, instead of learning principles so broad as to be applicable in all cases.

In the following chapters we shall try at all times to keep in mind our general objective, and to think as little as possible of methods per se. Any mathematically sound process of producing a perspective is good if it seems simple and quick to the draftsman who uses it. Experience alone brings confidence and speed, no matter what the method. No one can learn perspective drawing without study, followed by constant practice, but it is obviously wiser for the beginner to aim for the best form. Like the golfer who learns to swing correctly at the start, he who has the soundest technique is apt to go farthest—but what counts is the result, not the way it is achieved. This book aims to show clearly "what" and "why." It also tells "how," but leaves the details of that infinitely varied problem largely to the individual after he has been started on the right path.

[1] Ivins, William Mills, "On the Rationalization of Sight," Museum Papers No. 8, New York, Metropolitan Museum of Art, 1938.
[2] Taylor, Brook, "Linear Perspective," London, 1715 (many later editions).
[3] Monge, Gaspard, "Géometrie Déscriptive," Paris, An. VII (many later editions).
[4] *Cf.* Ivins, *op. cit.*

A

Woodledge Farm, Gloucestershire, England; drawn by Francis Adams Comstock.

B

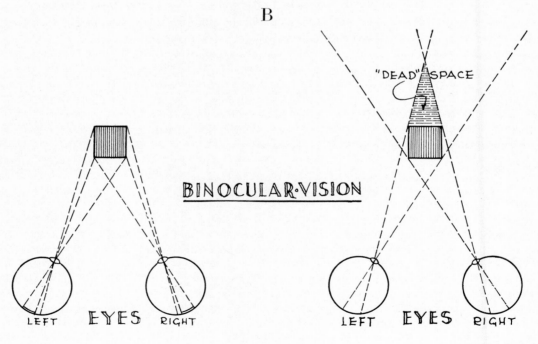

"DEAD" SPACE

BINOCULAR·VISION

LEFT EYES RIGHT

LEFT EYES RIGHT

ILLUSTRATION 1-3

Many painters have accused *linear perspective* of being impractical because they could not apply its rules strictly to their own problems. The artist working from nature sees many different perspectives as he looks intently first at one part of his subject and then at another. Even though he stands in one place without moving, he will turn his head (or at least his eyes) toward the particular spot which is attracting his attention at the moment. If he then attempts to record on one drawing the way that each separate part looks when he fixes his eyes directly upon it, he will produce a series of overlapping views in which each is the center of its own little perspective. This gives a representation of the whole which is often quite effective, but very difficult to work out graphically, for imaginary objects.

The wide use of photography today, both for individual prints and for many kinds of reproduction, has made modern man more conscious of how things look than were his predecessors. In magazines and newspapers, and on the movie screen, we see every day thousands of perspectives made by machines (cameras) and thus mechanically correct. Yet we know that many of them do not convey a true idea of the objects they are supposed to represent. This may be due to forcing the photographic process by using lenses of greater focal depth or wider angle than the human eye, or to a variety of professional tricks in exposure, development, and printing.

The camera has one greater and further limitation. It is an accurate machine for making perspectives but it can only record **existing** objects, while we can draw **imaginary** things as well as real ones. Perhaps the most important use of perspective today is to show what **would be** the appearance of things not yet in existence. Such a drawing (or better, a number of them) can tell a story more quickly and more dramatically than many words. It can often make intelligible a complex relationship of parts which would be confusing if presented in any other way. Best of all, it can be an **accurate** prophecy.

The architect who knows perspective can make pictures of your dream house in advance, and then build it later, exactly as he drew it for you. His sketches can be worked back to plans and elevations, and his more careful renderings will be exact representations in three-dimensional space of ideas which he has first recorded accurately in feet and inches by orthographic projection. There is something almost magical in his power to show in advance that which he can later construct. Such ability is well worth the time and study needed to acquire it.

Although the drawings and photograph in Illus. 1-4 were actually based on an existing building (instead of the building having been erected from drawings), the perspective was developed from the orthographic plan and elevations, and could have been projected before any construction had taken place. It looks as much like the building as the photograph because it was made with the limitations of human vision in mind.

In contrast to the elevation, notice how the true form of the building is made visually obvious by the perspective, because in it the central projecting portion stands out clearly from the main mass, whereas in the orthographic drawing the whole façade seems to be flat. Of course, the trained observer can read the difference by mentally transforming the elevation into its visual counterpart in space, but the layman will find the perspective much more revealing, despite the fact that it does not show true dimensions.

The use of perspective as a tool in design gives us not only a means of making others visualize what we propose, but an even more valuable power of clarifying our own ideas as we develop them. Quick perspective sketches can "see around the corners"—show us the relations between adjacent sides—and test the visual qualities of our designs. Nearly all great architects have mastered the technique of sketching quickly (and with over-all accuracy) in perspective.

A

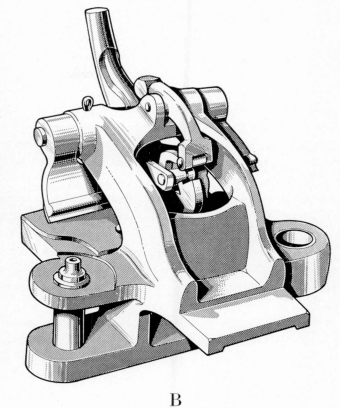

B

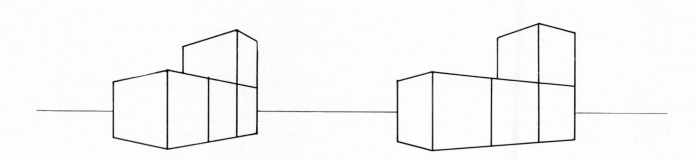

SAME FOUR CUBES

VISION DIRECTED TO SIDE.
(GIVES DISTORTED PICTURE OR
WRONG IDEA OF OBJECT)

VISION CENTERED ON OBJECT
(GIVES TRUE PICTURE OF REAL
FORM AND PROPORTION)

C

ILLUSTRATION 1-5

The Second World War gave perspective drawing a widened use in industrial production. When vast quantities of complicated machines, such as tanks and airplanes, had to be turned out with unprecedented rapidity, few workers were available who were experienced enough to understand the complex drawings required in their manufacture. It was soon discovered that perspective representations could save much time in explaining an elaborate part, or assembly, to relatively unskilled laborers. Such drawings could show clearly how complicated members were to be put together to make the final object. Much better results were obtained whenever the fabricators had such pictures before them as a guide. Drawings were found to be clearer even than photographs of actual completed assemblies, since the camera could not avoid shadows and could not see through intervening parts. A clever draftsman, however, could bring out forcefully exactly what was wanted by emphasizing important relationships and eliminating confusing or concealing detail (Illus. 1-5-A, 1-5-B).

The basic laws governing perspective procedure are, of course, identical whether we are drawing from nature or from our imagination. All representative drawings (not abstractions or willful distortions) must obey them. A painter working from a living model, or recording a landscape before him, uses the principles of perspective to lay out his picture as definitely as does an architect who is making a rendering of a building which exists as yet only in his plans and elevations. The manufacturers of animated cartoons for the movies use their knowledge of these laws very cleverly to make the audience see their characters in a setting which suggests three-dimensional space as successfully as though it actually existed.

Even sculptors, who always work in three dimensions, have to take perspective into account when their figures are intended to be seen only from certain angles. Ornamental sculpture high up on a building is often intentionally distorted to "look right" to the spectator in the street. The effect of his foreshortened point of view is corrected by leaning the figures forward, enlarging the upper parts, etc. The frieze of the Parthenon is very subtly handled in this way and looks its best only when seen from below. Though the Greeks never worked out the science of *linear perspective*, they took visual effects into account in all their monumental art.

After we have mastered the mathematical rules of perspective, there is always danger that we will overdo the graphical process and exceed the limitations of human vision, just as a camera can be made to do. Once a drawing is completed, it gives no sure indication of the viewpoint from which it was made, except the general relationship of the objects represented and the implied suggestion that the center of the picture coincides with the direction in which we are supposed to be looking. If we depict only a single object which is actually located at one side but whose true position is not made obvious, the observer will assume that he is looking directly at the figure that he sees on the paper. If the object is unfamiliar, he will consequently get an erroneous impression of its shape or will assume it to be drawn more or less foreshortened than it is actually shown. If the object is familiar, he will conclude that the drawing is "distorted" (Illus. 1-5-C). All perspectives are optical illusions in so far as they suggest to the spectator a third dimension (depth) which does not actually exist on the flat surface of the canvas or drawing board. Unless we are trying to deceive, we must be careful that we do not further confuse those who look at them (see Chap. 8, Sec. 7, Optical Illusions).

In architectural design there is the further risk that we may become so enamored of the pictorial qualities of a perspective as a drawing that we will forget the realities behind it and think of what is on the paper, rather than of what is represented. This subtle self-deception has certainly influenced many painters as well as architects. Some critics have accused the process rather than the man and complained of the shallowness of a *perspective age*, tracing many of the artistic ills that have developed since the Renaissance to the overfacility in representation which the new knowledge engendered, with consequent detriment to deeper thought and understanding.[1] Some contemporary architects maintain that a building can be truly studied only in the austerity of orthographic projection in line without perspective, shadows, or color. This seems like throwing out the baby to get rid of the dirty bath water. Each designer must decide such matters for himself after he has learned the advantages and limitations of the various means of representing space.

[1] See Giedion, S., "Time, Space and Architecture," pp. 33*ff*., Cambridge, Harvard University Press, 1941, but compare Ivins, *op. cit.*

DEMONSTRATION OF BLIND SPOT
CLOSE LEFT EYE, LOOK AT CIRCLE WITH RIGHT
AND MOVE BOOK NEARER AND FURTHER. AT
SOME POINT THE CROSS WILL DISAPPEAR.

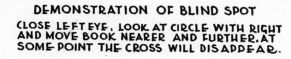

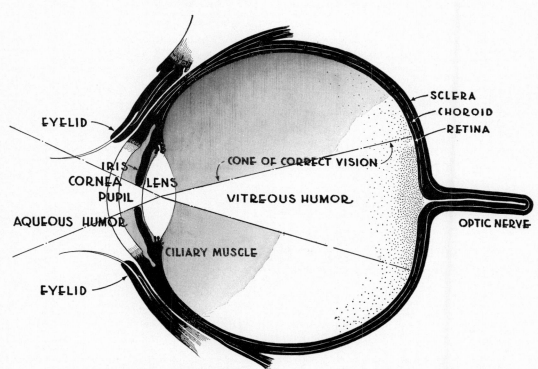

VERTICAL SECTION THROUGH THE PUPIL ENLARGED

THE EYE

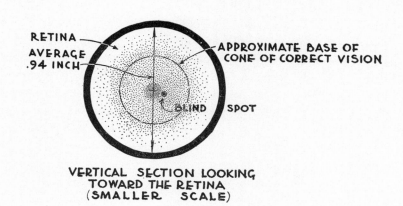

VERTICAL SECTION LOOKING
TOWARD THE RETINA
(SMALLER SCALE)

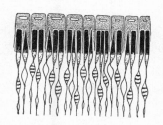

SECTION THROUGH THE
TERMINI (RODS AND CONES)
GREATLY ENLARGED

ILLUSTRATION 2-1

Chapter 2

BASIS OF LINEAR PERSPECTIVE

A PERSPECTIVE drawing represents an object (either real or imaginary) as it would appear to a person looking at it from a particular location in space. In order to make a successful perspective, we must therefore consider the mechanics of seeing (optics); the limits of the visual field of the human eye, and the effect of the concentration of attention on a part of it (focus); and the effect of color, distance, and atmospheric conditions on vision (aerial perspective).

The first two considerations are capable of exact analysis and may be reduced to scientific rules. They govern the theory and use of *linear perspective*, the graphical science by which the apparent size and shape of any object (its perspective picture) may be found accurately if its true dimensions and position are known. The third consideration affects the expressive treatment of the finished drawing. It is a matter of artistic choice rather than of geometrical construction, and determines the pictorial value of our work, as opposed to its mere correctness.

If we analyze the physical means by which the eye makes us aware of the three-dimensional space in which we live, we can understand how a similar impression may be conveyed to our minds by figures drawn on the flat surface of a piece of paper. When we have mastered the problem of drawing correct linear perspectives, we can go on to consider the pictorial treatment of the objects that we have thus outlined and the values and colors that may be added to a line drawing to give aerial perspective.

1. LIGHT RAYS AND THE EYE

We become aware of the world around us by means of the light reflected from illuminated objects to the retina of the eye. There the minute sensitive termini of the optic nerve respond to the reaction caused in the visual *purple*, and transmit a different stimulus to the brain for each of the different rays of light reflected from each of the millions of points which make up any object. Our brains have learned to interpret these stimuli and from them to construct a concept of three-dimensional space based on the patterns formed on the two-dimensional surface of the retina. In order that the impression caused by the light reflected from each point may be clear and distinct, nature provides us with a lens behind the pupil of the eye which concentrates on the retina the rays reflected from external objects, thus bringing in more light and producing more stimulus.

Illustration 2-1 shows the construction of the eye and the relation between its parts. In order to control its focus, the lens may be contracted or dilated by the ciliary muscles which hold it, and the size of the pupil (the opening which admits light) may be varied by the action of the iris (the complex of tiny muscles which is made completely opaque by the pigment which gives our eyes their color). These muscular adjustments take place under the shield of the cornea and are largely automatic and unconscious.

The eyeball behind the lens is a hollow spheroid filled with liquid (the vitreous humor) and completely enclosed by the sclera and choroid, which protect the sensitive inner surface or **retina.** This consists of a very fine and complicated network of nerve ends (they number many hundred thousand) whose form has brought them the names of *rods* and *cones*. Each type has its own special function in vision but for our purpose the distinctions are not important because both help to convey light stimuli to the brain.

They are most closely grouped on the axis of the eyeball opposite the pupil (some 500,000 there form a small yellow spot about $\frac{1}{8}$ in. in diameter) and become more scattered in the portions of the retina which are farther from this center. The region of most sensitive vision thus coincides with the circular area which is so placed as to receive the most direct light and be most nearly perpendicular to the rays entering the eye along the axis of vision.

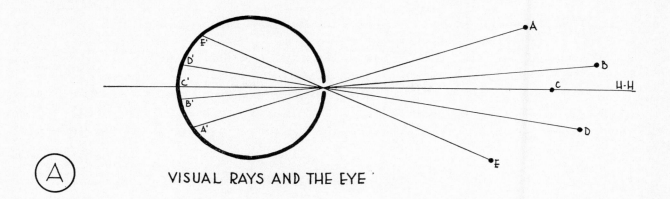

(A) VISUAL RAYS AND THE EYE

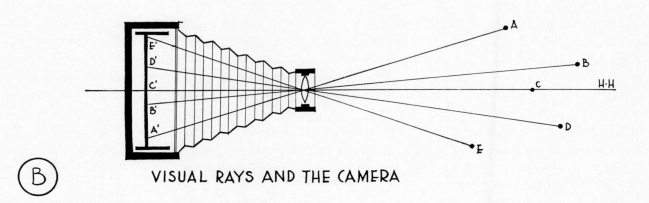

(B) VISUAL RAYS AND THE CAMERA

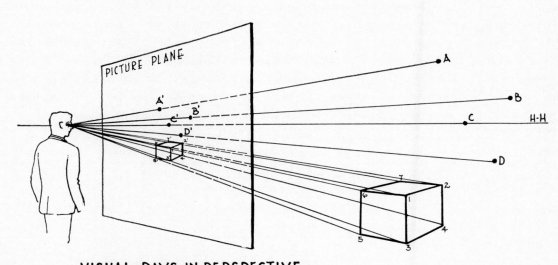

(C) VISUAL RAYS IN PERSPECTIVE

NOTE · THE PATTERN (2' 3' 4' ETC.) TRACED ON PICTURE PLANE BY THE VISUAL RAYS IS THE PERSPECTIVE IMAGE OF THE CUBE (1-2-3-4-5-6-7)

At the point where the optic nerve leaves the retina there are no rods and cones. Consequently each eye has a blind spot. We are normally unconscious of its existence because we move our eyes constantly and hence the light rays reflected from the same point in space never strike the blind spots of both eyes at the same instant. The diagram at the top of Illus. 2-1 will quickly demonstrate to you the presence of such spots in your own eyes.

We shall consider later how the focusing action of the lens limits the choice of our perspective point of view and the pictorial treatment of our drawings. Graphically the result is the same (only more powerful because more light is admitted) as if the eye had merely a pinhole opening through which only one ray could be reflected from each point in front of it.

2. PERSPECTIVE PROJECTION

We may thus say that the appearance to us of any point in space is due to a single ray of light which is reflected from that point through the pupil of the eye to the retina (Illus. 2-2-A). A line thus fixed from object through pupil to retina is called a *visual ray*. On the drafting board we can represent the retina by a plane, the pupil by a point, and the light rays by straight lines (Illus. 2-2-C).

A camera (Illus. 2-2-B) is a mechanical device for applying this principle, and its lens collects the light rays and concentrates them on the sensitive plate or film exactly as the lens of the eye does on the retina (except for the slight difference due to the flatness of the film and the curvature of the retina). This discrepancy between the retina and a photograph (or drawing) is negligible under most conditions, but becomes noticeable in certain cases (spheres, colonnades, etc., not in the center of the picture) (see Illus. 3-6). A system of projection onto a cylindrical surface has been worked out to meet these conditions, but its technical complexity makes it of doubtful value for any but the specialist (see Chap. 9, Sec. 8). The selection of a proper point of view can nearly always be made so as to obviate the need for such a process.

In projecting onto a flat plane, we make the apparent length of a line in perspective depend on an oblique intersection of the angle subtended at the eye, whereas it should depend on the angle itself. Under certain conditions the difference becomes noticeable and produces distortions, especially as the distance of the object from the center of the picture increases (see Illus. 3-7).

In both cases, the **appearance** of the object is the pattern formed on a plane surface by lines drawn from every point of the object through another fixed point to the surface. As we are trying to duplicate this process, we may define a perspective graphically as **the projection of an object on a *fixed* plane from a *fixed* point.**[1]

We must always remember, moreover, that we are concerned with the reproduction of a physiological phenomenon which has very definite natural limitations. The result of our drawing may be geometrically correct but pictorially unsuccessful, if we limit ourselves merely to graphic projection without regard for human vision. Perspectives which are accurate mechanical drawings but distorted pictures may easily be produced.

Certain groups of contemporary delineators have used this possibility to achieve striking and unusual effects. While intentional distortion is a powerful means of expression in the hands of competent artists, it is rarely of use in the representation of architecture. We are concerned with telling the pictorial truth about a building (actual or proposed) and must be careful that we do not convey a false impression of its scale or proportions.

[1] Leonardo da Vinci recognized this phenomenon at least partially. In his notes on perspective he says: "Perspective is a rational demonstration whereby experience confirms how all things transmit their images to the eye by pyramidal lines. By pyramidal lines I mean those which start from the extremities of the surface of bodies and by gradually converging from a distance, arrive at the same point; the said point being, as I shall show, in this particular case, located in the eye, which is the universal judge of all objects." (Lubschez, Ben Jehudah, "Perspective," 4th ed., p. 116, New York, D. Van Nostrand Company, Inc., 1926.) In another place he calls perspective "the bridle and rudder of painting," but he never worked out the mathematics for representing accurately any objects except those parallel to the picture plane.

ILLUSTRATION 2-3

3. STATION POINT

The point from which we view an object is called the *station point* (symbol S). The pictorial success of our perspective depends primarily on a wise choice for its location. Many considerations must be taken into account before it can be fixed to the best advantage. A painter or photographer will walk round and round looking at his chosen subject from many different angles and many different distances before he decides on the spot from which the very best view will be obtained. We must do the same in imagination before locating our station point.

An orthographic plan (if available) provides the easiest means of trying different possible choices of position, and most perspectives are begun by determining on such a drawing the horizontal relation of S to the object to be represented. The reasons for deciding on a particular location for S are brought out fully later in Chap. 4, Sec. 1, and are summarized as Proposition I of Chap. 10.

4. PICTURE PLANE

The location of S gives us our *fixed point*. We must also have a *fixed plane* upon which to project our object. Such a projection will be identical (except for size) on any vertical plane which the visual rays intercept, whether behind the point like the retina, or between it and the object like a window glass (Illus. 2-3-A). Anyone who has used a camera with a ground glass behind the lens for focusing has seen his picture-to-be as it is projected on the retina—upside down (Illus. 2-3-B)! But just as we can later turn the photograph around until it is right side up, so can our brains interpret visual images correctly by a mental turn of which we are unconscious, because we have always thus turned everything that we have ever seen since first we opened our eyes. It is startling to realize that we have always seen the world upside down—and never known the difference! In drafting, it is much more convenient to work out a picture right side up, so we place our fixed plane **between** our fixed point and the object.

The plane onto which we project our object we call the *picture plane* (symbol PP). It is our window glass; when we hold it before us we see the object on it just as we would see it through the window. When we make a perspective we consider the surface on which we draw (our paper or canvas) to be this plane.

We thus create on the drafting board the same situation that occurs in real life when we look through a window at an object (Illus. 2-3-A). The rays from it to our eye will trace out on the glass an image identical to that which they will trace on the retina, although not the same size, and right side up instead of inverted. Dürer and other great early students of perspective often traced out a picture on an actual piece of glass held between them and the subject selected. You can do the same on the window of your own room, using a china-marking crayon and a pin hole in a card held by a stick tied to the back of a chair. The figure formed on the glass is the perspective image of the objects beyond. (Remember that *perspective* comes from the Latin *perspicere*, meaning "to see through.")

The visual experiences on which we base our pictorial judgments are made up of countless memories, the great preponderance of which consists of mental pictures of our surroundings projected onto an approximately **vertical** plane. No matter where we are located on the earth, we feel the pull of gravity and stand upright. Hence we are constantly reminded of verticality by a physical reaction, and commonly bring our retinas into a vertical position when looking around us (whether standing or sitting). This applies particularly to looking at large objects (like buildings) which we see from some distance and in a natural setting. Every wall, every body of water, most tree trunks, etc., serve to remind us of the necessarily vertical relationships of a world conditioned by gravity. Hence, for normal architectural representation, **the picture plane should be vertical.**

It is hard for us to accept a picture projected onto an inclined picture plane, unless we hold the drawing above (or below) our eyes, until we are looking at it from the angle assumed in the perspective. Inclined picture planes produce results which are abnormal (though accurate), and hence often seem "distorted" to those who look at the drawing. A camera can easily be tilted so as to produce effects of this sort. It is possible to project perspectives onto an inclined picture plane, but the process is laborious and seldom justified by the results. Such so-called *three-point perspectives* are discussed later (Chap. 9, Sec. 3).

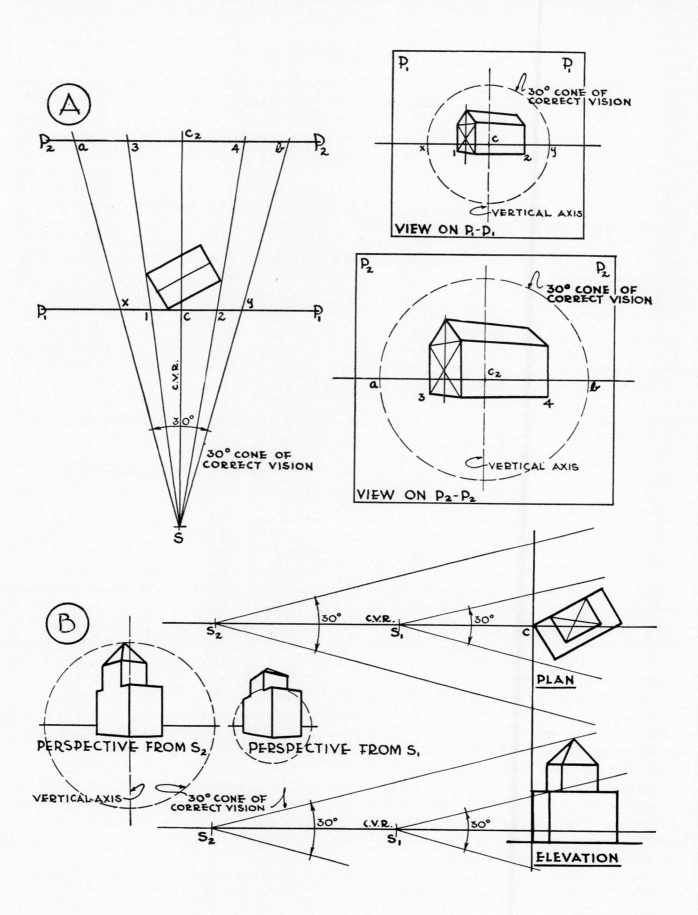

ILLUSTRATION 2-4

5. CONE OF CORRECT VISION

The width of the perspective representation of any object is governed by the distance between the points in which the picture plane is cut by the visual rays drawn to the extreme corners of the object. We can thus find out very quickly how large a picture will result from any combination of S and PP. In Illus. 2-4-A the points 1 and 2 in plan show immediately how wide the picture of the building will be if P_1P_1 is used, and points 3 and 4 give the same limits on P_2P_2.

The sensitive field of the retina of the eye embraces a maximum of 50° to 70° vertically (angle centered in the pupil) and as much as 100° horizontally, but most people can distinguish forms clearly only when they are projected onto the central 30° of this area and thus contained within a cone of rays which, when extended into space outside the pupil, is called the *cone of correct vision*. Light rays reflected from objects outside it strike the less effective portions of the retina, which is most sensitive at its center and loses reacting power rapidly near its periphery. In life we move our eyes constantly so as to bring successively to the center of the field of vision the objects in which we are interested and which we wish to see clearly. A drawing, however, can only "look" in one direction, and so must avoid trying to represent more than the eye can see accurately at **one** time, from **one** point, and looking in **one** direction.

The possible spread of the cone of correct vision varies with different people, but rarely exceeds 45° at the apex (S). For a normal architectural drawing it is better to reduce it to 30° or even less. Painters usually limit their canvases to between 10° and 20°. Landscapes in which natural forms predominate may be extended to as much as 60°, provided that geometrical objects such as buildings, etc., are kept near the vertical axis or in the background. During the Second World War it was demonstrated that the size of the cone of correct vision can be greatly increased by training. Airplane observers, pilots, etc., were able, after intensive practice under controlled conditions, to recognize planes seen at extremely wide angles. Previously these observers would have been conscious only of a blur.

Be careful, in the case of tall objects such as buildings with towers, to test S in section as well as in plan, in order to be sure that all parts of the object are inside the cone of correct vision. In Illus. 2-4-B, S_1 should be moved back to S_2 so that the whole tower is in the cone, not only in width and breadth, but also in height. The plan of a church spire (or of a skyscraper) may easily be well within our cone horizontally, and yet its upper (and usually most interesting) parts may be completely outside the limit of correct vision from our chosen station point.

6. CENTRAL VISUAL RAY

The axis of the cone of correct vision is called the *central visual ray* (*C.V.R.*). It is the line along which we are looking, and the point C in which it strikes the PP is the center of our attention and hence should be the center of our picture. In order to make a perspective which will conform to our visual experience, it is therefore essential to locate both S and $C.V.R.$ so that the object and its accessories will be within the limits of the resulting cone of correct vision. The trace of this cone on PP is, of course, a circle with its center at C. We must confine our final picture within this border if we wish to get a correct image.

Since our eyes are usually attracted to the nearest corner of a large object like a building, it is ordinarily best to draw the $C.V.R.$ to such a corner and to locate the picture plane passing through it. This gives the easiest projection, but PP may be moved backward and forward along $C.V.R.$ in order to secure a larger or a smaller image, just as one moves a magic lantern screen back and forth to control the size of the picture (Illus. 2-4-A).

PP **however, must always remain perpendicular to** $C.V.R.$ because the retina of the eye is fixed by nature in that relation to its pupil and hence to its $C.V.R.$ We must always recall in making perspectives that we are limited to reproducing the human mechanism for seeing, and may not determine graphic relationships merely by geometrical possibilities. It is perfectly possible to project an object onto a plane which is **not** perpendicular to the direction of vision, but the result will **not** be a perspective because it will not be a reproduction on paper of the image produced on the human retina by light rays passing through the pupil of the eye.

For a normal perspective, with a vertical PP, **the** $C.V.R.$ **must be horizontal** because it must be perpendicular to PP. That is why we learn to "hold the camera level" when we take a photograph.

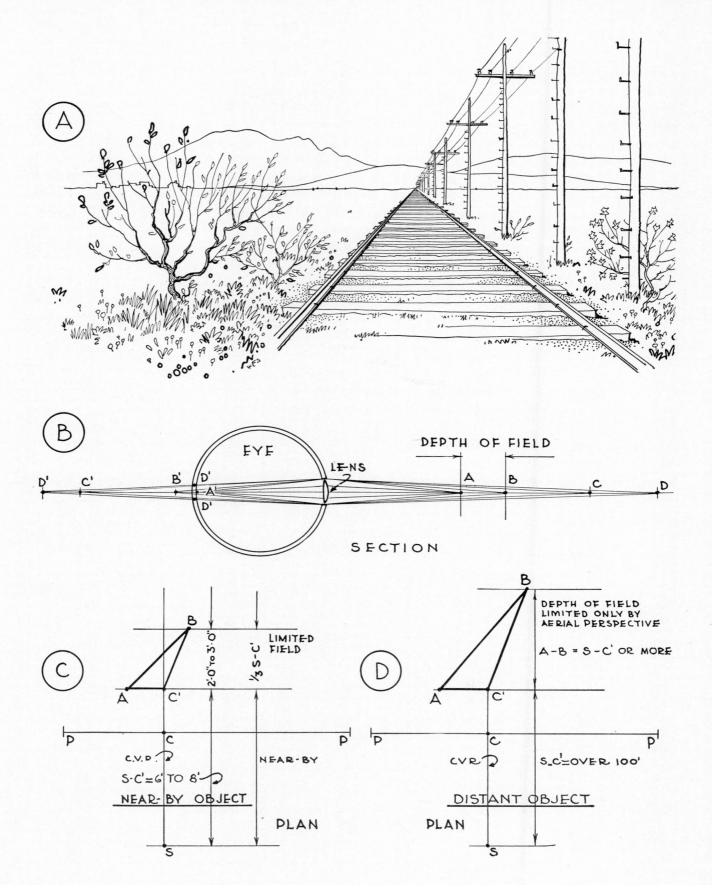

A

B

EYE
LENS
DEPTH OF FIELD

D' C' B' D' A' A B C D

SECTION

C

B
2'-0" TO 3'-0"
⅓ S-C'
LIMITED FIELD
A C'

P C P

C.V.P.
S-C'=6' TO 8'
NEAR-BY OBJECT

NEAR-BY

PLAN

S

D

B
DEPTH OF FIELD LIMITED ONLY BY AERIAL PERSPECTIVE

A-B = S-C' OR MORE

A C'

P C P

CVR
S-C'=OVER 100'
DISTANT OBJECT

PLAN

S

22

ILLUSTRATION 2-5

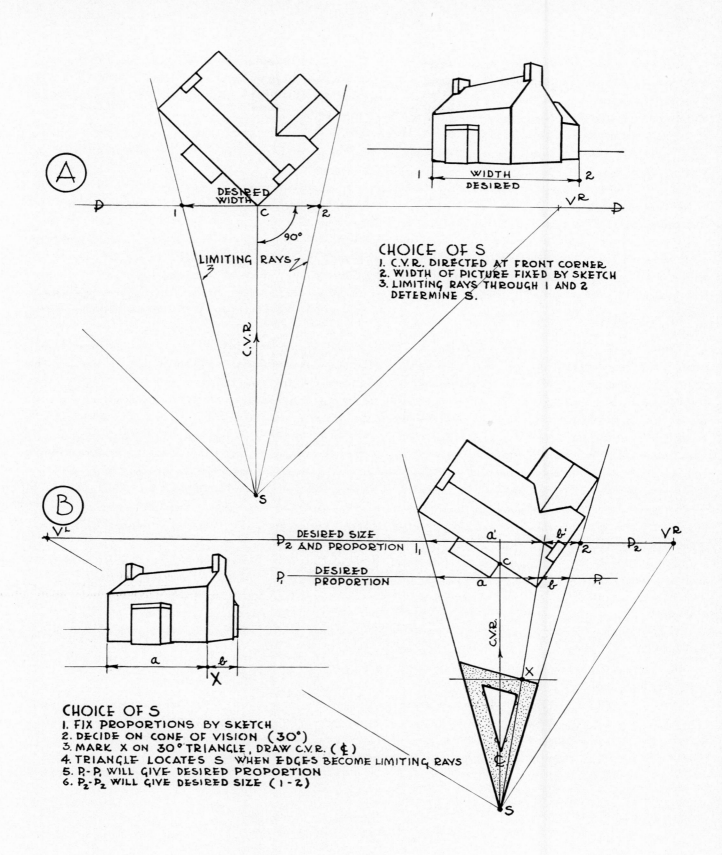

A

DESIRED WIDTH

WIDTH DESIRED

90°

LIMITING RAYS

C.V.R.

S

CHOICE OF S
1. C.V.R. DIRECTED AT FRONT CORNER
2. WIDTH OF PICTURE FIXED BY SKETCH
3. LIMITING RAYS THROUGH 1 AND 2
   DETERMINE S.

B

VL

DESIRED SIZE AND PROPORTION

DESIRED PROPORTION

VR

C.V.R.

X

S

CHOICE OF S
1. FIX PROPORTIONS BY SKETCH
2. DECIDE ON CONE OF VISION (30°)
3. MARK X ON 30° TRIANGLE, DRAW C.V.R. (℄)
4. TRIANGLE LOCATES S WHEN EDGES BECOME LIMITING RAYS
5. P_1-P_1 WILL GIVE DESIRED PROPORTION
6. P_2-P_2 WILL GIVE DESIRED SIZE (1-2)

7. FOCUS

Besides including the object to be represented within the cone of correct vision, we must be careful to locate S so that our picture will not require a greater *depth of field* than would be possible for human vision. By this term we mean the extent (in the direction away from S) of the visible portions of the object to be drawn. This restriction is necessary in order to limit what we draw to what our eye can focus clearly.

For instance, let us suppose that we are making a perspective looking down a straight railroad track which stretches away from the observer for many miles over a level plain. Theoretically, it is possible to project onto our picture plane any number of crossties no matter how distant they may be. Practically, it is impossible to draw so many lines so close together. Pictorially, it would be an error to attempt to do so because the eye cannot clearly distinguish remote objects at the same time as nearer ones. This is because the pupil of our eye is not a point, but an opening provided with a lens which has the optical properties for making light rays converge. Many visual rays are reflected through the pupil from any point of the object which it sees, and are brought to focus again on the retina, thus concentrating more light there and giving a sharper stimulus to the optic nerve.

Nature has given us muscles to adjust the optical qualities of our eye lenses so as to be able to see clearly objects at different distances. Although the size of the eyeball fixes the dimension from pupil to retina (Illus. 2-1) the shape of the lens can be changed by the action of the eye muscles, so that the light rays from objects at various distances may be brought together on the retina. When we focus on any particular one, all those nearer or farther away will of course be less accurately perceived and those beyond a certain distance will be completely blurred. The limits of clear vision, before and beyond the point of focus, fix our depth of field in any particular case.

Cameras having a single unchangeable lens are manufactured so that the distance from lens to film can be varied, and thus the focus changed to suit the position of the object. In perspective drawing, we can make no such adjustments as can eye or camera. All that we can do is to locate S and to limit the resulting projection so as to include only that which the eye would normally find clearly visible when looking in that one direction from that one point of view.

Illustration 2-5-B shows that if we focus on any particular point all others will become increasingly out of focus as they approach or recede from the eye. A and B could be shown in the same perspective, because they can be focused by nearly the same adjustment of our lens, but A and C can never be seen distinctly at the same time. Point D would be completely blurred, and would look like a circle of diameter $D'D'$ to anyone whose pupil was adjusted for looking at A. In order to focus on C or D, the eye would have to change the shape of the lens. This would prevent clear vision of A or B.

The focus of the human eye can be varied sufficiently to see clearly objects that are within a few inches of us, or those that are as much as several miles away. This flexibility is accomplished at the expense of depth of field for the nearer positions. When the distance from the lens to A (see Illus. 2-5-C) is small (not over 6 or 8 ft.), nothing nearer than A or farther than B can be seen clearly at one time, and their distance apart cannot exceed 2 or 3 ft. A safe rule for most drawings is that the depth of field should be kept as small as possible in relation to the distance from the station point to the nearest part of the object.

This limitation is expressed geometrically by the rule of thumb that $A'\text{-}B' \leqq \frac{1}{3} S\text{-}C'$. However, when $S\text{-}C'$ exceeds 100 ft. everything will be in focus from A to the limit of vision possible under the prevailing atmospheric conditions.

Since most perspectives are drawn at a scale smaller than the object to be represented, and we can vary this size relationship at will, we must be particularly careful to think of the true size of the object when we are locating S. The permissible depth of field depends on the construction of the human eye and hence on the actual dimensions involved, no matter what the scale of the picture.

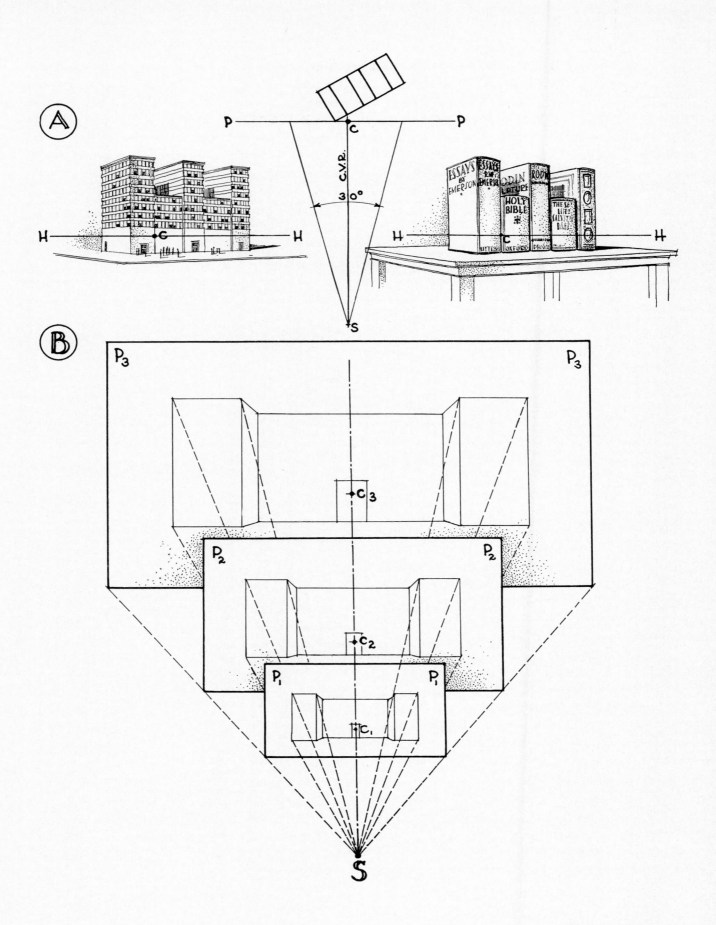

ILLUSTRATION 2-6

Taking care to think of the true length of S-C' will also help us to decide on our use of aerial perspective to bring out the true size of the object. Although the science of linear perspective will show us how to represent accurately any point inside the cone of correct vision, the result of thus recording everything without discrimination would be misleading. Only a small object held near the eye is seen in full detail. Its depth of field covers only inches, and hence there is no atmospheric difference to affect our perception of its parts. Large objects, like most buildings, have to be seen from such a distance in order to include all of them in a normal cone of vision, that the visual field may be several hundred feet in depth. This true size may be brought out by emphasis of nearer parts, elimination of detail, variation in colors and value, etc., as is discussed in Chap. 8.

The two objects shown in Illus. 2-6-A have exactly the same outline in perspective. Only the difference in the amount and kind of detail makes it clear that one is a near view of a row of books, and the other a distant view of a large building. The plan diagram is the same for both perspectives but the scale is different, making the true value of S-C several hundred **feet** for the left-hand drawing, and less than forty **inches** for the one on the right.

A photograph taken with a telescopic lens thus often conveys a false impression, especially when printed very clearly. We are shown objects in a relationship which is only possible when viewed from a distance, while the special lens brings out full details such as we could see only from nearby. Our sense of the true sizes involved (the quality architects call *scale*) is thus confused and is apt to be upset. The relative distance between objects is particularly affected, and becomes very difficult to judge. A building several hundred yards from a lake can be made to seem to stand directly on the shore, etc.

8. CENTER OF PICTURE

The point at which the $C.V.R.$ strikes the object is the center of interest of our drawing. Psychologically, it is the *projection* of the observer into the picture—the reference point around which he groups all things represented to form an understandable picture of a real three-dimensional world. Graphically it usually is made to coincide with the point at which the object strikes PP. This is another reason for locating PP so that a corner of the object lies in it, but whether or not the two points coincide in plan, their perspective is the same. This point is very important to us. We call it C—the *center of the picture*.

The length of the line from S to PP was formerly considered to be all important and was called the *distance* of the picture. While it is true that any perspective representation of space relationships will seem most satisfactory if the drawing is looked at (with one eye) from a point in front of it equal to the distance between the PP and the S from which it was projected, the advantage gained is very slight if S has been wisely chosen. It is much more important for the artist to realize the true distance between S and the object, and to be guided by this fixed actual relationship between observer and object when rendering a linear perspective according to the principles of focus and of aerial perspective.

It will be shown later (see Chap. 9, Sec. 2) that one of the first methods ever discovered by which the apparent diminution of distant objects could be accurately determined, was based graphically on the length of S-C. We now have many other ways of solving this problem, and hence no longer attach exaggerated importance to this distance— realizing instead that PP may slide back and forth along $C.V.R.$ with no other effect than changing the **size** of the picture (Illus. 2-6-B). The appearance (shape) of any object will be proportionately the same for any position of PP, once S and $C.V.R.$ have been determined. PP must of course always be perpendicular to $C.V.R.$ since that is the way in which our eyes are constructed.

In the graphical methods used later, when we refer to C we mean the point where $C.V.R.$ strikes PP whether or not this is also a point of the object. Its representation in perspective is the datum from which all other points are located geometrically. Wherever we put it on our drawing, the horizon and the vertical axis must then be drawn through it and the rest of our perspective built up around it. Only points in PP can be measured off directly (since only those in PP will appear at their true relative size). All others must be found by construction, as is demonstrated later, and all such work is determined by using C as a point of departure.

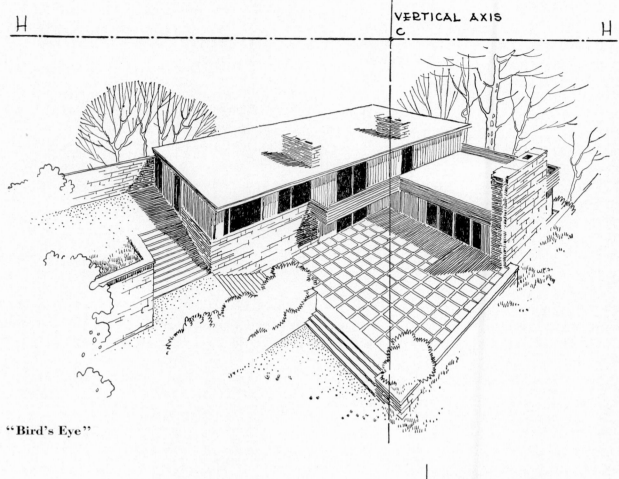

VERTICAL AXIS

H   C   H

"Bird's Eye"

VERTICAL AXIS

H   C   H

"Worm's Eye"

ILLUSTRATION 2-7

9. THE HORIZON

The vertical line through C is the *vertical axis* of the drawing. It fixes the direction of gravitation for the picture. The horizontal line through C fixes the level of the observer's eye in relation to all objects represented. We call this horizontal line the *horizon* (symbol HH).

Before beginning a perspective, HH must be decided definitely in order to complete the exact location of S in space, by fixing its height. The decision as to the level of HH is a matter of our choice. It corresponds to deciding whether to hold the camera low or to raise it by climbing up on a ladder, after S has been located on the ground.

If we assume an observer of normal height, standing at the same level as the object to be represented, then HH will average about 5'-0" above the ground line, which shows pictorially the relation of objects to the surface of the earth. This is what the person seeing our picture will expect, and we must be careful not to mislead him by changing the normal height of HH only a little. Such a change may interfere with the scale of our drawing, unless there are many other indications of the true size of a man—the measure of all things.

If we wish to look down on our object, HH should be taken 25 ft. or more above $G.L.$ (the ground line), thus producing a true bird's-eye effect. The increasing use of airplanes will make such views more and more intelligible and useful, because people will be more accustomed to them (see also Chap. 9, Secs. 3 and 4).

When we go up in an airplane, our horizon seems to rise with us, and our view extends until haze blurs the distance, or mountains interrupt. What we call the horizon in such cases is really a false one marking the profile of the earth, and is considerably below the true vanishing line of horizontal planes, which depends on the height of the eye, but is not marked in the sky. Observers have to be specially trained to understand photographs taken from great heights.

If our object stands on a hill, the condition opposite to the bird's-eye view is created. Our picture is a worm's-eye view, in that the observer's eye is below the level of the ground at the object. Such unusual assumptions of HH are capable of producing very striking results, and present no difficulties as far as linear perspective is concerned. They must, however, be carefully handled pictorially with regard to conveying the true sense of scale. Either very high or very low HH's require relatively distant station points. The final drawing must be rendered to convey the correct impression as to distance.

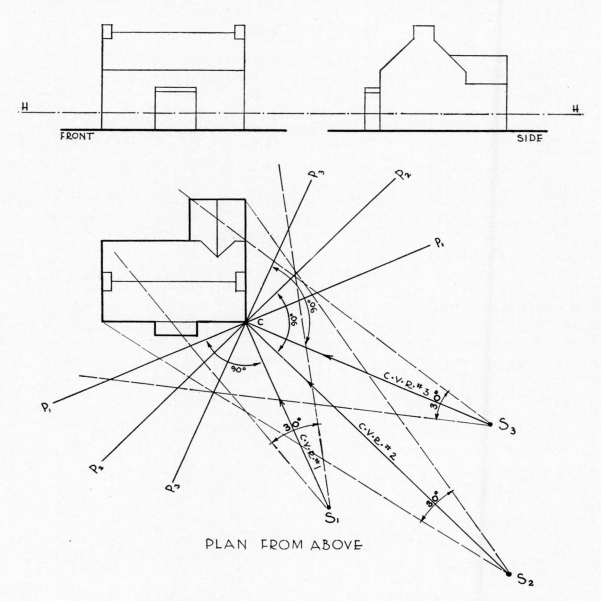

FRONT

SIDE

PLAN FROM ABOVE

C.V.R. #3

C.V.R. #2

C.V.R. #1

P_1 P_2 P_3 P_1 P_2 P_3

S_1 S_2 S_3

90° 90° 90° 30° 30° 30°

PERSPECTIVES FROM THREE DIFFERENT S's

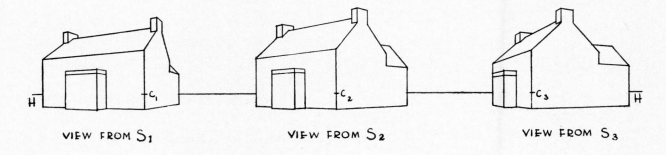

VIEW FROM S_1 VIEW FROM S_2 VIEW FROM S_3

10. SUMMARY

Once S, $C.V.R.$, and HH have been selected, everything else follows by geometrical projection, as surely as the photograph follows when we take the camera to a chosen spot, point it at our chosen subject, and decide how high to hold it. Of course we still have to master the technical drafting process involved in making a perspective, just as the film has to be exposed, developed, and printed under proper procedures, but the result is inevitable if we carry out correctly the consequences of our decisions to date.

Since the most effective selection of S, $C.V.R.$, and HH are all important, the principal considerations on which our choice of them should be founded are summarized in Proposition I, Chap. 10, and discussed fully in Chap. 4, Sec. 1. Of course, these are only general guides for the beginner. They are "don'ts" rather than "do's." Observance of such rules will prevent failures, but only experience and imagination will bring success. Within the area to which Proposition I limits us, there is still tremendous opportunity for choice, permitting every result from the merely satisfactory to the really distinguished. The rules only start us in the right direction. Study and practice will determine how far we shall advance along the road.

Illustrations 2-8 to 2-10 explain how the choice of S, $C.V.R.$, and HH affect the resultant picture. They show the same small house first from three different station points; then using three different $C.V.R.$'s from the same S, and finally from three levels (HH changing accordingly) after both S and $C.V.R.$ have been fixed. The way in which the perspectives are worked out in each case is explained in Chap. 4.

The choice of S_1 and S_3 in Illus. 2-8 has intentionally been made to violate to some extent our rule about the limitation of the cone of correct vision. Hence, somewhat "distorted" effects are produced. Too great a depth of field also results from these unfortunate decisions and this contributes to the unpleasant appearance. The view from S_3 has the further disadvantage that the edge of the entrance vestibule lines up with the left end of the house.

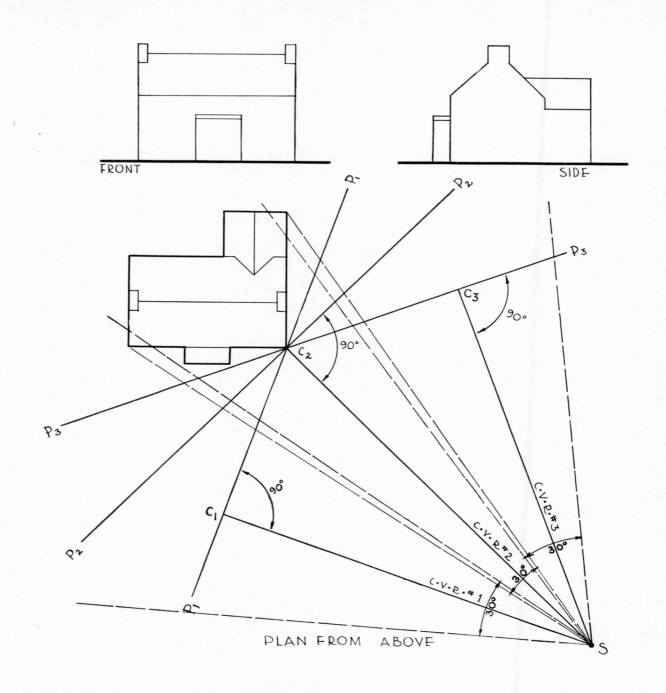

FRONT

SIDE

PLAN FROM ABOVE

THREE PERSPECTIVES FROM SAME "S", WITH DIFFERENT "C·V·R·s".

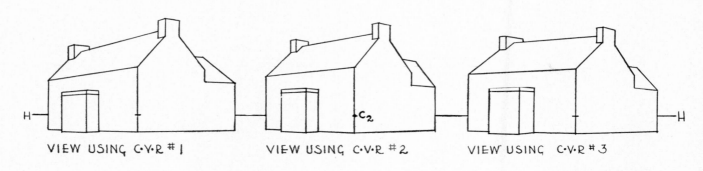

VIEW USING C·V·R #1

VIEW USING C·V·R #2

VIEW USING C·V·R #3

ILLUSTRATION 2-9

In Illus. 2-9 the visual changes due to the choice of $C.V.R.$ are not as apparent at first glance. However, notice the proportions of roof to wall, of height to width, and especially of the chimneys. These show the effect of the unnatural choice of a $C.V.R.$ not directed at the object, and thus throwing it far to one side of the cone of correct vision.

The person seeing such a drawing infers that he is doing the natural thing, and looking at the object, whereas in each case he is seeing it as it would look if his attention were centered on the corresponding C. Since he does not know the building, he concludes mentally that it is a different design having the same general disposition of parts, but less agreeable proportions.

In Illus. 2-10 the changes in HH are not great enough to involve the disagreeable effects encountered in the other cases. If HH were raised or lowered sufficiently, unpleasant "distortions" would begin to appear as soon as the house got out of the cone of correct vision.

Note that all vertical lines lie the same distance to right or left of C in all examples of Illus. 2-10. Since S and $C.V.R.$ do not change, this is inevitable. Note also that lines actually horizontal are drawn sloping **down** if they are above HH, and **up** if they are below it, and that they tend to converge toward the points on each HH that are marked V. The reasons for these phenomena are explained in the next chapter.

QUESTIONS

1. Explain how the human eye perceives objects in space.
2. Compare a perspective drawing to a photograph.
3. Define the following: S, $C.V.R.$, PP, HH.
4. How does the cone of correct vision affect the location of S?
5. What determines the direction of $C.V.R.$?
6. Why is PP usually vertical?
7. Why must PP be perpendicular to $C.V.R.$?
8. What and where is C?
9. What limits our *depth of field*?
10. What are the first three steps in making a perspective?

PROBLEMS

1. Criticize the choice of S, $C.V.R.$, and HH in each example of Illus. 2-8, 2-9, and 2-10.
2. Using Illus. 2-11-A locate S, $C.V.R.$, HH and PP to meet the following requirements, and mark the depth of field permissible in each case.
   a. Normal view from southeast, so as to make perspective view of building 2 in. wide.
   b. Bird's-eye view from north and 100 ft. above ground.
   c. Worm's-eye view from southwest to show both wings of building.
3. Locate the necessary data to begin a perspective of Illus. 2-11-B.

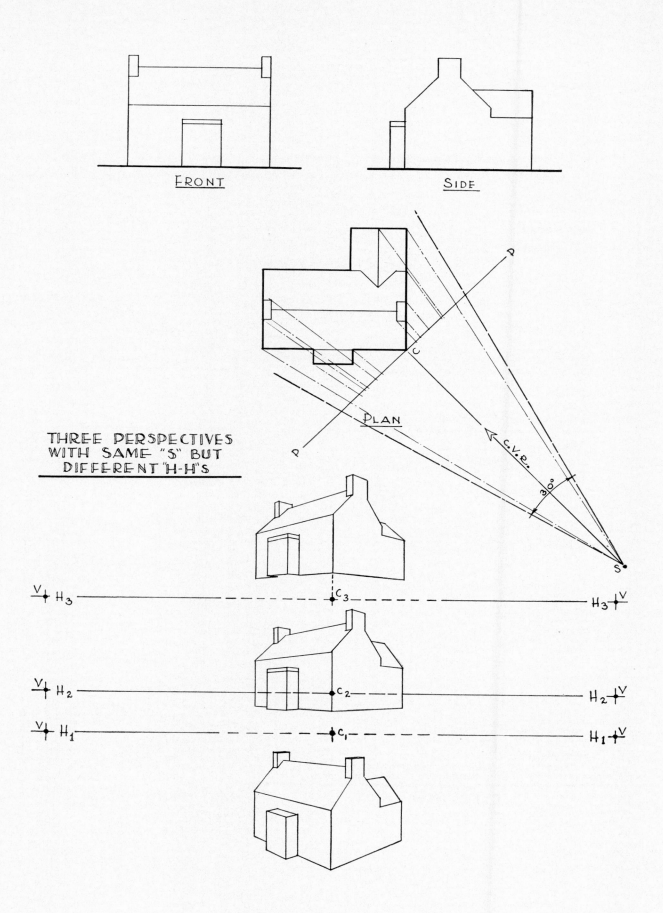

FRONT

SIDE

P

C

C.V.R.

30°

S

PLAN

THREE PERSPECTIVES
WITH SAME "S" BUT
DIFFERENT "H-H"S

$\frac{V}{H_3}$ ———————————— C_3 ———————————— $H_3 \frac{V}{}$

$\frac{V}{H_2}$ ———————————— C_2 ———————————— $H_2 \frac{V}{}$

$\frac{V}{H_1}$ ———————————— C_1 ———————————— $H_1 \frac{V}{}$

ILLUSTRATION 2-10

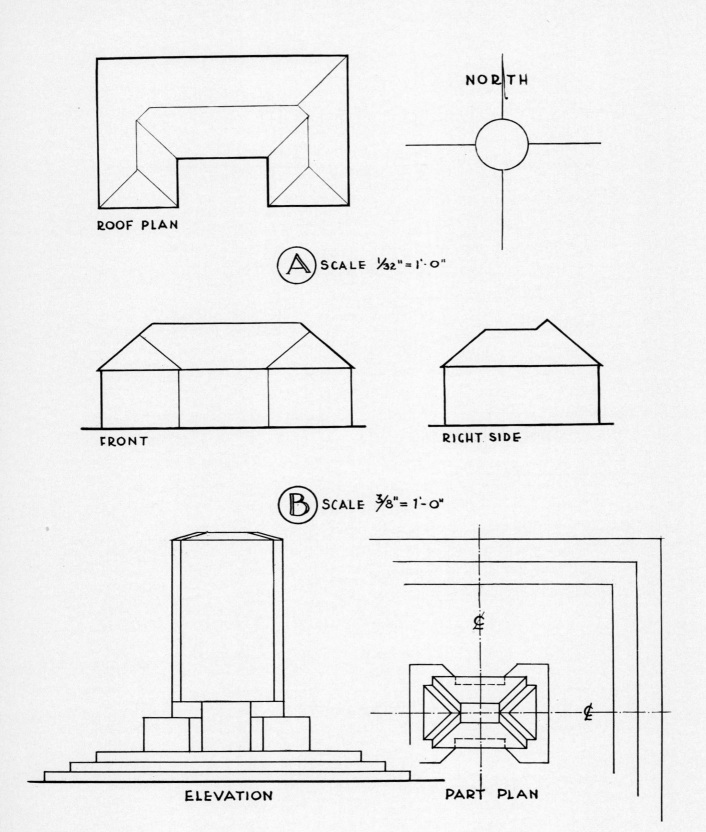

ROOF PLAN

NORTH

(A) SCALE ⅟₃₂" = 1'-0"

FRONT

RIGHT SIDE

(B) SCALE ⅜" = 1'-0"

ELEVATION

℄

℄

PART PLAN

ILLUSTRATION 2-11

33

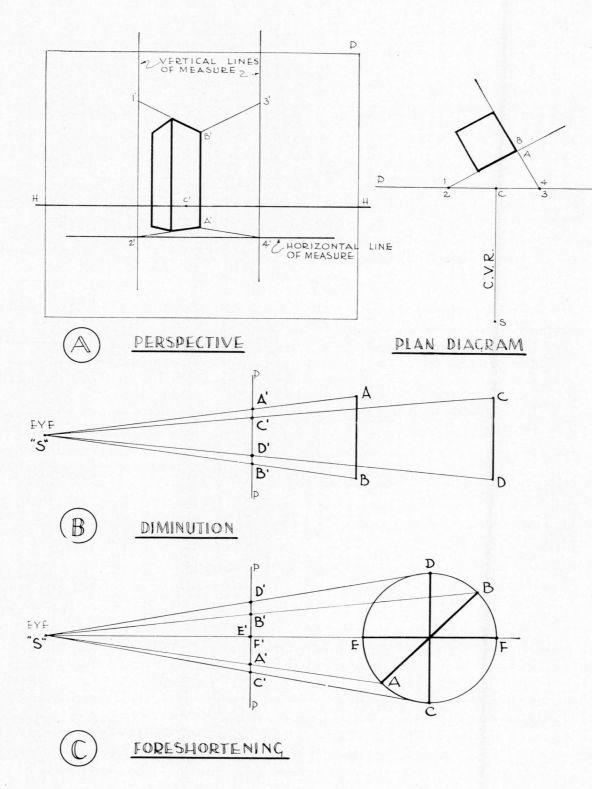

(A) PERSPECTIVE

PLAN DIAGRAM

(B) DIMINUTION

(C) FORESHORTENING

ILLUSTRATION 3-1

Chapter 3

FURTHER PERSPECTIVE PHENOMENA

1. THE PLAN DIAGRAM

Since we must first establish *S*, *C.V.R.*, *PP*, and *HH* before we can make a perspective drawing of any object, it is easiest to begin with an orthographic plan of the object to be represented, and on this diagram to locate our *S*, and our *C.V.R.* Before final location, they must be checked for the considerations discussed in Chap. 4, Sec. 1. This can be done quickly, but usually requires several trials before a satisfactory decision is made. Then *PP* is placed perpendicular to *C.V.R.* and usually through a vertical corner of the object.

2. LINES OF MEASURE

No part of the object (unless it lies wholly in the *PP*) will appear in its true (scaled) size, because we are using a converging projection which makes the apparent size of everything depend on the angle subtended at the eye. Hence, we cannot determine the apparent length of any line of the object by laying off its true scaled dimensions.

Only when the line happens to lie wholly in *PP* are perspective dimensions equal to true dimensions. For all other parts of the object (whether situated beyond *PP* or between *PP* and *S*), **we must make all our measurements on the picture plane,** and reduce (or increase) them to find the size, in perspective, of the part concerned. Such reference lines are called *lines of measure*. We use them especially for determining heights, and these are called *vertical lines of measure* (abbreviation *V.L.M.*). Horizontal lines of measure, however, are also commonly used. Lines of measure are merely lines lying in *PP*, and hence drawn at their true length in perspective.

Thus, in Illus. 3-1-A the length of A-B cannot be measured off in perspective directly. Its true height can only be laid off (in *PP*) as at 1'-2' or 3'-4', after 2' and 4' have been located laterally by measurement from *C'*, and 1' or 3' laid off by measuring the true length of *A-B* in relation to *HH*. (Since 2'-4' also lies in *PP*, its length is the same as that of 2-4 in the plan diagram.) Then, if we know the **direction** of lines 1'-B' and 3'-B' we can draw them and find *B'*. We shall see later how this is done.

3. DIMINUTION

In order to find the perspective length of any line except those lying in *PP*, we must understand the *law of diminution*. This governs the phenomena which we have all observed—that objects seem to grow smaller as they are moved farther away from us.

When a line originally in the picture plane is moved back (away from *S*) without being turned, it looks smaller as it recedes because our converging projection makes its length on *PP* depend on the angle subtended at the eye. Thus, of two equal lengths, the one nearer the eye will give the longer projection or apparent length, because it subtends a larger angle (see Illus. 3-1-B). A-B and C-D are actually equal in length, but their projections onto *PP* (*A'-B'* and *C'-D'*) are different. *A'-B'* is longer than *C'-D'* because *A-B* is nearer the eye and subtends a larger angle.

Once the reason for diminution is understood in relation to the other basic concepts of perspective, the whole problem of perspective representation boils down to the question of finding **how much** smaller a given dimension will appear due to its distance from the observer. Every perspective method that has ever been developed is an attempt to find the simplest solution for this problem. The law of diminution proves that lines behind the picture plane will be represented as shorter than their true length. The question is how to find the exact dimension to which they will be reduced. Since a straight line is located exactly when its two terminal points are known, the basic problem can be simplified further into that of finding specific points.

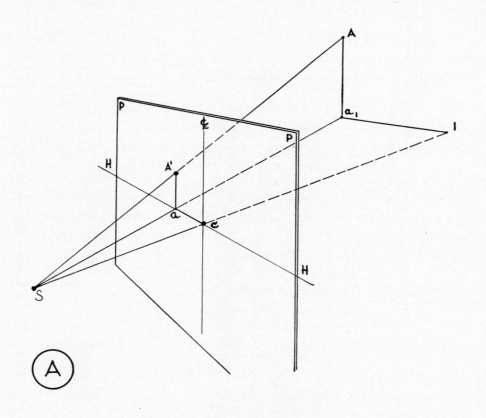

36

ILLUSTRATION 3-2

If we can evolve a method of finding the perspective image of **any** point, we can find any straight line by locating its terminal points. By lines we can bound planes, and by planes we can represent the surfaces of three-dimensional objects. The whole problem of linear perspective thus boils down to that of finding enough points.

4. FORESHORTENING

When a line originally parallel to the picture plane, and hence seen in a certain proportion of its true length, is revolved, it gradually looks smaller and smaller until it assumes the position of pointing directly toward the eye; then it seems to become a point and to have no length at all. This is called *foreshortening* (Illus. 3-1-C).

Both diminution and foreshortening affect the perspective appearance of lines at an angle to PP, making each one a special case requiring a separate solution by locating its end points, but the basic problem of finding such points (or any other points) remains the same. We need not bother with innumerable particular cases if we grasp this fundamental fact.

The perspective image, A', of any point A, whose position in space is known, may be calculated from its vertical and horizontal relation to C and HH. In Illus. 3-2-A, we are given S, C, PP, and point A. In order to find A', project A vertically onto the horizontal plane through S-C (at a_1), and draw through a_1 parallel to HH, to find 1 on S-C prolonged.

Draw the visual rays from A and a_1 to S, piercing PP at A' and a respectively. Then triangles S-C-a and S-1-a_1 are similar (parallel and common sides). So $\dfrac{C\text{-}a}{1\text{-}a_1} = \dfrac{S\text{-}C}{S\text{-}1}$ or $C\text{-}a = 1\text{-}a_1 \dfrac{S\text{-}C}{S\text{-}1}$

Since the location of point A is stated, its distance 1–a_1 to the left of C and its distance C-1 behind PP are known, and so is S-C. Hence, since S-1 = S-C plus C-1, C-a can be calculated by substituting in the above equation. In like manner a-A' can be found from the similarity of triangles S-a-A' and S-a_1-A. So, having located a in the perspective by horizontal measurement from C, A' may be determined by laying off a-A' along a vertical from a.

Thus the perspective of any point can be found by laying off its calculated distances, vertical and horizontal, from C, but in practice such a procedure would be exceedingly tedious and open to error unless the computations were made mechanically (see Chap. 9, Sec. 7). Hence this construction is rarely employed except by the painter who is drawing from nature and uses a quick approximation of the method. He holds his pencil at the same distance from his eye as his canvas (usually arm's length), measures the apparent distance of a point right or left and up or down from the center of his scene in terms of the pencil, and marks off the same length on his picture from its center. His pencil thus becomes a means of finding rapidly the distances C-a and a-A' and gives him graphically points whose perspective position he would find it boring to calculate (even if he knew how).

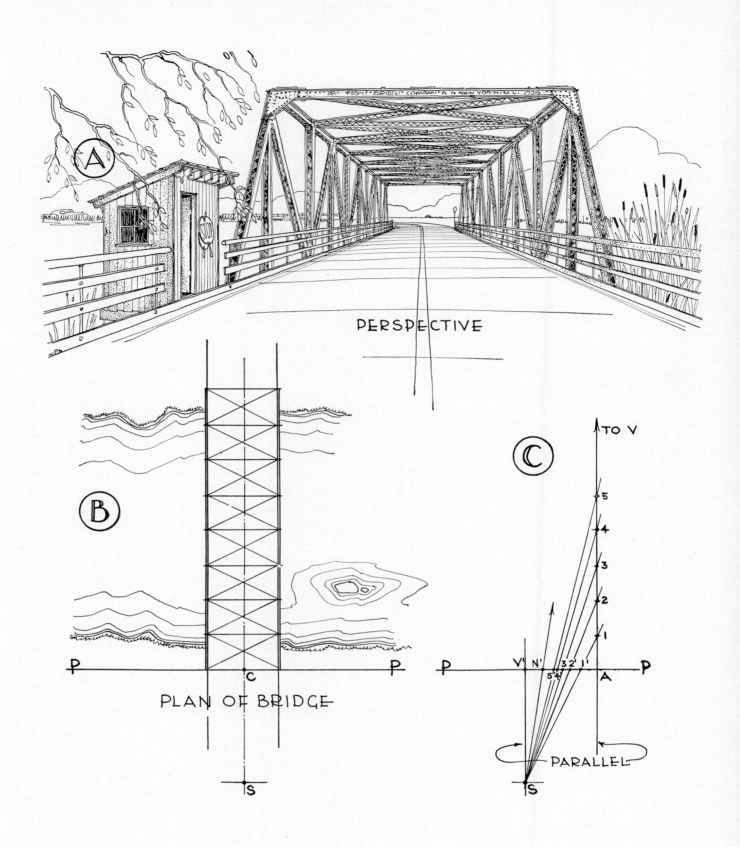

A

PERSPECTIVE

B

PLAN OF BRIDGE

C

TO V

5
4
3
2
1

P V' N' 3'2' 1' A P
5'4'

PARALLEL

S

ILLUSTRATION 3-3

5. VANISHING POINTS

Since parallel lines are by definition always the same distance apart, then if the lines are prolonged away from us, this fixed equal distance must, in perspective, constantly seem to us to become smaller because of diminution. Such lines will therefore appear to converge as they are continued farther away from us through space. At an infinite distance they will seem to meet. Nearly everyone has verified this phenomenon in his own experience by looking down a straight railroad track and noticing how the rails seem to converge as they get farther away from us (Illus. 2-5). Yet we know that they remain always the same distance apart. The perspective (made from a photograph) of a bridge (Illus. 3-3-A) illustrates very clearly this apparent convergence of actually parallel lines.

In perspective this point of apparent meeting is called the *vanishing point* (symbol V) of the series, and like any other point, can be represented on our picture plane. However, since it is mathematically at infinity, a vanishing point should never be used as part of the final picture. The eye can only see a short distance under the most favorable conditions and never more than a few miles. We need vanishing points to control and simplify the **construction** of a perspective, but in our finished picture we must never draw lines all the way to them, if we want our drawings to duplicate what the eye sees.

Since one line of any series of parallels (infinite in number) can be assumed to pass through the eye, this line will be seen as a single point; and since all the lines of the series must tend to converge to a common vanishing point, the line which has only one point must have as that point the vanishing point of the rest of the series. Hence, **to find the V of *any* series of parallel lines, draw the one of the series which passes through the eye. Where this line pierces the picture plane is the V of the series.**

Thus, in Illus. 3-3-B the plan shows that the vanishing point of the receding side rails, the longitudinal struts connecting the trusses, etc., must be at C, because the parallel to these lines, drawn through S, strikes PP at C.

This theorem is basic to most linear perspective drawing. Another way of demonstrating it is given in Illus. 3-3-C. This shows a plan view of the observer, the PP, and the given line A-V (extended to infinite length away from PP). If we lay off on A-V equal distances 1, 2, 3, 4, 5, etc., and join them to S by visual rays, these subdivisions will appear in perspective at $1'$, $2'$, $3'$, $4'$, etc. Each such successive point, all the way to the one drawn to V at infinity, will appear nearer to V' until we finally reach it. Since V' will then represent V, which is at infinity, the lines S-V' and A-V can meet only at infinity and are therefore parallel in geometry. Hence the perspective of point V, which represents the ultimate extension of A-1-2-3, etc., to infinity, could have been found by drawing a parallel to A-V, through S, to intersect PP at V'.

Obviously, if the lines of the given series are horizontal, a parallel to them through S must strike PP at the level of S—i.e., somewhere on HH (see Sec. 8 below). Any other series will require a special construction to find where the parallel through S strikes PP. However this problem is never difficult of solution graphically.

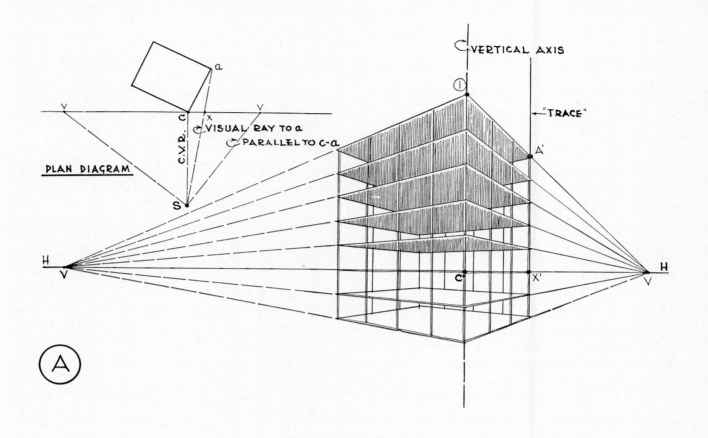

PLAN DIAGRAM

VERTICAL AXIS

"TRACE"

VISUAL RAY TO a

PARALLEL TO C-a

C.V.P.

(A)

(B)

ILLUSTRATION 3-4

8. V'S OF HORIZONTAL LINES

The horizon is graphically the trace on the picture plane of a horizontal plane passing through the eye. Therefore, **the vanishing points of all horizontal lines lie on the horizon,** because all horizontal lines lie in horizontal planes, and all horizontal planes must vanish on the horizon.

We can now complete the process of finding the V of a series of horizontal lines whose location in space is fully fixed by their orthographic projections. We begin with the following plan: After determining S, $C.V.R.$, and PP, draw a parallel to the series through S; and prolong it to intersect PP at V. Then in the perspective drawing, we decide on C', draw HH through it, and locate the required V on HH, the same distance from C' as V is from C, the plan of C' (see Illus. 3-5-A).

If we wish to put the given horizontal into perspective, we can use the system suggested in Sec. 6, because we have now learned how to find V. Prolong the plan of the given line to intersect PP at x. Lay off C'-X' equal to C-x. On a vertical through X', locate X from its known height above HH (2 units). The line X'-V now represents in perspective the entire extent of our given line, from the picture plane to infinity.

Of course only the portion of the line that lies within the cone of correct vision will be used as part of any perspective picture. The rest would be too far away from (or too near to) the observer to be visible by the human eye —either because of extending too far to either side, as in this case, or because of exceeding the permissible depth of field, if V happened to lie within the limits of the cone of correct vision.

Since the vanishing points of **all** actually horizontal lines must lie on HH, it follows that those lines lying **above the eye** in reality, must be represented in perspective as sloping **down,** and those **below** the eye level as sloping **up.** It is even possible for lines which actually slope up to appear in perspective as lines sloping down, and vice versa, particularly if they lie well above (or below) the eye.

9. V'S OF OTHER LINES

Since V's are found by drawing from S to PP, parallel to the series concerned, there will be no V if the parallel through S does not intersect PP. Any such series of lines will be represented in perspective as parallel rather than converging. For this reason **lines parallel to PP in reality do not vanish in perspective.**

The most common case of this phenomenon is that of vertical lines. Since PP is ordinarily assumed to be vertical, they are parallel to it. Hence, unless PP is inclined, **vertical lines do not vanish in perspective** but are drawn vertical (and hence parallel).

Since the horizon of any series of planes is found by passing through the eye a plane parallel to those in the series and thus finding a trace on PP, which is the horizon desired, the horizon of vertical planes is a vertical line (as long as PP is vertical).

Since a line and its plan, by definition, together determine a vertical plane, the horizon of this plane will be a vertical line. This horizon must contain the vanishing point of the line (since it contains the trace on PP of a plane parallel to the line, and passing through the eye), and hence **the V of every line must be on a vertical line through the V of its plan.**

The commonest example of this is the raking line of a gable, which must vanish on the vertical through the V of the horizontals of the gable wall (Illus. 3-5-B). The method of determining such V's quickly and exactly is given as Proposition VII, Chap. 10. For proof of the construction required see Chap. 6, Sec. 1.

A

Redrawn from "The School of Athens" by Raphael.

B

ILLUSTRATION 3-6

10. DISTORTION

As long as we confine our use of the graphic processes just described to delineate objects within a reasonable cone of correct vision, the results will be accepted readily by those who see them as an understandable representation of three-dimensional objects in space. If we forget that our process is not merely geometrical, but must be limited also by the physical function of the human eye, it is all too easy to produce "distortions." These are not so much the fault of our theory as of our failing to be bound by its postulated limitations.

Linear perspective, by definition, can produce results which will be entirely acceptable **only** to a person who places his eye at the position assumed for S in the drawing. Everyone else sees the picture itself in perspective and hence somewhat foreshortened, except for objects in the exact center. In addition we move our eyes (and often also turn our heads) whenever we look at a drawing more than a few inches in diameter. When we are confronted with large pictures, like murals, we even move about, and thus assume several different S's. Knowing that the public will thus, if possible, insist on violating the basic conditions of linear perspective, the artist must not attempt to apply a rigid perspective projection unless he can be sure in advance of the position from which his picture will be viewed (a very rare situation).

Special care must be taken with objects that are situated far from the axis of the cone of correct vision. The size of the latter must be severely cut down when certain types of geometrical forms are to be represented toward its edges. Circles, cylinders, and spheres particularly must be watched. Few people realize that a ball actually looks slightly ellipsoidal except when we are looking directly at it. Yet such is the case. The balls at the side of Illus. 3-6-B seem "distorted" until we hold the paper so that our eye is at the point chosen for S. Then all looks right again because the eye sees the spheroids projected onto the retina as true spheres.

Since the draftsman knows that he cannot thus control most observers, he is forced to avoid the issue. Either he must choose a new S far enough away to get his required subject within so small a cone that the change of shape will be negligible, or he must knowingly abandon strict observance of perspective rules, and correct his drawing so that it will accord with the visual experience of the observer.

The latter process really consists of breaking up the perspective into a multiple series of slightly different views drawn so as to merge into one another. Each part is shown as though the eye were looking directly at it, making a new C for each—without changing S but as though rotating $C.V.R.$ to point toward various important parts of the object in succession. Thus all spheres are represented by circles, just as we expect to see them, and all circles will seem to lie in their proper planes. Human figures (which can be abstracted into cylinders supporting spheres) will also thus avoid the apparently "wrong" distortion which would result if they were represented accurately just as they would appear from a single S.

Examination of a large painting such as Raphael's "School of Athens" will show how this problem was handled by the old masters. The figures at the right side carry spheres represented by true geometrical circles (not projected as ellipsoids) and are drawn almost as though seen from in front. Since the size of the painting precludes anyone from taking it all in at one glance, such a treatment agrees with the action of the observer, who turns his eyes (or even moves to a new position) as he looks at each part of the composition in turn. When he is looking at any single portion particularly, his eye is fixed directly on it and he finds the figures before him treated accordingly. Of course great skill is required to blend all these views into one another so that the whole picture seems consistent in perspective. Fortunately our visual memories are not so exact that this cannot be done, but obvious clashes between whole and parts must be avoided.

Such disagreements are most apt to occur if free forms are allowed to contrast with geometrical shapes whose perspective is clearly shown by lines or details. Thus if a checkerboard floor is fully drawn without interruption, all figures standing on it in a row will have to place their feet in accord with its vanishing lines, and thus cannot be "frontalized" as recommended above. Such conflicts can only be avoided by changes in composition. The perspective difficulty cannot be corrected.

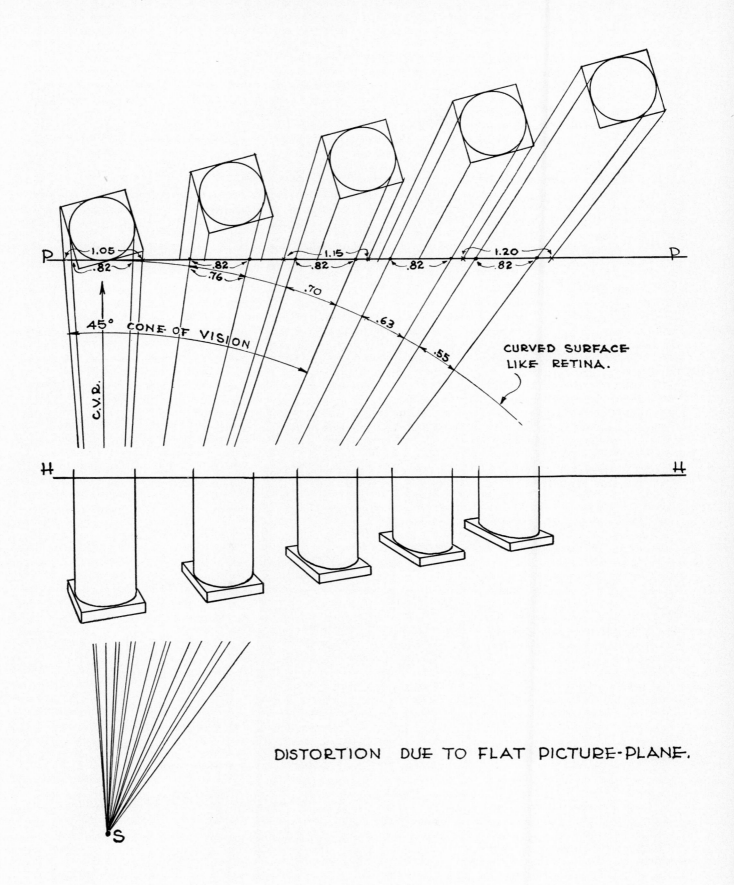

P   1.05   1.15   1.20   P

.82   .82   .82   .82   .82

.76

45° CONE OF VISION   .70

C.V.R.

.63

.55

CURVED SURFACE
LIKE RETINA.

H   H

•S

DISTORTION DUE TO FLAT PICTURE-PLANE.

ILLUSTRATION 3-7

An even more serious difficulty arises when repeated objects (colonnades, etc.) are continued too far across a large cone of vision, particularly if they are parallel to the picture plane or nearly so (Illus. 3-7). The law of diminution requires the most distant column to appear the smallest, but the angle of projection makes it intersect an equal portion of the picture plane. The square bases even **increase** in over-all perspective dimension as they recede. That of the third column makes a noticeably larger intersection with PP than does the first, although it is inside a 45° cone of vision. If the front edges of the bases were placed so as to be in a flat PP, all would project as identical lengths, no matter how far away they were.

In actual vision, the perspective image on the curved surface of the retina depends on the angle at S between the limiting rays, and always gives a smaller perspective for the more distant object, as is shown in the figure. It is our assumption of a flat picture plane that has caused the trouble here. The foreshortening of the nearer objects adds to the confusion by making the left sides of the bases more visible as the columns are farther away.

Should we correct this apparent conflict between our rules? Many older texts[1] so advised. A better solution would be to change S so as to include the colonnade within a smaller cone of vision, or place it at a sharper angle to PP. Then the discrepancy would not be so evident, and could be adjusted.

QUESTIONS

1. Which points in a perspective drawing can be found by measurement? Explain why and how.
2. Explain the laws of diminution and of foreshortening.
3. What is a vanishing point? Why is it important?
4. Which series of parallel lines do not vanish? Why?
5. What is the horizon of a series of planes? How is it found?
6. Why must all horizontal lines have their V's on HH?
7. How does the V of any line relate to the V of its plan? Why?
8. How is the perspective of a horizontal line found?
9. What causes "distortion" in a perspective?
10. How is the perspective of any given point found? Illustrate.

PROBLEMS

1. Find the V's of the following series of horizontal lines of unlimited length beyond PP:
    a. 30° to PP (either slope).   b. 45° to PP (either slope).   c. 90° to PP.
2. Find the perspective images of the following horizontal lines of unlimited length beyond PP:
    a. 60° to PP and 4 units above HH. b. 45° to PP and 3 units below HH. c. 90° to PP and 5 units above HH.
3. Find the perspective images of the following points:
    a. 3 units right of C, 4 units behind PP, 5 units above HH. b. 3 units left, 5 units behind PP, 4 units below HH.
    c. 5 units right, 5 units behind PP, at same level as HH.
4. At the scale of ⅛ in. = 1 ft., draw the top and front views of a cube measuring 12'-0" on each side and surmounted by a regular pyramid whose apex is 6'-0" above the top of the cube. Choose S about 10'-0" away from one corner so that the sides make angles of 30° and 60° with PP in plan, when $C.V.R.$ is directed at that corner and PP passes through it. Make perspectives (assuming object standing on level ground) with (1) horizon at normal height, (2) horizon level with bottom of cube, (3) horizon level with apex.
5. A painter is standing 30 ft. from the water's edge looking out to sea over a flat sand beach. Ten feet to the left of his central line of vision a single gull is flying 20 ft. above the waves and 28 ft. from the shore. A little to the right of C, a steamer is nearly "hull-down." Make a plan diagram and a perspective of this scene, locating the gull accurately (as a point) and showing the shore line, and the true horizon (dotted). Estimate the apparent HH and the steamer, and draw them, adding a palm near the hightide mark (if you wish).

[1] For an example see Ware, William Robert, "Modern Perspective," pp. 256–257, The Macmillan Company, New York, 1914.

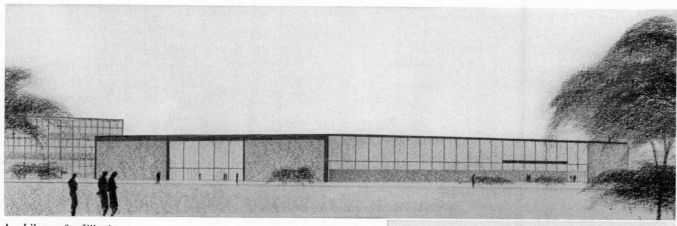

A—Library for Illinois
    Institute of Technology.

ARCHITECTURAL STUDIES
BY MIES VAN DER ROHE.

B
Promontory
Apartments,
Chicago.
Steel and glass
version.

C—Chemical Engineering Building
    for Illinois Institute of Technology.

Chapter 4

THE OFFICE METHOD

THIS METHOD of making a perspective is simple to understand, gives excellent graphic intersections which help to make drafting accurate, and is easy to check. Because of these advantages, the beginner should master it before undertaking more difficult constructions, although there are many situations where it is not the most effective procedure.

Its disadvantages are that it requires large drafting tables, long T squares, big-scale orthographic drawings, and careful draftsmanship to avoid soiling the final picture with construction lines. In rendered drawings it makes the casting of shadows difficult.

The procedure in making a perspective by the *office method* is listed step by step later in this chapter (page 63). For the beginner, the order of the steps is important, and should be followed rigidly in order to avoid confusion. Later, several steps may be combined for convenience. Be sure, however, that you understand the reason for each step. In order to represent an object in perspective (no matter what method we intend to use), we must first know definitely what the object is. This is often fixed by drawing plans and elevations in orthographic projection, where most dimensions can be scaled to their true proportional size. **It is impossible to make an accurate perspective of an indefinite object.**

This seems obvious, yet most difficulties in perspective are due to the fact that the draftsman has not decided exactly what it is that he is trying to draw. An eighteenth-century cook book began its instructions for making rabbit pie by advising, "First catch a rabbit." Let us follow this excellent precept and be sure that we know where any desired point actually is before we try to put it into perspective. Until we have a definite "rabbit," we cannot make a picture of it. Remember that three coordinates are required to fix a point in space. A plan tells us only two of them. In addition, heights must be noted, or shown by an elevation.

1. CHOOSE S

Having complete data about our object, we must next set up our perspective apparatus. This is most easily done by reference to the orthographic plan, where we can imagine ourselves to be moving about seeking the best location for S and C.V.R., much as a photographer would try to find the best place from which to take a photograph. Having made our decision, we test it by blocking in the main masses of our object, and adjust, if necessary. The selection of the **very best** place for S can be made in advance only by the expert, but we can be sure of good results by following certain simple rules.

So far, in discussing the choice of S, we have considered only the basic limitations (cone of correct vision and depth of field). Experience will show that more specific directions can be developed to help us in making a wise decision. The following suggestions are intended for that purpose. They are not rules in any specific sense, but rather hints to help the beginner to work in the right direction. Like all attempts to make fixed precepts for art, they tend to produce an unexciting, middle-of-the-road type of result. Sometimes a more dramatic and exciting effect can be produced by flouting them completely, but at the outset, it is well to consider the following:

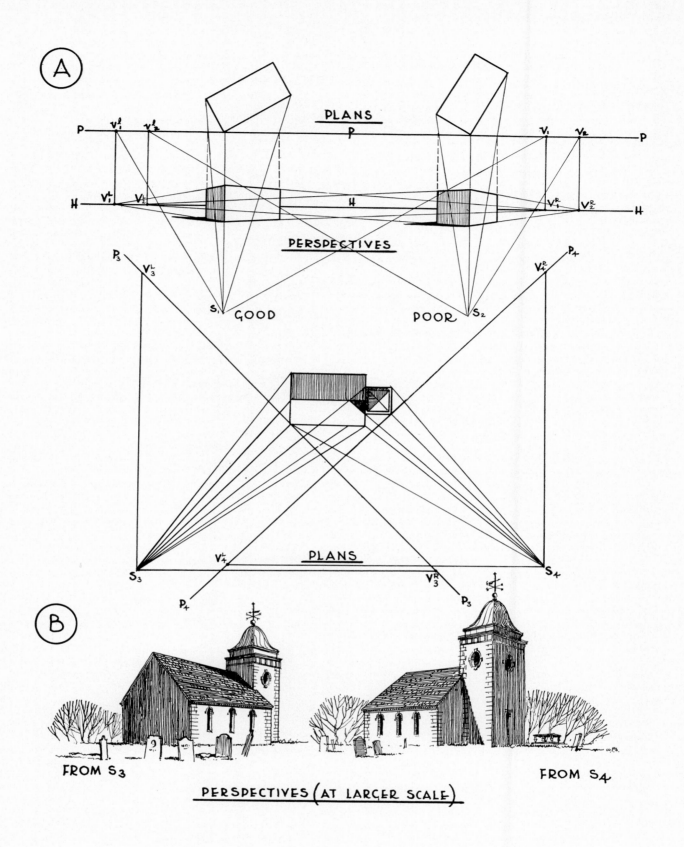

PLANS

P — V_1^ℓ V_2^ℓ — P — P — V_1 V_2 — P

H — V_1^L V_2^L — H — V_1^R V_2^R — H

PERSPECTIVES

P_3 V_3^L V_4^R P_4

S_1 GOOD POOR S_2

S_3 V_4^L PLANS V_3^R S_4

P_4 P_3

FROM S_3 FROM S_4

PERSPECTIVES (AT LARGER SCALE)

Emphasize the basic proportions of the object. If it is a rectangle, turn the long side at a flat angle to PP, and the short side will consequently be at an acute angle, and hence more foreshortened. The perspective will thus immediately convey the idea of an object with one long and one short side. The opposite arrangement is apt to confuse a spectator who has never seen the drawing before. Worst of all is the choice of a setup which makes really unequal sides so foreshortened as to appear equal (Illus. 4-2-A).

Note that in this figure the perspectives have been placed on top of the plans. This is a common method of "saving paper," and permits transferring working points from plan to perspective by short (hence quick and accurate) projections, rather than by measurement. As is emphasized again in Sec. 2 of this chapter, the perspective drawing may be made **wherever convenient,** and does not have to be placed in **any** special relation to the plan on which it is based. Illustration 4-2-B illustrates this freedom of placing to fit drafting conditions. The perspectives are placed side by side for comparison. Each has a different relation to its plan layout.

Proper emphasis also results if we choose S near the big things so that they will look largest through having the least diminution, *e.g.*, a church tower is usually more effective in the foreground (Illus. 4-2-B).

Stand as near as possible. One would instinctively stand as near as possible to a real object because we naturally want to see as clearly as possible and yet grasp the whole subject at a glance. Telescopic effects are hard to make self-explanatory and difficult to handle graphically.

It has been explained already that one should not place S so close as to require proportionately too great a depth of field in order to show the whole object. Since the inexperienced draftsman is apt to err on the side of putting S **too** near, in order to make the construction easier and "keep the V's on the paper," the advice given here is often phrased conversely—"stand as far away as possible"—meaning "as far as will still permit easy drawing." It seems, however, more logical to think of **what** we are drawing, and to place S accordingly, rather than to base our choice on our own technical convenience.

Since the V's will move farther away from C as the distance from C to S is increased, it is usually desirable to keep them well apart. This will insure a large cone of correct vision and an undistorted perspective. The width of the picture should rarely exceed one-third of the distance between V's, as long as the main faces of the object are at right angles to each other as in most buildings.

Check the size of your picture. This can be done very quickly by drawing the limiting visual rays in plan and then noting how much of the picture plane is included between them (refer back to Illus. 2-4-A). Moving S a little may change the width of the perspective considerably and thus produce more nearly the desired result. It may also serve to avoid the technical difficulty of having the V's fall off the board.

Beginners are usually disappointed at the small perspectives that come out of their setups. It obviously saves time to find this out in advance before a lot of work has been done to little purpose. Move PP back to get a larger perspective, or vice versa.

In Illus. 4-3-A it is assumed that the desired effect is to have a picture width equal to 1-2, with $C.V.R.$ directed at the nearest corner of the building. PP must be perpendicular to $C.V.R.$ and the limiting rays must pass through the outside limits of the object, and through points 1 and 2, before meeting at S.

If a pair of perpendiculars representing $C.V.R.$ and PP are drawn on tracing paper, and the desired width marked, a few trials will soon locate S so as to meet the imposed conditions. So we put our tracing paper over the plan of the object, with C on the front corner, and revolve it until the limiting rays are seen to converge on $C.V.R.$ A triangle laid to draw these rays will show quickly how accurate our assumption has been. Further adjustment will easily make our guess into an exact decision. In some cases it may be necessary to move PP (always keeping $C.V.R.$ through C).

Consider the proportions of your picture. Often it is desired to have the picture show a predetermined relation between the sides of a building. This may have been fixed by a thumbnail sketch which gave the desired effect. The approved proportion can be maintained by locating S so as to secure the same result.

Having decided on the proper cone of vision (say 30°), locate by trial a position of S where the limiting rays will cut the desired proportion on a line (PP) perpendicular to the axis of the cone ($C.V.R.$). Any parallel to this line may be used as a picture plane, depending on the size of the picture desired. In trying locations of S under these conditions, a transparent triangle with a line drawn across it perpendicular to its axis, and marked at X in the chosen proportion, will be very helpful. By looking along its edges and the line S-X (which must go through the point which divides the sides of the object into the approved proportions) the desired location will soon be found (Illus. 4-3-B).

To sum up the criteria for choosing the location of S, test a proposed decision to be sure that:

1. Object is within cone of correct vision. Outdoors this may be as large as 30° to 45° for buildings—but always make it as small as possible.

2. $C.V.R.$ is directed at center of interest of object. Normally this is the nearest corner of a large salient object, such as a building. Feature the best and most interesting part of your object.

3. Angle of object to picture plane makes big things look big (remember that PP **must** be perpendicular to $C.V.R$).

4. No important parts of the object are obscured by the projection of other parts, and no important corners "lined up."

5. Depth of field of reentrant objects is not more than one-third the distance from S to C. The less, the better, especially for interiors.

6. Given conditions of site (orientation, existing buildings, etc.) are respected. **Stay inside room** for interiors.

7. HH is taken about two feet above the ground level for exteriors, thus suggesting that the ground slopes gently away from the building—a normal condition. If bird's-eye or worm's-eye effects are desired, move HH well above or below (20 ft. or more) and check whether upper parts of object are in cone of vision.

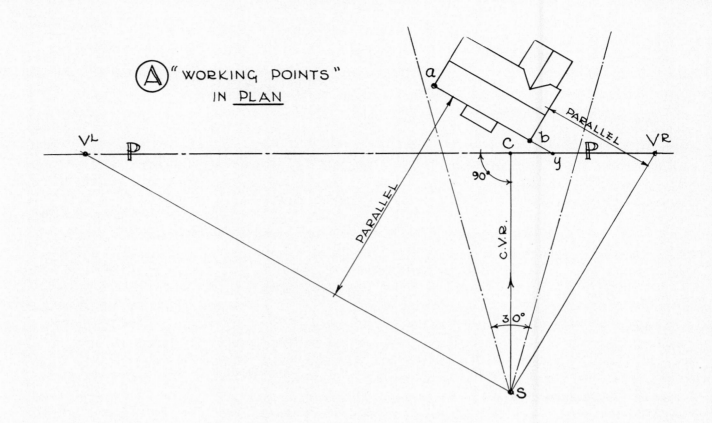

"WORKING POINTS" IN PLAN

LAYING-OUT A PERSPECTIVE

B TRANSFER "WORKING-POINTS" TO PERSPECTIVE

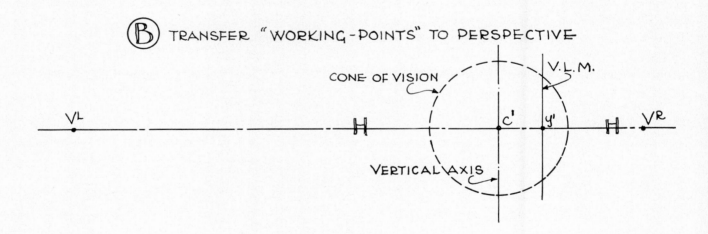

ILLUSTRATION 4-4

2. FIND WORKING POINTS IN PLAN

Taking as our problem the small house shown in plan in Illus. 4-4-A, locate S and $C.V.R.$ and draw PP perpendicular to $C.V.R.$ Mark C and draw parallels through S to the principal lines of the object. This gives us the plans of the V's that we are likely to need and establishes our *working points* for the perspective.

Note that there is no fixed number of V's. Their number depends upon the object. There are as many V's as the object has sets of parallel lines. The vertical walls of buildings are usually at right angles to each other and this relationship establishes two main systems of horizontals in most architectural perspectives. Their V's are called V^R (right-hand V) and V^L (left-hand V), but this notation is merely a convenience for handling a common situation involving two vanishing points. It must not be considered a special type of perspective problem having its own special rules. A triangular prism, for example, would have three V's, and an octagonal tower might require four.

3. LAY OFF WORKING POINTS ON THE PERSPECTIVE

Only now are we ready to start our perspective drawing, and again let us be careful to avoid a common misconception. It is often convenient to draw the perspective directly below the orthographic plan and thus to be able to project points from PP onto HH, rather than having to measure them. But this may require a very large drafting board, and the plan must be on a loose sheet which can be turned at an angle. Neither may be available. So at first we had better place our perspective to one side of the plan, rather than below it—or put it on another board. This is almost as easy and will help us to keep our construction accurate by avoiding the mental misconception that a perspective **must** be projected from plans pinned down above them at an angle. Such a mistaken idea has confused many beginners.

Having decided where we want to draw our perspective (perhaps on a different table from the plan), we locate HH and C' so that our picture will come out where we want it to on the sheet. From C' we can measure off the location of the V's by making C'-V^R on HH, equal to C-V^R on PP (in plan). Other points on HH, such as V^L and y' are similarly located (Illus. 4-4-B).

If PP cuts the object, this point will locate a $V.L.M.$, or a convenient $V.L.M.$ may be found by prolonging one of the main lines of the object to PP in plan and measuring off this point (y' on HH), as we did for the V's.

Again we must be on guard against a common error. The object does not have to be situated so that one corner of it coincides with C in plan. This is often not desirable with salient objects, and almost never so with reentrant ones. The rule is to **start the perspective with a point in the** PP, so as to be able to draw to a known V a horizontal which will pass through the point whose perspective we wish to find. If the choice of PP does not place a real line of the object so that it intersects PP, we must imagine some line to be extended until it does.

At last we can start to determine our "picture," but time is well expended in making wise preliminary decisions and locating accurately the working points which result from our choices. Everything depends on them. A mistake in their selection or location may cause all our later work to be wasted. Stop now, and check them carefully.

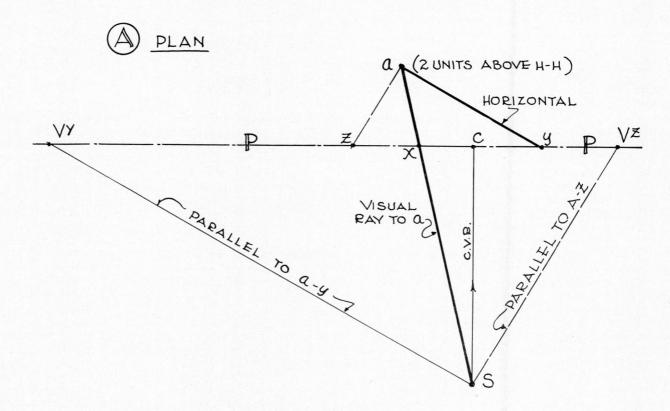

a (2 UNITS ABOVE H-H)

HORIZONTAL

VY — P — z — X — c — y — P — VZ

PARALLEL TO a-y

VISUAL RAY TO a

C.V.B.

PARALLEL TO A-Z

S

PERSPECTIVE OF ANY POINT – A.

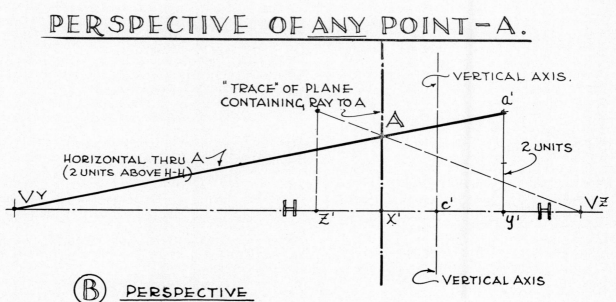

VERTICAL AXIS.

"TRACE" OF PLANE CONTAINING RAY TO A

A

a'

2 UNITS

HORIZONTAL THRU A
(2 UNITS ABOVE H-H)

VY — H — z' — X' — c' — y' — H — VZ

VERTICAL AXIS

Ⓑ PERSPECTIVE

4. DRAW VISUAL RAYS

In Chap. 3 we learned that the office method has as its basic theory the finding of any point in perspective as the intersection of its visual ray and a horizontal through it. This is usually quicker than finding two horizontals and gives a better intersection to establish the point exactly.

It is not even necessary to find the complete perspective of the visual ray, which is nearly always a sloping line and hence would involve graphical difficulties. All that is required is the trace on PP of the vertical plane determined by the plan of the ray.

In the orthographic plan (Illus. 4-5-A), we have merely to draw from S to a (the point to be found), and mark the intersection of S-a and PP, point x. In the perspective drawing, x' can be laid off on HH by its relation to C. A vertical through x' will be the trace on PP of a vertical plane containing the visual ray S-A. This trace will therefore contain A', the perspective image of A (Illus. 4-5-B).

5. FIND DEFINITE POINTS

Having made sure that our layout is correct, let us start our perspective drawing by finding the perspective of one definite point. If we can do this successfully, we can solve any problem by repeating the process often enough. Of course, we shall not be able to see one point as a "picture," unless we imagine our subject to be small enough to count only as a point (such as a single sea gull flying over a calm, empty ocean). But if we grasp clearly the process involved, we shall be able to proceed confidently to build up, step by step, perspectives of more interesting objects.

In Illus. 4-5-A we are given the plan position (a) of our gull or single point A, and its true height above the horizon (2 units). We find its perspective by drawing the visual ray to A in plan, and then transferring to perspective at x' on HH the point x in which the ray cuts PP. A vertical through x' gives the **trace** on which A', the perspective of A, must lie.

Next choose any horizontal line through A, draw its plan and mark the point y in which it pierces PP. Find its V by drawing a parallel to it through S and lay off V^y in perspective on HH (Illus. 4-5-B). At y' on HH, measure the true height (above or below HH) to find a'. The line a'-V^y is the perspective of the chosen horizontal extended from PP to infinity, and its intersection with the trace gives us the desired perspective A'. A similar procedure using any other horizontal through A will of course give the same result (as at z).

Complete procedure under the office method is summarized on page 63. Refer to this, and check the construction of Illus. 4-5 with your solution of Prob. 5, Chap. 3.

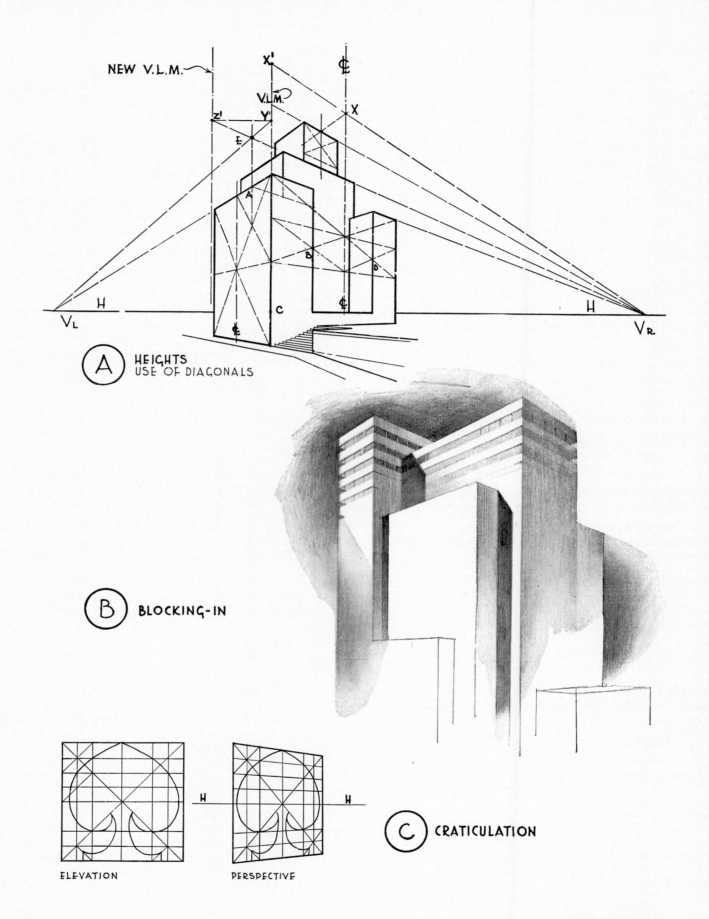

NEW V.L.M.

X'

℄

V.L.M.

X

Z'
Y'

E

A

B

D

H

C

℄

℄

H

V_L

V_R

(A) HEIGHTS
USE OF DIAGONALS

(B) BLOCKING-IN

(C) CRATICULATION

ELEVATION   H   H   PERSPECTIVE

58   ILLUSTRATION 4-6

6. HEIGHTS

Note that while the traces of the visual rays locate immediately the distance of any point to right or left of C', its perspective height above HH must be found by intersecting the traces with a horizontal line (real or assumed) which passes through the point. This horizontal is determined by joining its V with the point on its $V.L.M.$ in which it intersects PP.

Thus the height of the central tower in Illus. 4-6-A was laid off at X' on the $V.L.M.$ through the nearest corner (lying in PP), and a line was drawn to V^R to intersect the center line of the right side of the building (found by the diagonals) at X. The line from X to V^L is the perspective of a horizontal line which will pass through the top center point of the tower.

Similarly the true height of the central block is laid off at y'. The line from y' to V^L represents a horizontal which intersects at E the vertical through A on the left side, at the level of the top of the central mass. The upper edge of the latter can now be found by drawing from E to V^R. Of course the same result could have been obtained by finding a new $V.L.M.$ in plan for the upper edge and laying off its true height on this directly as at Z'.

7. DIAGONALS

Particular attention should be paid to the use of diagonals to determine the perspective center of a rectangle. This is a very quick and simple device and a great timesaver. Thus, in Illus. 4-6-A, if it is known that the central block is set back one-quarter of the depth of the left side, the diagonals drawn on this side (once its over-all dimensions have been worked out from plan) will fix the amount of the setback in perspective, point A, without referring again to the plan. Similar subdivision of the right façade will determine the location in perspective of the wings if their edges come at the "quarter-points" B and D. Note that the diagonals divide the façades not only vertically but horizontally.

8. BLOCKING–IN

By the use of short cuts such as diagonals, an experienced draftsman can reduce to surprisingly few the points which have to be worked out in full. He obtains at once both speed and accuracy. Usually he boxes in all irregular shapes by fitting around them the nearest equivalent geometric solid—cube, sphere, prism, pyramid, etc. These "envelopes" are easily put into perspective, and the irregular form can then be "carved out" of its envelope. Such "cubistic" generalization is very helpful in many problems (Illus. 4-6-B).

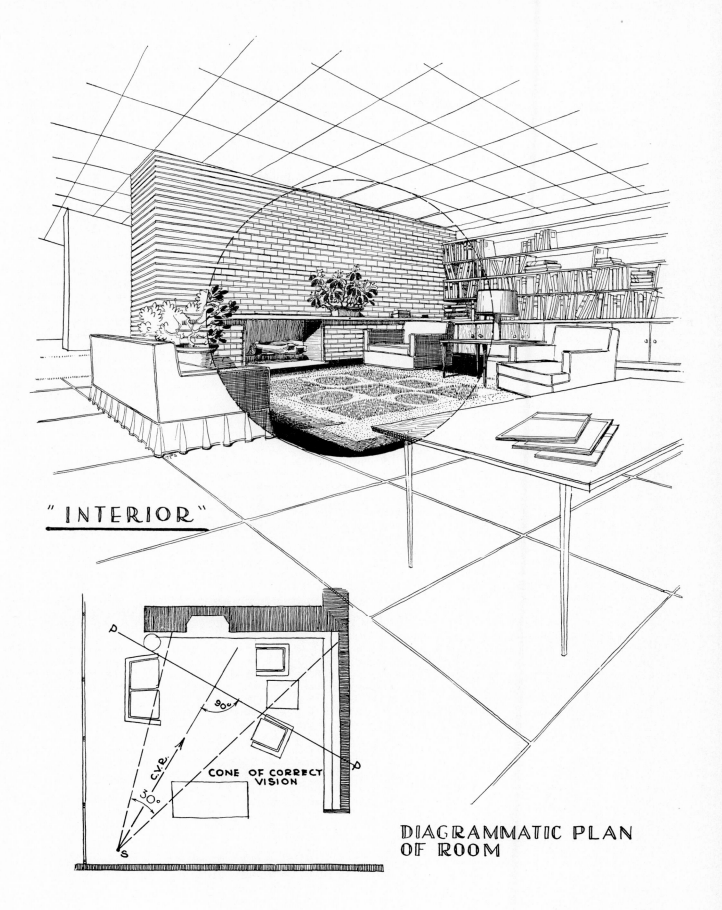

"INTERIOR"

90°

c.v.e.

30°

s

CONE OF CORRECT VISION

P

P

DIAGRAMMATIC PLAN
OF ROOM

ILLUSTRATION 4-7

Curves lying on plane surfaces (arches in a wall, carving on architraves, etc.) may be similarly approximated by reference to rectangular subdivisions (usually squares) superimposed on the surface in plan or elevation, and then used in perspective as a reference network. This process is also useful in enlarging a drawing, and has been given the name of *craticulation* (Illus. 4-6-C). Diagonals may be used to simplify the task of putting the subdivisions into perspective. It is rarely worth while to memorize special constructions for separate shapes, although some very ingenious graphical methods have been worked out for finding the perspective of circles and other geometric forms (see Chap. 6, Sec. 8).

When we have become confident of our ability to find **any one point,** no matter what, we are ready to learn how to apply our skill most effectively to block in the picture. Key points will fix the most important lines, and these lines in turn will bound planes, and thus delimit volumes. By knowing which points and lines to choose, the graphical process can be greatly shortened. Only experience based on analytical observation will tell us how to make the best selection, but a general suggestion may be helpful in putting the beginner on the right track.

The making of a perspective should **proceed by subdivision.** That is, the most important parts should be determined first, and their component elements worked out as subdivisions of the larger whole. This precludes carrying mistakes forward, and assures control by preventing us from getting lost in our own constructions. This approach may be summarized in the advice—**always have a picture.**

There should never be (at any stage of a drawing) a tangled mass of construction lines, or a scattering of unrelated elements, each more or less complete but unorganized as a whole. Instead, one should block in the principal masses first with as few lines as possible, and then check the points by which these masses were located. Thus our eyes will help us to avoid confusion, and we shall see clearly all through the development of our drawing what we have accomplished and what to do next.

9. INTERIORS

As far as theory (and practice) are concerned, there is no difference in the making of perspectives between interiors and exteriors. The procedure is exactly the same. Do not let the fact that lines on the left of the picture vanish toward the right, and vice versa, confuse you. Our rules have no exceptions. They apply to points in front of the *PP* as well as to those behind it, to reentrant objects like interiors as well as to salient ones.

However, even more care is required in choosing *S* when an interior is involved. Common errors are too large a cone of correct vision and too great a depth of field. We are all familiar with the false sense of scale that is produced by a photograph of a long narrow space (like a railroad car) when the whole length of it is shown clearly by means of a special lens—or when a wide-angle lens has been used to show too great an area.

If a true picture is desired (not just a diagram) do not try to include too much in one interior perspective. Remember that we look **at** a building but **around** a room. Thus our common speech suggests that an interior view is necessarily limited and that several views are needed to tell a complete story.

Another common error is to forget the walls and locate *S* outside them in order to get a larger picture without too wide an angle of vision. This can sometimes be done successfully but it is usually better to "stay inside the room" if the real effect of its size and scale is to be conveyed to the spectator.

In Illus. 4-7 notice how rapidly the objects in the room lying outside the cone of correct vision seem to become "distorted" if they are included in the perspective.

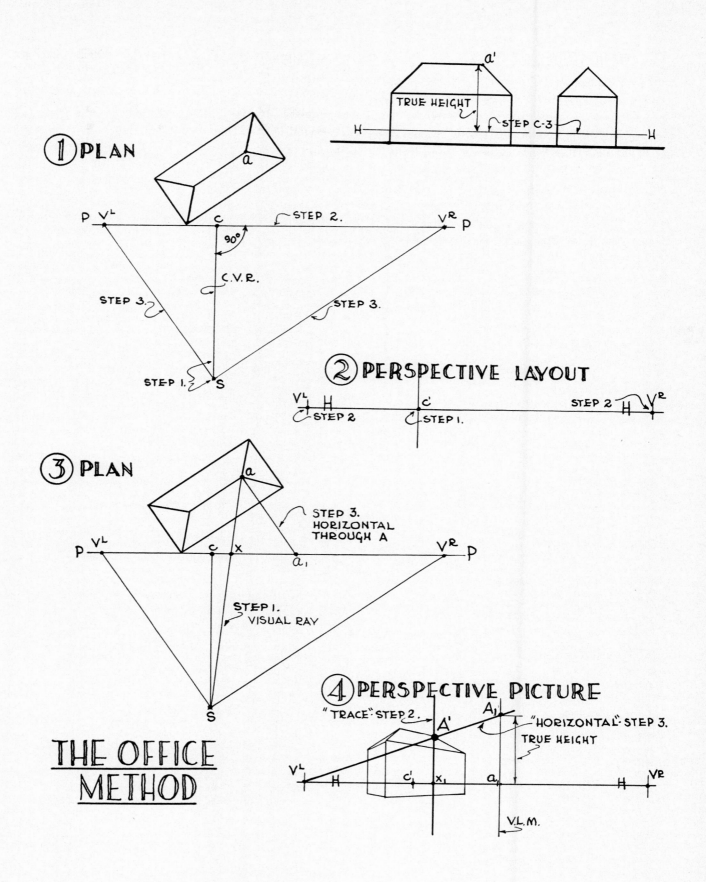

① PLAN

STEP 2.

90°

C.V.R.

STEP 3.

STEP 3.

STEP 1.

P V^L   c   V^R P

S

TRUE HEIGHT

STEP C-3

② PERSPECTIVE LAYOUT

V^L H   c   V^R

STEP 2   STEP 1   STEP 2 H

③ PLAN

STEP 3.
HORIZONTAL
THROUGH A

P V^L   c x   a_1   V^R P

STEP 1.
VISUAL RAY

S

THE OFFICE METHOD

④ PERSPECTIVE PICTURE

"TRACE" STEP 2.   A'   A_1   "HORIZONTAL" STEP 3.
TRUE HEIGHT

V^L H   c' x_1   a   H   V^R

V.L.M.

62   ILLUSTRATION 4-8

10. *HOW TO MAKE A PERSPECTIVE*[1] *BY THE OFFICE METHOD*

Given: Orthographic plan and elevations of object.

A. *Find working points* on the orthographic plan (Illus. 4-8-1).

    1. Locate S and draw $C.V.R.$

    2. Locate PP perpendicular to $C.V.R.$

    3. Find V's by drawing parallel lines through S to PP.

B. *Transfer working points* to perspective (Illus. 4-8-2).

    1. Draw HH and locate C (where desired).

    2. Locate V's by relation to C.

    3. Locate $V.L.M.$'s (always in PP, not always at C).

C. *Draw picture* (Illus. 4-8-3 and 4). For each point (as A'):

    1. Draw visual ray to a in plan. Mark x on PP.

    2. Lay off x on HH in perspective at x_1. Draw vertical trace through it.

    3. Assume horizontal through a. Find its V, and its $V.L.M.$ Locate HH on orthographic elevation. Measure true height of a' from HH and lay off on its $V.L.M.$ at A_1. Draw A_1-V^L to intersect trace at A'.

[1] Normally only two drawings are used in making a perspective. Figures 3 and 4 are further developments of Figs. 1 and 2, separated in Illus. 4-8 to show procedure instead of drawn consecutively on the same framework.

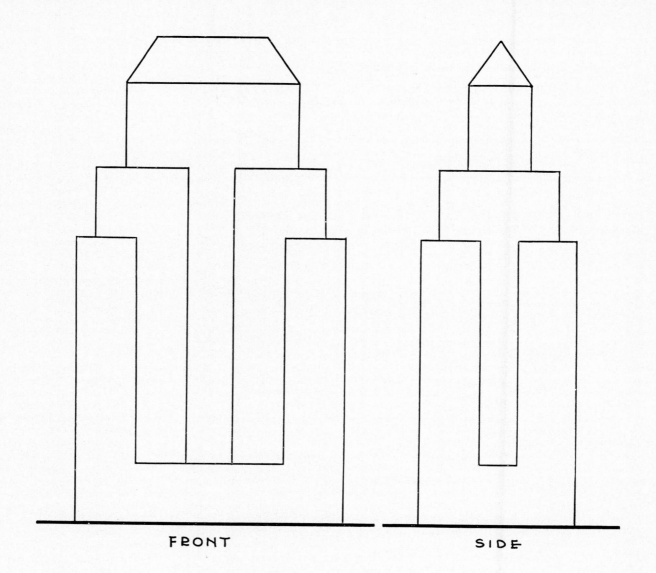

FRONT   SIDE

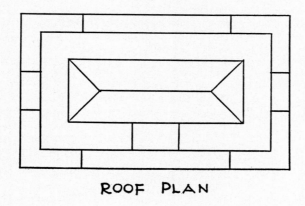

ROOF PLAN

A SKYSCRAPER

SCALE 1/64" = 1'-0"

1

QUESTIONS

1. List in your own words the most important considerations for choosing S.
2. Explain the general method by which the perspective of **any** point may be found.
3. What lines are used to find points by the office method?
4. Where should the perspective be drawn in reference to the orthographic plan?
5. How many V's are used in the office method? $V.L.M$'s?
6. How are heights determined by the office method?
7. Must the picture plane be placed through the nearest corner of the object?
8. Explain the use of diagonals in a perspective drawing.
9. Why is it important to block in a drawing?
10. How can the size and proportions of a perspective be assured in advance?

PROBLEMS

Illustrations 4-9, 4-10, and 4-11 give the orthographic drawings necessary to make perspectives of typical architectural problems. Special conditions may be applied to each as suggested below, or the complete choice of layout may be left to the student.

1. Office building, normal view and HH. Redraw with HH at center of object and compare results.
2. Make both bird's-eye and worm's-eye views of this pyramid.
3. Make an accurate perspective to preserve the proportions of the thumbnail sketch.
4. Assume the long dimension of the room to be twice that of the fireplace end.
5. Make perspective at double scale. Use figure as diagram to choose S, etc., and then make new plan layout. Do not redraw elevation.

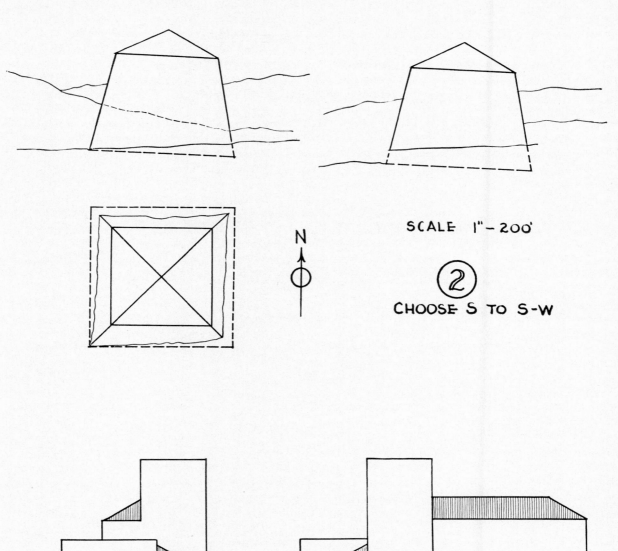

SCALE 1"- 200'

② CHOOSE S TO S-W

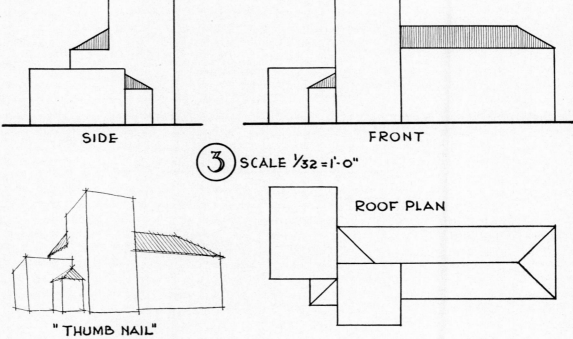

SIDE

FRONT

③ SCALE 1/32 = 1'-0"

"THUMB NAIL"

ROOF PLAN

ILLUSTRATION 4-10

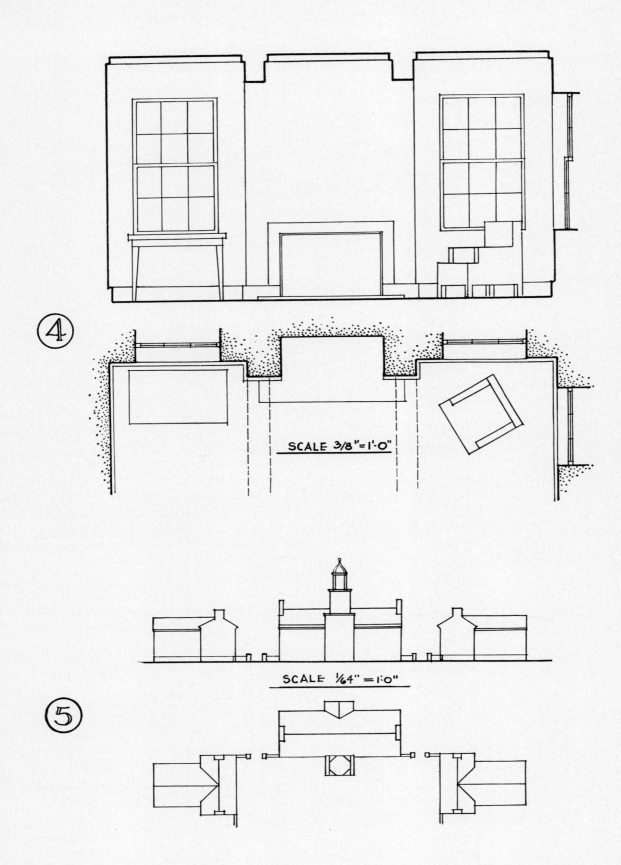

SCALE 3/8"=1'-0"

SCALE 1/64" = 1'-0"

ILLUSTRATION 4-11

67

Study for Ohio Steel Foundry, Lima, Ohio; Albert Kahn & Associates, architects; drawn by Hugh Ferris.

ILLUSTRATION 5-1

Chapter 5

PERSPECTIVE PLAN—MEASURING POINTS

IN USING the office method, one is soon impressed by the amount of paraphernalia involved in producing even a modest result. Projection from a fairly large orthographic plan yields only a small picture out of a welter of construction lines. It is tedious to try to clean up the paper for rendering and difficult to cast shadows (as we shall see later). A larger picture can be obtained only by putting the picture plane behind the object. This should not be confusing (no new principles are involved) but often seems so, especially to beginners.

The *perspective plan method* meets all of the above objections at the cost of learning an additional idea and its application. Unless you are ready to make this effort, skip this chapter and Proposition VI—but be prepared to have those who have mastered this method produce much quicker and more useful perspectives than you will ever achieve. Besides eliminating the difficulties already noted, they will also be able to progress to inverse perspective by which true dimensions can be determined from photographs and sketches. This powerful tool in design will never be available to you.

1. THE PERSPECTIVE PLAN

The new idea involved is merely the extension of our familiar use of vanishing points in order to find the perspective of the **plan** of an object. This we use as a construction drawing from which to develop later the **picture** of the **whole** object. The graphic process is exactly similar to that of drawing a plan as the basis for an elevation in orthographic projection. The perspective plan may be at any level that we choose, above or below our object. Usually it is taken well below so as to improve accuracy by providing sharp intersections, and so as to keep the construction lines off the part of our paper where the picture will later appear. After determining the plan, we can build the picture from it by projection. Illustration 5-2-A will show the basic relationship.

The farther below (or above) the picture that one places the perspective plan, the sharper the intersections of its construction lines will be and thus the more accurate the projections made from them. Of course this will make the perspective plan look distorted, because it will be far out of the cone of correct vision. Since it is used only for construction and not as a final picture, such queer effects are of no importance and should cause no artistic concern.

Often several perspective plans are drawn at various levels in order to precise special parts of the object which would overcomplicate the drawing if all were made at the same level. This corresponds to drawing several orthographic plans to explain a building.

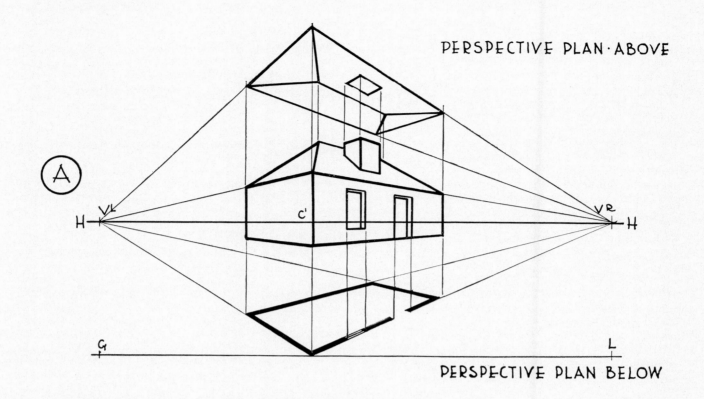

PERSPECTIVE PLAN·ABOVE

Ⓐ

VL   H   C'   VR   H

G   L

PERSPECTIVE PLAN BELOW

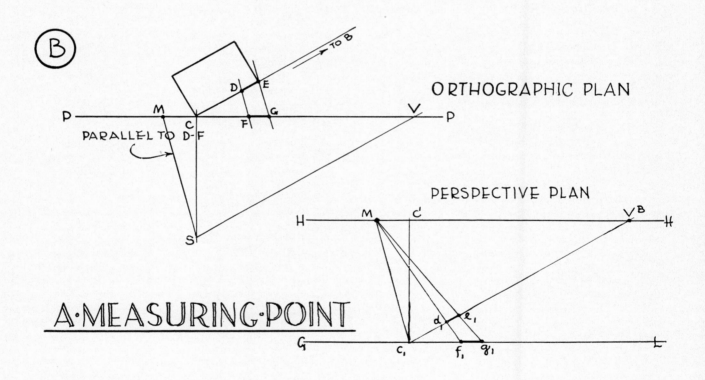

Ⓑ

TO B

ORTHOGRAPHIC PLAN

P   M   C   F   G   V   P
D   E

PARALLEL TO D-F

S

A·MEASURING·POINT

PERSPECTIVE PLAN

H   M   C'   VB   H

d₁   ℓ₁

G   c₁   f₁   g₁   L

ILLUSTRATION 5-2

2. MEASURING POINTS

Since a plan is by definition a two-dimensional figure on a horizontal plane, we do not have to consider heights in putting it into perspective. All the lines involved are horizontals whose V's will lie on HH. Thus, in Illus. 5-2-B we can easily find the perspective of C-B, as an infinite length extending from PP to V. How can we locate definite points on it such as D and E? The answer is, of course, by using other horizontals through them drawn from PP to their own proper V.

In the orthographic plan of Illus. 5-2-B, line F-D is so drawn that C-$F = C$-D. Find the V of F-D in the normal way by drawing a parallel through S striking PP at M.

Now start the perspective establishing HH, C', V^B and M. Drop down any convenient distance to C_1, which fixes the level of the plan to be drawn. Draw a **ground line** (*horizontal line of measure*, abbreviation $H.L.M.$) through C_1 and lay off f_1 so that c_1-$f_1 = C$-$F = C$-D.

Lines drawn from C_1 to V^B, and from f_1 to M, will give the perspective plan of D at their intersection d_1.

Now if in the orthographic plan we lay off F-$G = D$-E, and draw G-E, it will be parallel to F-D by geometry. Hence the perspective of G-E will have the same vanishing point as F-D, *i.e.*, M.

Therefore we can in *perspective plan* on G-L lay off f_1-$g_1 = F$-$G = D$-E by their relations to C_1, draw from g_1 to M, and find e_1, on C_1-V^B.

In other words, we can lay off true dimensions from C_1 on G-L, and by knowing M can draw lines to it which will cut off corresponding perspective lengths on C_1-V^B.

Similar M's can be found for as many other series of lines as are important to the final picture. They are very easy to locate because in every case V-S will equal V-M in plan (see Sec. 5 for proof).

M's are the basis of our new method, so we must be sure to know what they are besides learning to call them *measuring points*. It follows from the above construction that:

A measuring point is the V of a series of parallel lines which cut off equal distances on another series of parallel lines and on the picture plane.

Learn This Definition.

It will interest the student to check this method by drawing the visual rays to D and E in the orthographic plan, and thus prove to himself that the resulting traces on PP will give the same locations for d_1 and e_1 by the office method as have just been found by using a measuring point.

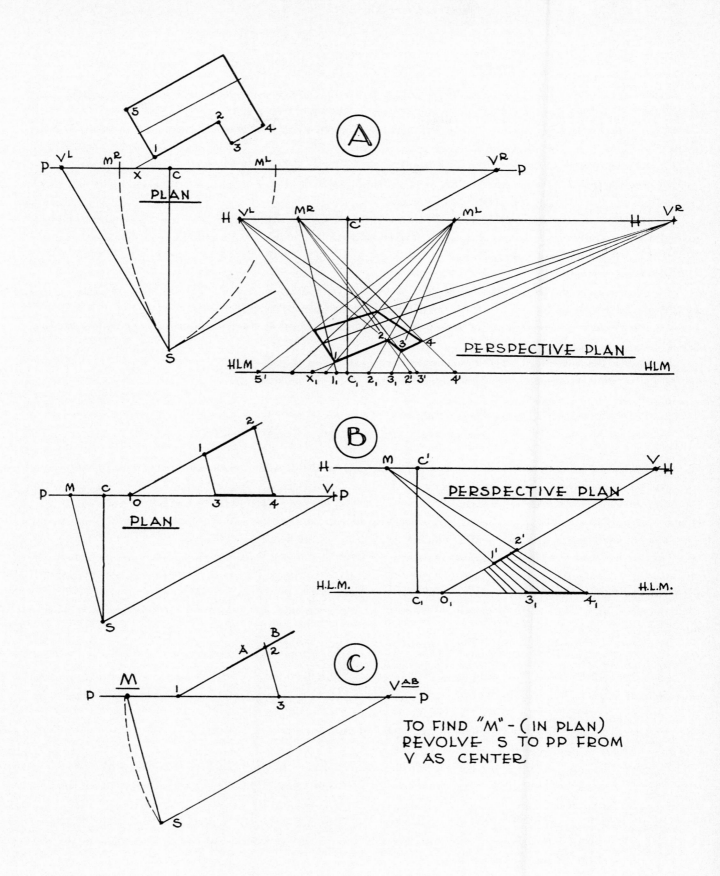

PLAN

PERSPECTIVE PLAN

HLM   HLM

PLAN

PERSPECTIVE PLAN

H.L.M.   H.L.M.

TO FIND "M" - (IN PLAN)
REVOLVE S TO PP FROM
V AS CENTER

3. PUTTING A PLAN INTO PERSPECTIVE

Given the plan of a small house as shown in Illus. 5-3-A, we set up our perspective apparatus as usual, except that when V^R has been located we use it as a center, and swing S to PP to find M^R. V^L similarly gives us M^L.

Then in perspective we choose C', draw HH, and lay off the V's and M's. Since no part of our plan touches PP, we extend one side (as 1-2) **in order to start at** x, **a point in** PP. Next x_1 is located on $H.L.M.$ by measurement from c_1 and joined to V^R. Then x_1-1_1 is laid off on $H.L.M.$ equal to x-1, and 1_1-M^R is drawn, finding 1 in perspective.

In order to find 2, the distance 1-2 in the orthographic plan is laid off from 1_1 in the perspective plan to $2'$. A line from $2'$ to M^R locates the perspective of 2.

The location of 3 involves one more step. Since 2-3 vanishes at V^L, we cannot draw the line at once, because finding 3 will require the use of M^L instead of M^R. Therefore 2 is first referred to $H.L.M.$ by a line through it and M^L, then the true length of 2-3 is laid off on $H.L.M.$ at 2_1-3_1, and another line drawn to M^L which will cut V^L-2 at 3, the point desired.

Similarly 4 is located from 3, by first drawing 3-V^R, then referring 3 to $H.L.M.$ by a line from M^R, thus getting $3'$, laying off the true distance on $H.L.M.$ ($3'$-$4'$), and drawing back to M^R to locate 4.

All other points are worked out in the same manner. Their construction has been omitted for the sake of clarity. In each case, the procedure is as follows:

1. Be sure which V controls the line on which the measurement is to be made.
2. Refer the starting point to $H.L.M.$ by a line from the corresponding M.
3. Lay off the true distance on $H.L.M.$
4. Draw to M to cut off the perspective distance.

4. ISOSCELES TRIANGLES

Another way of understanding the measuring point process is to think of it as the putting into perspective of the isosceles triangles seen in plan as O-1-3 and O-2-4 (Illus. 5-3-B). One of the equal sides (O-3 and O-4) of each of these triangles lies in the PP, and will appear in its true length. Hence 3_1 or 4_1 can be found by **measurement** from O_1, on $H.L.M.$ The other two sides can then be found by drawing to their vanishing points—V and M respectively. The sides intersect at the points $1'$ and $2'$ which are the perspectives desired.

Thus by using M's, we are putting into perspective a series of isosceles triangles which have one side lying in PP on $H.L.M.$ We know the vanishing points of the other two sides. According to the geometrical theorem that a parallel to a side cuts the other two sides of a triangle proportionately, lines drawn to the vanishing point of one side (M) represent lines that are really parallel and hence cut the other side into perspective distances equal to the true dimensions laid off on the side in PP.

5. HOW TO FIND AN M

The use of M's in laying out perspectives is greatly facilitated by the ease with which they can be found. All that we have to do in order to find the M corresponding to any V, is to use that V as a center in the orthographic plan, and revolve S up to PP. This construction can be proved as follows (Illus. 5-3-C):

Given: An orthographic plan in which S, PP, and horizontal line A-B are shown.

To Find: The M of A-B.

Construction: Find the V of A-B by drawing a parallel to it through S to PP. Prolong A-B to PP at 1. Lay off 1-2 = 1-3, and draw 2-3. Find V of 2-3 by drawing a parallel to it through S to PP, thus locating M.

Proof: 2-3 is a measuring line and its V is the M required, because, by definition, **a measuring point is the vanishing point of a measuring line, i.e., a line that cuts off equal distances on the** PP, **and on a line in perspective.**

Since triangles 1-2-3 and S-M-V are similar (parallel sides), V-S is to V-M as 1-2 is to 2-3. But 1-2 is equal to 2-3 by construction; therefore V-S is equal to V-M.

Hence M can be found by revolving S to PP from V as a center (Q.E.D.).

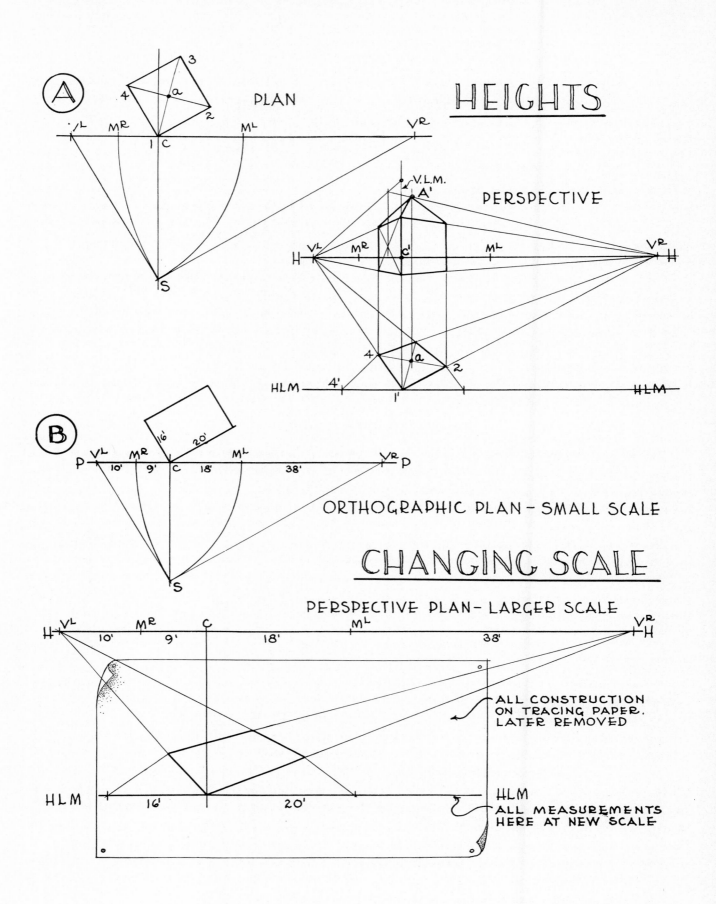

A PLAN

HEIGHTS

PERSPECTIVE

V.L.M.

B

ORTHOGRAPHIC PLAN — SMALL SCALE

CHANGING SCALE

PERSPECTIVE PLAN — LARGER SCALE

ALL CONSTRUCTION
ON TRACING PAPER.
LATER REMOVED

HLM

ALL MEASUREMENTS
HERE AT NEW SCALE

6. HEIGHTS

The height of any point is found (exactly as in the office method) by finding the perspective of a horizontal through the point at the proper level. Such a line locates the point A' by intersection with a vertical projected from the perspective plan (instead of a trace from a visual ray). See Illus. 5-4-A.

7. APPLICATION OF THIS METHOD

The perspective plan method seems to most beginners to involve an unnecessary step which adds another complication rather than simplifies the drawing. Until they have tried it often enough to judge fairly, novices should accept the opinion of those more experienced. The proof of this pudding (like most others) is in the eating. Many things that seem difficult or unpalatable when first tried turn out after longer acquaintance to suit us better than others which have more appeal at first taste.

After a few trials it will seem natural to those who are accustomed to develop orthographic plans to scale, to build up perspective plans by measurement. A whole façade can be quickly "ticked off" from its orthographic plan on a strip of paper which can then be laid along H.L.M. Points may be marked in perspective very rapidly by putting a pin at M and revolving a triangle along the strip without drawing the full lines. All the standard short cuts can also be used.

The only real difficulty is to avoid confusion between M's and V's, both in locating and using them. In order to help the student maintain control in applying this method the several steps have been listed in order at the end of this chapter on page 77.

8. ADVANTAGES

The student who has fully understood the above explanations and has made at least a dozen perspectives from plans, will begin to appreciate some of the advantages claimed for this method. He will see that it permits a cleaner picture by relegating much of the construction to a lower part of the sheet (which can later be cut off), or to a piece of superimposed tracing paper which can be removed (Illus. 5-4-B). It will also occur to him that since the picture is made from exact dimensions, changes in it can be made if desired and the true measurements necessary to effect the altered proportions can be determined exactly by referring the changes back to the H.L.M. This is of great value in studying a design, and can even be applied to a photograph (see Chap. 9, Sec. 10, Inverse Perspective).

The value of knowing M's in finding the V's of sloping lines is explained in Chap. 6, Sec. 1. The advantage of the perspective plan in casting shadows will become obvious in Chap. 7, but the really great advantage of the perspective plan method is the opportunity that it offers to **change the scale of the picture** from that of the orthographic drawings.

9. CHANGING SCALE

In the M method we need an orthographic plan merely as a small-scale diagram on which to make our perspective setup. Having located S, $C.V.R.$, PP, and the V's and M's, we use this diagram only to fix their relative positions on any HH that we select. We can even locate our working points on a sheet of tracing paper, and thus have to interrupt only for a few minutes the further development of the orthographic plan by another draftsman. We can make our picture on another table **and at a different scale** (Illus. 5-4-B).

Of course, our working points must be laid off on our horizon **at the same graphic scale as we will use to make our measurements on** H.L.M. Otherwise we should be changing the assumed relation between the observer and the object, on which the accuracy of our perspective depends. In order to avoid any possibility of confusion the best practice is to mark the distances from C to the V's and M's, **in feet at the scale of the plan diagram.** Corresponding dimensions can then be laid off in perspective at any scale that we wish to use (Illus. 5-4-B).

Quite commonly we shall find that the desired increase in the size of the picture will so increase the actual dimension between vanishing points at the new scale that one of our V's will fall beyond the limits of our available drawing board. The procedure in this case is explained in Chap. 6, Sec. 5.

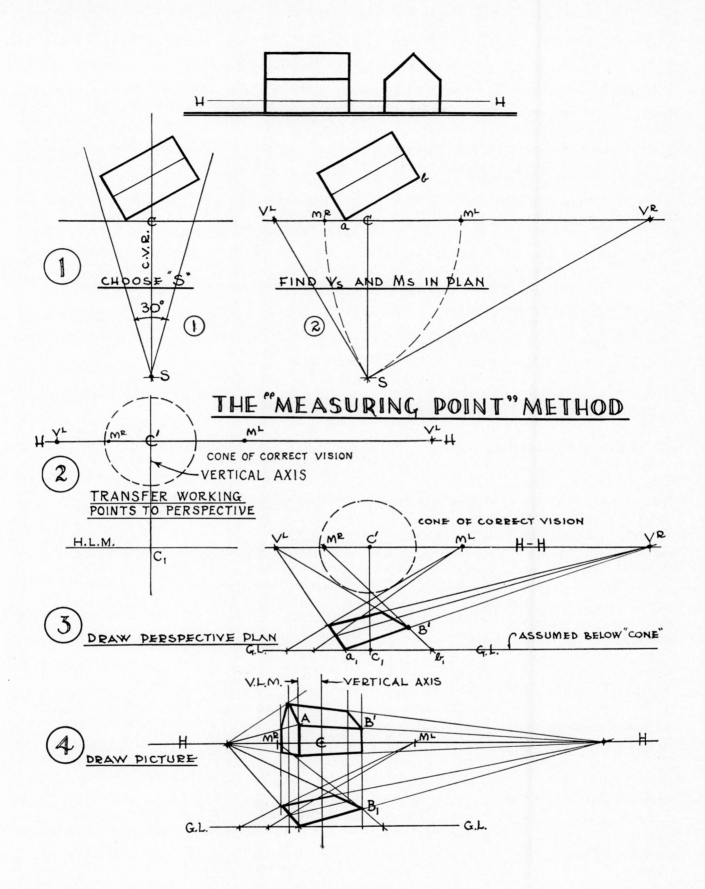

THE "MEASURING POINT" METHOD

① CHOOSE "S"

30°

② FIND Vs AND Ms IN PLAN

② TRANSFER WORKING POINTS TO PERSPECTIVE

CONE OF CORRECT VISION

VERTICAL AXIS

③ DRAW PERSPECTIVE PLAN

CONE OF CORRECT VISION

H.L.M.

ASSUMED BELOW "CONE"

④ DRAW PICTURE

V.L.M.

VERTICAL AXIS

ILLUSTRATION 5-5

10. HOW TO MAKE A PERSPECTIVE
BY PERSPECTIVE PLAN AND MEASURING POINTS

A. *Find control points* on the orthographic plan (Illus. 5-5-1).

    1. Locate S (keep building in cone of correct vision) and draw $C.V.R.$

    2. Draw PP perpendicular to $C.V.R.$ thus fixing C.

    3. Find V's by drawing parallels through S to PP. Revolve V's to locate M's.

B. *Transfer working points* to the perspective (Illus. 5-5-2).

    1. Draw HH, and locate C' where desired. Draw circle limiting picture to cone at scale selected.

    2. Locate V's and M's at proper scale by relation to C'.

    3. Locate $H.L.M.$ (far enough below HH so that plan will not overlap picture) and c_1.

C. *Draw perspective plan* (Illus. 5-5-3).

    1. Start with point in PP (prolong lines if necessary), as a_1. Draw to V^R.

    2. Lay off a_1 to b_1 equal to a-b at proper scale on $H.L.M.$

    3. Draw b_1-M^R. Intersection is B'—the perspective plan of B.

D. *Draw picture* (Illus. 5-5-4).

    1. Locate HH on orthographic elevation.

    2. Lay off true heights on $V.L.M.$ (in PP) by relation to HH.

    3. Draw to V's to locate points on verticals projected from perspective plan.

QUESTIONS

  1. What is a perspective plan?

  2. At what levels may perspective plans be drawn?

  3. Define a measuring point.

  4. How many M's are there in a perspective drawing?

  5. How is an M found? Prove this construction.

  6. Can a perspective plan be drawn without using M's?

  7. Explain how the use of M's permits changing the scale of a perspective from that of the plan diagram.

  8. State the advantages of using M's as compared to the office method.

  9. How are heights in perspective found when using M's?

10. For lines parallel to PP, how does the distance S-C compare to C-M? Why?

PROBLEMS

Make perspectives by the M method of the objects shown on Illus. 5-6 and 5-7.

1. View showing apse, with end wall parallel to PP, scale $\frac{1}{8}$ in. = $1'$-$0''$.

2. View from southwest, HH level with stylobate, scale enlarged one and one-half times.

3. Normal perspective from southwest, scale $\frac{1}{8}$ in. = $1'$-$0''$.

4. Bird's-eye from northeast, scale $\frac{1}{16}$ in. = $1'$-$0''$.

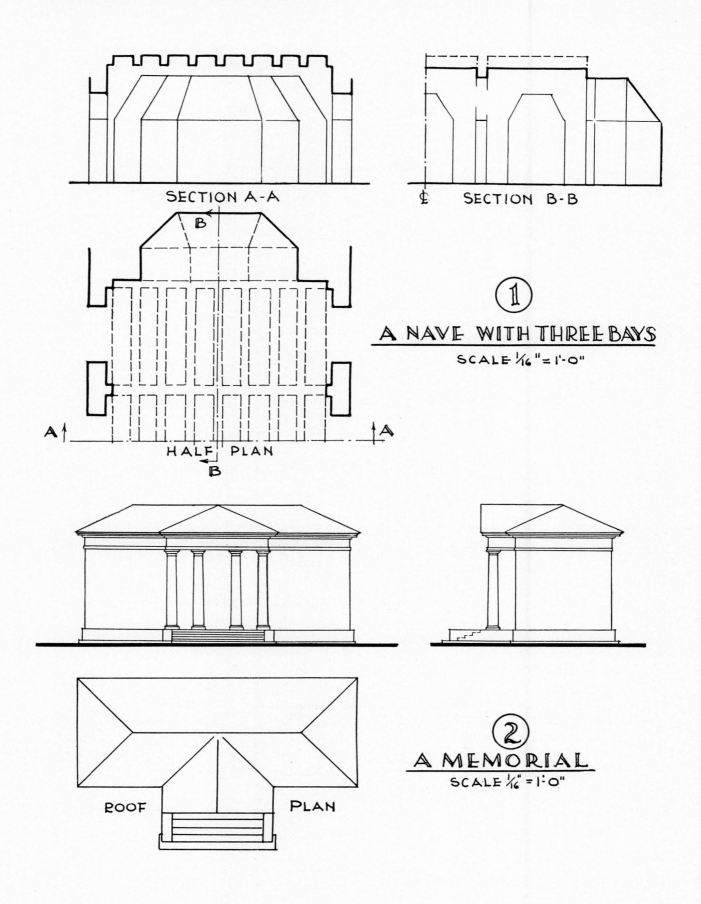

SECTION A-A

SECTION B-B

B

HALF PLAN

B

A ↑   ↑A

① A NAVE WITH THREE BAYS
SCALE 1/16" = 1'-0"

② A MEMORIAL
SCALE 1/16" = 1'-0"

ROOF PLAN

③

SCALE 1/16" = 1'-0"

NORTH

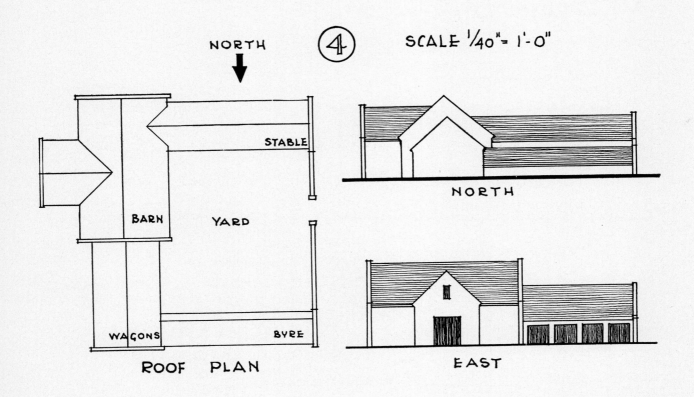

NORTH ④ SCALE 1/40" = 1'-0"

STABLE

BARN   YARD

WAGONS   BYRE

ROOF PLAN

NORTH

EAST

ILLUSTRATION 5-7

79

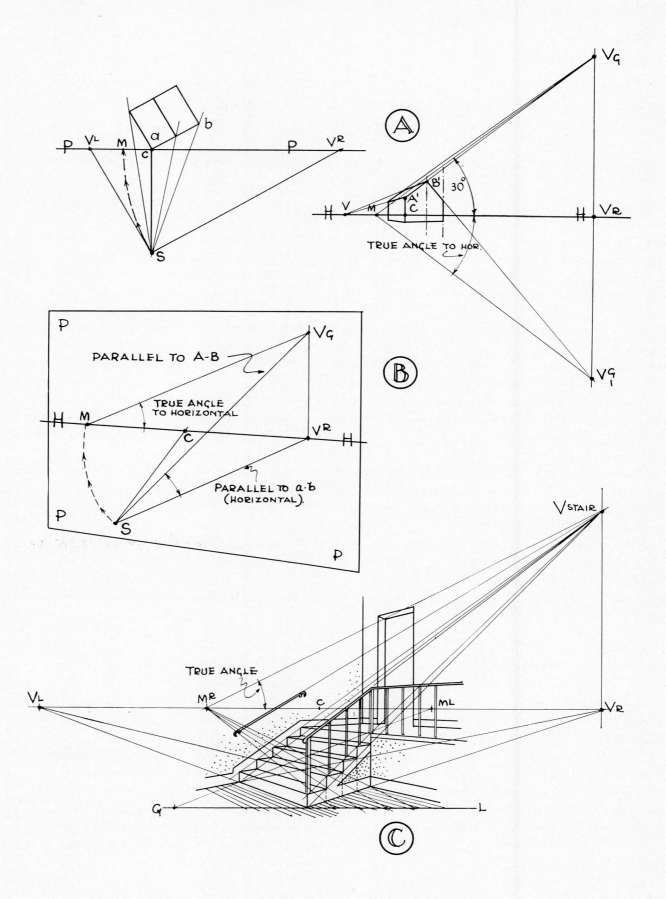

A

TRUE ANGLE TO HOR.

B

PARALLEL TO A-B

TRUE ANGLE
TO HORIZONTAL

PARALLEL TO a-b
(HORIZONTAL).

C

TRUE ANGLE

ILLUSTRATION 6-1

Chapter 6

AIDS IN DEVELOPMENT OF THE PICTURE

1. VANISHING POINTS OF SLOPING LINES

So far we have used the V's only of systems of **horizontal** lines, but the law of diminution applies also to all other systems of parallels, either existing in the object which is to be shown in perspective or assumed for purposes of construction. The actual equal distance between any two lines of **any** series of parallels tends constantly to look smaller as the lines are prolonged away from the observer and hence the lines seem eventually to converge at the V of the series.

Like the V of a series of horizontals, the V of any other system (no matter what its inclination) can be found and represented on the picture plane as a control for drawing the perspective projections of the lines which compose the series. This can be done by finding where that member of the series, which can be assumed to pass through the station point, strikes PP. Since such a construction involves a line which is at an angle to HH, we must first define this angle. The simplest way to show such an inclination graphically is to draw the **plan** of the line, and then fix its angle with the horizontal either in elevation or by a notation. Again we must "first catch our rabbit" before we "make a pie." Usually any difficulty in finding the V's of sloping lines comes from not having exact data to determine the problem.

If then (see Illus. 6-1-A) we are given the plan a-b of a line A-B which makes a 30° angle with the horizontal plane (such as the gable of a small house), we first treat this plan (which is by definition a horizontal projection) like any other horizontal line and find its V by drawing a parallel through S to PP. Then we locate this point V^R in perspective on HH by its relation to C.

A vertical through V^R will determine the trace on PP of the vertical projecting plane containing the parallel to A-B which passes through S. The trace of this plane on PP therefore contains the point in which this parallel through S pierces PP. This point is by definition the V of A-B which we are seeking. Now if we revolve this vertical plane around its trace on PP until it lies in PP, we will see the angle of A-B to the horizontal in its true size as the angle between A-B revolved and HH.

When we make such a revolution S will fall at the M of a-b (which being a plan is therefore a horizontal line and has its M in the usual location on HH.) Lay off this point M on HH in perspective and at it erect the true angle of 30° to intersect the trace at V^G, which is the point desired. The diagram in Illus. 6-1-B shows (in perspective) how this construction looks in space, and should make the reasoning visually obvious.

Note that under our given conditions this angle will be above HH because our line was shown by the arrow to **rise** as it is prolonged away from S. If instead it had gone **down** as it was extended, we would have laid off the true angle **below** HH. This would have given us the V of the other slope of the gable.

When the angle between the given line and the horizontal is large, V^G may fall off the paper. We have, however, a very valuable check if we know its location, even approximately. Whenever the object includes a number of lines which vanish at such a V, we do not have to locate it exactly, but we can use an approximation of it to control the results, even though we find the lines by other means. In sketching from nature the knowledge of where such V's lie is of great assistance in assuring the approximate correctness of freehand drawings. We can sum up this theorem in a form easy to remember by saying: **the V of every line must be somewhere above (or below) the V of its plan.**

The treads, railings, strings, etc., of staircases are most readily constructed, and the risers most easily found, by determining the V of the slope of the stair. Illustration 6-1-C should make this construction clear.

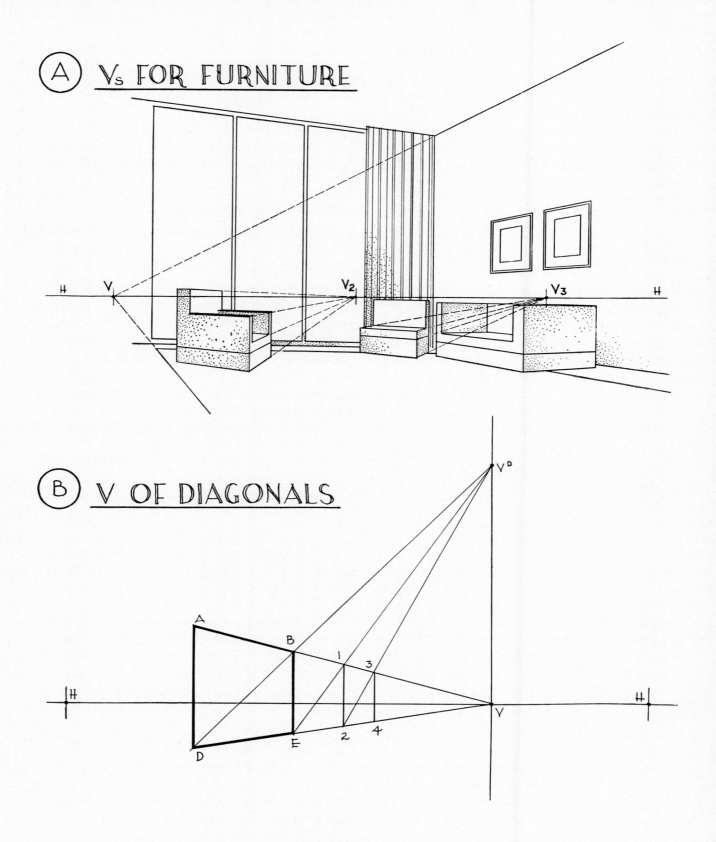

Ⓐ Vₛ FOR FURNITURE

H · V · V₂ · V₃ · H

Ⓑ V OF DIAGONALS

Vᴰ

H · A · B · 1 · 3 · V · H
D · E · 2 · 4

2. AUXILIARY VANISHING POINTS

Extra vanishing points are especially useful for furniture placed irregularly in an interior. Chairs, etc., can be turned as desired and their arms, backs, etc., drawn rapidly by remembering that their feet must rest on the floor and hence form a horizontal pattern whose bounding lines must vanish on *HH*. Having assumed the position of two feet, prolong the line through them and find the *V* where it pierces *HH* (Illus. 6-2-A). This *V* will control the drawing of the other parallel parts of the object and another *V* can be found for the sides at right angles to the first set. This *V* should be checked approximately in plan, or definitely constructed, except by the experienced draftsman who will "feel" its location with uncanny accuracy.

3. PROPORTIONAL DIVISION

The basic graphic principle of "big things first, then subdivide" has already been stressed as being of primary importance in the development of a perspective drawing. This idea has been combined with the use of the *V*'s of inclined lines in what has been called *proportional division*. It has been very fully worked out by Prof. Morehead.[1] Every draftsman should be familiar with the underlying principles involved and will be well repaid to study its further possibilities as a tool in his own work. The practical limits of the process are fixed by the size of the available working space in relation to the given conditions and to the time available. Those who have thoroughly mastered the full procedure will find it a quick and well-controlled method, while those who have not practiced it enough to have become expert will only be confused by trying to remember the additional graphic construction required to apply it.

We have already noted the importance of using the diagonals of rectangles as a quick way of finding the perspective centers of plane areas. Since we normally know the *V*'s of the horizontals bounding such figures above and below, we have only to prolong the diagonals until we find their own *V*'s at the points where they intersect the vertical through the *V* of their plans. These new *V*'s enable us to draw parallels to the original diagonals, and thus to establish the perspective of new rectangles, actually equal to those first found by some other (and more lengthy) method.

In Illus. 6-2-B,

> *Given:* The perspective *A-B-D-E* of a rectangle.
>
> *Required:* A series of equal rectangles in perspective.
>
> *Construction:* Find *V* by prolonging *A-B* and *D-E* to meet *HH*. Draw *D-B* to meet vertical through *V* at V^D. Draw E-V^D cutting *A-B* at 1, and 1-2 vertical. Draw 2-V^D to find 3, etc.

Of course *A-E* could have been used similarly by finding its *V* below *HH*.

If the given rectangle *A-B-D-E* is a square, *D-B* will make a true angle of 45° with both vertical sides, and V^D could have been found from knowing its *M*, and erecting the true angle. Distances scaled vertically on *A-D* (assuming it to be in *PP*) can then be foreshortened into perspective along *A-B* by drawing to V^D.

[1] Morehead, James C., "A Handbook of Perspective Drawing," Pittsburgh, The author, 1941.

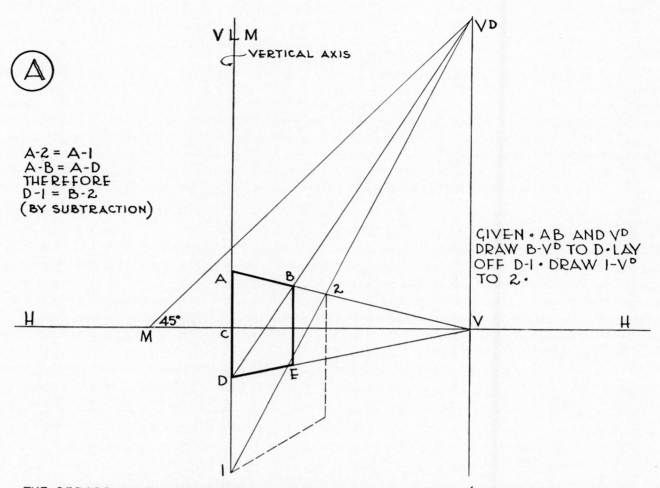

A-2 = A-1
A-B = A-D
THEREFORE
D-1 = B-2
(BY SUBTRACTION)

GIVEN · AB AND V^D
DRAW B-V^D TO D · LAY
OFF D-1 · DRAW 1-V^D
TO 2 ·

THE PERSPECTIVE OF A KNOWN HORIZONTAL DISTANCE (B·2) MAY BE FOUND
BY THE USE OF THE DIAGONAL OF A VERTICAL SQUARE WHOSE SIDE LIES IN V·L·M·

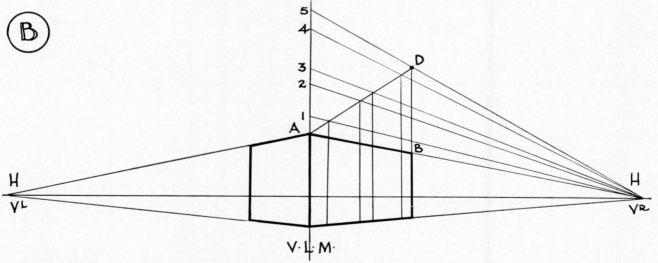

HORIZONTAL DIMENSIONS MAY BE LAID OFF ON V·L·M· AND PUT INTO PER-
SPECTIVE BY THE DIAGONAL OF A RECTANGLE

ILLUSTRATION 6-3

In Illus. 6-3-A,

Given: V and M on HH and A-D on $V.L.M.$

Required: To draw a square of which A-D is one side.

Construction: Draw 45° from M to V^D above V, then D-V^D to get B. The vertical B-E gives the required square in perspective.

V^D may also be used, to find the perspective of a known length along A-V.

Given: The true length of B-2.

Required: To find its perspective.

Construction: Lay off D-1 equal to the length required and draw 1-V^D to get 2. (A-1 and A-2 are sides of squares, and so are A-D and A-B. Hence B-2 = A-1 minus A-D. Therefore D-1 = B-2.)

Clever draftsmen have long made use of a variation of this construction by scaling a required dimension and its subdivisions above (or below) one vertical side of a rectangle. A new rectangle is then completed and its diagonal drawn. Lines to V will cut the diagonal proportionately (by geometry) and intersections may be projected to mark the desired subdivisions. The limitation of this procedure is the skill of the draftsman in determining flat intersections exactly (see Illus. 6-3-B). Often it is necessary to control the graphical result by our knowledge of perspective law. A series of windows of equal width must be made to diminish regularly, even though our drawing will not be accurate enough to produce this effect, if we merely draw lines where we have projected points.

Thus in Illus. 6-3-B,

Given: The perspective block of a building.

Required: To subdivide the façade so as to have two windows regularly spaced.

Construction: Lay off the desired parts (1,2,3,4,5, etc.) along the vertical through A at any convenient scale. Complete the rectangle by drawing 5-V^R and B-D (vertical) and draw the diagonal A-D. Draw lines to V through points 1,2,3, etc. Project intersections with A-D onto façade. (A-D is divided proportionately to 1-5 by the parallels drawn to V, and A-B is divided proportionately to A-D by the vertical parallels to D-B.)

Both of the above short cuts avoid the necessity of repeating for every subdivision the whole basic process of finding points in perspective. Their most valuable employment is in designing or sketching. Various treatments of a façade may be tried quickly without the tedium of making orthographic drawings which then have to be put into perspective, only to be discarded. No plans are required, and yet accurate measurements may be represented and if necessary worked backward to true dimensions.

In most cases, however, only major geometrical subdivisions are thus tested. We want to know whether to use three windows or four, wider ends or wider centers, etc. When such decisions have been tested in perspective and a choice has been made, the exact division, on a similar graphical basis, can be made directly on the elevation.

Ⓐ "ONE-POINT" PERSPECTIVE

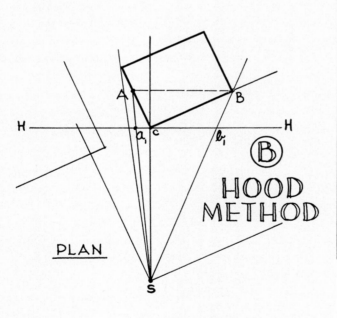

Ⓑ HOOD METHOD

PLAN

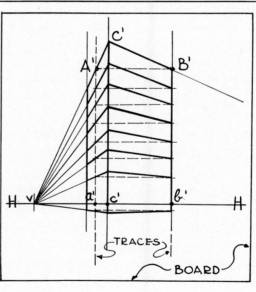

TRACES

BOARD

ILLUSTRATION 6-4

4. LINES PARALLEL TO PP

The fact that lines parallel to the picture plane remain parallel in perspective may be used to advantage in several ways. So-called *one-point* or *parallel* perspectives are simply cases in which an object, defined largely by two sets of lines in a vertical plane and a third set perpendicular to both others, is parallel to PP. Then the perpendicular lines will have the only V necessary (hence the name *one-point*) and this will of course coincide with C. M's may be found either to the right or to the left, since in plan S-C is perpendicular to PP and may be revolved either way. Those who have occasion to use this type of setup regularly (it is particularly adapted to reentrant objects such as interiors or street scenes) will find it worth while to remember and employ many such special constructions. Most of us can get results more surely, and almost as quickly, by sticking to our basic rules.

The late Raymond M. Hood of New York (architect of the Daily News Building, the McGraw-Hill Building, and of much of Radio City) developed a very useful short cut for drawing the perspectives of skyscrapers. It avoided the necessity of a very large and clumsy layout by using lines parallel to PP.

I found him in his office one day working on a small board, but producing a good-sized perspective of a multi-storied building. He was not using any of the mechanical devices explained in Sec. 5 of this chapter—only a T square and triangle in the normal way. Yet one side of his subject was placed at so flat an angle to PP that the V of its horizontals was obviously many feet distant—not only beyond the surface of his board, but probably not even in the same room! Nor was he drawing freehand. At each story at least one line was carefully worked out as a guide. This study was not merely a rough sketch, but was based on exact representation.

Mr. Hood was kind enough to explain his procedure to me and to give his permission for me to use it in any way that I wished. The "Hood method" is important as an illustration of how the man who knows basic principles can apply them to any special conditions that may arise. When Mr. Hood wanted to draw a skyscraper on a small board, he did not have to know in advance how to meet all the possible technical difficulties that may confront the perspective draftsman. He knew the fundamentals thoroughly and so could solve **any** problem.

He explained his reasoning about as follows:

The building which I want to draw in perspective will be situated on the corner of a main avenue and a side street. I therefore want my drawing to show the avenue side at a flat angle to PP, so as to be the most important part of the picture. This means that one principal V will fall far off my board, and will be unavailable for constructing the drawing. On the other hand, the V of the sharply foreshortened street elevation will be close in, and can be located on even a small board. If I cannot locate and use the other V, is there any way that I can proceed without it?

Mr. Hood had now a specific problem. He had "caught his rabbit." He continued:

Any vanishing point is used primarily to find one of the two lines necessary to locate the perspective of a point. For one of the lines required I can use a visual ray (*i.e.*, I shall employ the office method). The traces of these rays on PP will all fall on my drawing board and can be located easily. What other lines, rather than those which will require drawing to an inaccessible V, can I select to intersect the traces? The easiest will be those parallel to PP, which do not vanish and can be drawn with my T square.

So, through the most distant avenue corner B of the building I assume in plan a parallel to PP, and draw the visual ray for the point A where my parallel cuts the street façade. This will give me a trace in perspective which will intersect all the floor levels vanishing to V^L (the V on the board) and already accurately located. A horizontal through these intersections can then be drawn to locate the floors on the avenue side by cutting the trace (through b_1) for such points.

I was careful to check that the successive floors made smoothly increasing angles with HH. I had no V to control this relationship, but I knew that control was more important than the results of merely geometrical drafting. If I had found any one point so inaccurately as to give too steep a perspective to correspond to that of the floors above or below it, I should not have hesitated to adjust it. I tried to be careful, and actually had no trouble, but the success of any graphic process depends on the skill of the eye and hand that execute it, as well as on its geometrical correctness. The results of human attempts to apply geometrical formulas must always be checked against the higher law from which the procedure is deduced. In perspective the law of diminution is more important than the method used to apply it, and the final drawing must conform to basic truth, which is not subject to human error, rather than to drafting technique.

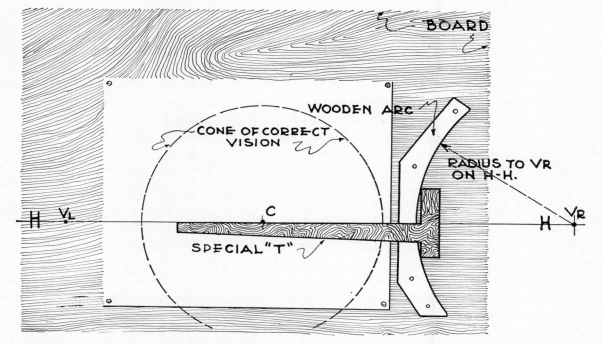

BOARD

WOODEN ARC

CONE OF CORRECT VISION

RADIUS TO VR ON H-H.

H   VL   C   H   VR

SPECIAL "T"

DRAWING TO V OFF THE BOARD

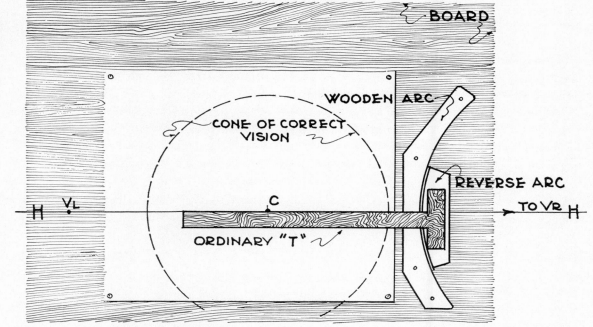

BOARD

WOODEN ARC

CONE OF CORRECT VISION

REVERSE ARC

H   VL   C   TO VR H

ORDINARY "T"

5. DISTANT VANISHING POINTS

The use of vanishing points in drawing perspectives has one serious technical difficulty which has already been mentioned. This often arises to plague the draftsman who seeks to apply our rules for locating S. When he selects a station point far enough away from his subject to get the best effect, he often finds that his equipment is inadequate to draw the lines required, and that his drawing board is too small to contain the points needed for his work. It is expensive to buy larger apparatus, in addition to the delay and inconvenience involved for all concerned. At best such bigger tools will only increase the scope of our results slightly. We have already noted several times that even a large perspective layout may produce a comparatively small picture. If we want a larger image, we shall soon reach the practical limit of using bigger triangles and T squares.

Above all we must **not** change our station point in order to get our working points on the board. Better not to make a perspective than to make a bad one. The person who sees it will not take into consideration whether or not the author had an easy job in making it. Distortions will not be excused even if there is a written apology under the title, such as "Excuse this bad view; my drawing board was too small to allow a good one." The observer has the right to expect a competent performance and is uninterested in poor technique or ill-considered presentations.

Several ways have been found to overcome such mechanical difficulties. The problem in essence is a simple one geometrically and can be solved by applying the principle that the perpendicular bisectors of the chords of a circle will all pass through its center. The blade of a T square whose head is guided against the edge of a circular arc (instead of against the straight edge of a drawing board) will meet these conditions mechanically, if the drafting edge of the blade is in the center of the head. Such an arc may be cut from plywood, or even stiff cardboard, and fastened down temporarily with small brads, permitting later removal without damaging the board more than do thumbtacks (see Illus. 6-5-A).

The late Charles Z. Klauder drew perspectives so regularly—both for study of his designs and for presentation drawings—that he found it worth while to own a set of permanent arcs of different radii. These were well-made wooden templates that were in such constant use that it was important to have them as exact as his other drawing instruments. For each perspective he would calculate the true distance to the inaccessible V from a plan diagram, and then select the arc from his set which best fitted the radius required and the drawing board available. His outfit thus saved him from having to locate a center in order to draw a segment of a circle whose radius might often be larger than the dimension of the room in which the work was to be done. This latter difficulty is often greater than that of making the actual arc.

Since the T squares required for this construction are uncommon, the need for them can be eliminated by retaining the convex portion of the arc and fastening an ordinary T square to it. In this way one is not dependent on unusual equipment and has a smoother sliding combination, particularly when cardboard is used. Schell Lewis, the brilliant architectural renderer, always employs this simple and effective device. He cuts a new pair of arcs for every drawing, thus preventing wear and consequent inaccuracy; his equipment always is flexible to meet particular conditions (see Illus. 6-5-B).

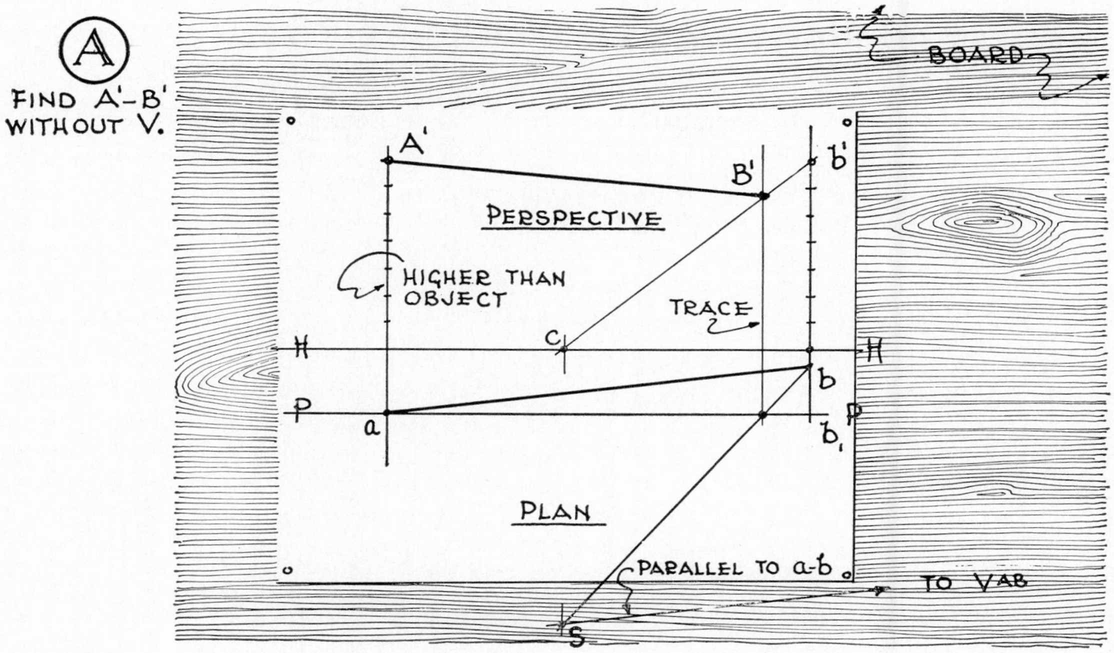

A
FIND A'-B' WITHOUT V.
BOARD
A'
B'
b'
PERSPECTIVE
HIGHER THAN OBJECT
TRACE
C
H
H
b
P
a
P
b1
PLAN
PARALLEL TO a-b
TO VAB
S

USING STRIPS FOR "V"-OFF-BOARD.

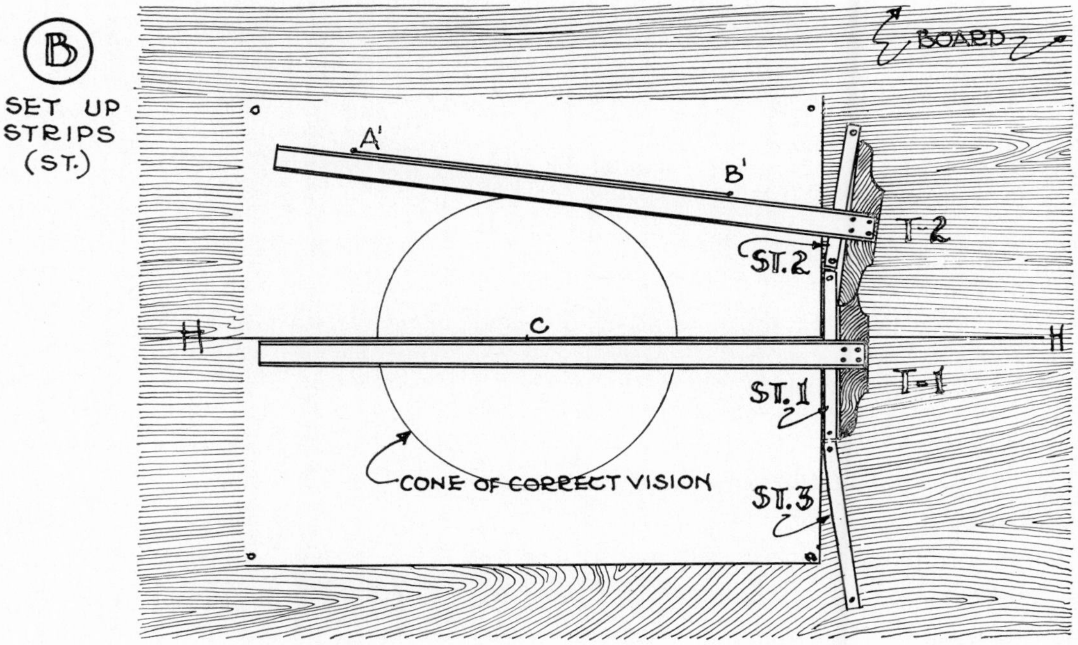

B
SET UP STRIPS (ST.)
BOARD
A'
B'
T-2
ST.2
C
H
H
T-1
ST.1
CONE OF CORRECT VISION
ST.3

Another method of setting up a mechanical means of drawing to a remote V requires us neither to draw a circle of large dimensions nor to cut out the arc thus determined. No special apparatus is needed, except some wooden (or stiff cardboard) strips and some brads. There is a distinct practical advantage in using strips instead of curves, because straight pieces are always easier to obtain and do not have to be cut to radius. But to place our strips correctly, we have to know how to draw a line without using its V.

In Illus. 6-6-A the plan a-b is given so that the V of A-B is off the board. In the perspective we first locate HH and C and then point A' by measurement (since it lies in PP). We must now determine A'-B' without using its inaccessible V, so we find B' from the trace of its visual ray and the line through b perpendicular to PP in plan. In perspective this line will begin at b' and vanish at C. Any other line through B' would of course do as well, but we should have to find its V as well as its intersection with PP, in order to draw it.

We have thus, without actually finding the distant V, drawn the perspective of a line which would go to it if continued, and which is higher than the object that we wish to represent. We now set a normal T square so that its blade will draw HH and tack down strip 1 (see Illus. 6-6-B). Note that this strip must be exactly as long as the head of our T square.

We then slide our T square with its lower corner against strip 1, until its blade lies along A'-B'. Strip 2 is now tacked down so as to have its lower corner touching the upper corner of strip 1, and its edge against the upper corner of our T square in its second position. Since we will use no lines above A'-B' the length of strip 2 does not matter. Strip 3 can now be added for lines below HH. It makes the same angle with strip 1 as does strip 2.

In large drawings it may happen that our T square will not slide far enough to draw A'-B' when its lower corner still lies against strip 1. In that case an intermediate line C-D—actually parallel to A'-B' and hence vanishing at the distant V—must be used for placing strip 2 which must be cut the exact length of the T square head. Strip 3 is added from strip 2 in the same manner that the latter was placed.

Prof. Clarence Martin first published several variations of the "strip method" in 1920, with the warning that "this procedure is accurate for practical purposes, though there is a theoretical error in mathematics. Under usual working conditions this error is infinitesimal and less than the errors due to the imperfections in even the best drafting paraphernalia."

Unless particular circumstances prevent, the draftsman will find it more convenient to locate S so that the right-hand V is the distant one, thus keeping his strips (or arc) out of the way of the normal position of the T square. Thus horizontals, verticals, and lines to V^R can all be drawn mechanically without interference of apparatus. A victrola needle driven lightly but firmly at V^L, and a second T square to slide through the guides at the right, will enable perspectives to be drawn almost as quickly and just as surely as are orthographic elevations. There is practically no new equipment with which to become familiar, and no new drafting habits have to be acquired. Most draftsmen will produce quicker and more accurate results by such setups than if they were to use more elaborate installations.

Complete geometrical accuracy in drawing to remote V's can be attained theoretically by such instruments as the centrolinead, introduced by Peter Nicholson as early as 1814. This consists of three arms held together by a central set screw. When adjusted to any combination of the three points necessary to determine a circle, the drafting arm (used like any straight edge) will always point to the center of the circle when the two other arms touch two of the defining points and the adjusting point is placed on the third. Despite the introduction of several minor improvements the centrolinead has never become popular. Its sprawling legs are always in the way and are constantly getting knocked out of adjustment. Time is lost resetting it, and even more time is wasted erasing errors made in all innocence through not noticing that the setting had unintentionally been changed. Unless pins are driven at the two control points, each line drawn requires careful placing of the two arms—a slow process. If pins are used they interfere with free use of the T square in drawing horizontals or to other V's. So practical objections overthrow theoretical exactitude, and simple devices which give special control over familiar instruments prove more effective than a new and special tool.

(A) BY INTERPOLATION

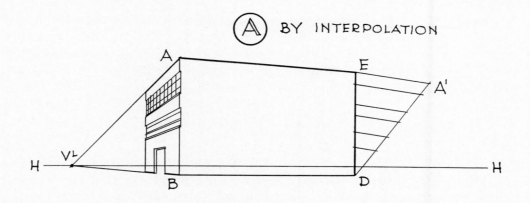

FINDING LINES WITHOUT USING "VS-OFF-BOARD"

(B)	(C)
BY PLANE PARALLEL TO P-P	BY "FRACTIONAL" V.

GIVEN - A-B AND POINT X

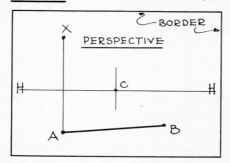

REQUIRED - PARALLEL TO A-B THROUGH X.

SOLUTION - DRAW A-C AND X-C, HORIZONTAL THRU B TO E, VERTICAL TO Y, HORIZONTAL TO W.

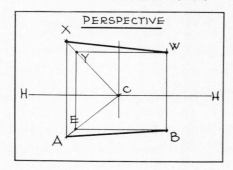

GIVEN - POINT A ON AXIS

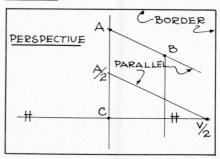

REQUIRED. LINE AB TO V.

SOLUTION. IN PLAN, DRAW FROM S/2 PARALLEL TO A-B, TO V/2 IN PERSPECTIVE, DRAW A·B PARALLEL A/2-V/2.

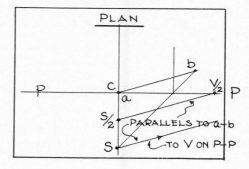

ILLUSTRATION 6-7

6. INTERPOLATION

In most perspective drawings, as has already been emphasized, only the most important lines are found accurately by complete graphic procedure. The details are interpolated by their relation to the main framework. Parallels are controlled by knowing their V's, and proportional division is used to establish intermediates when the V concerned is far off the board.

A common case of this sort occurs when the mass of a building has been blocked in and it is desired to mark off floor levels, window sills, and heads, etc. (Illus. 6-7-A). Since V^R is inaccessible we cannot subdivide the principal façade directly by drawing horizontals as we can on the left side. If, however, we subdivide D-E in the same proportions as A-B and join the corresponding points, we will get our interpolated parallels without using their V.

The geometrical principle involved in finding the points on D-E is the theorem that lines parallel to the base of a triangle divide the sides proportionately. In order to make the divisions that we want, we have only to draw D-A' (equal to A-B) at any convenient angle to D-E; divide D-A' into the same parts as A-B; join A' and E to form the triangle, and then find the other divisions on D-E by lines parallel to A'-E. The points thus determined on D-E now can be joined to the corresponding points on A-B.

In sketching from nature the divisions are usually first made by eye as halves (or thirds). A series of reference lines is thus established to which smaller divisions can be referred with reasonable accuracy.

In order to use the above device it is necessary to establish upper and lower limiting lines. Often only one is known fully, and one point on the other. The question then arises as to the easiest way to determine the required second line. We can always fall back on fundamentals, select a point known to be on the line, and find its perspective by Proposition IV, Chap. 10, but this may involve considerable graphic manipulation for which data is lacking.

Consider the following situation: in Illus. 6-7-B,

> *Given:* HH, C and A-B, but the V of A-B on HH is "off the board."
>
> *Required:* Through X draw X-W to the V of A-B to establish limits for interpolation of many minor lines.
>
> *Solution:* If we pass a vertical plane parallel to the picture plane through B, it will cut the line from A to C at point E which can be found in perspective by drawing a horizontal through B. A vertical from E to X-C will then give point Y from which a horizontal can be drawn to intersect the vertical through B at W. X-W will therefore be the perspective of a parallel to A-B, *i.e.*, it will if prolonged go to the same inaccessible vanishing point.

7. FRACTIONAL V'S AND M'S

Large drawings, such as murals which may occupy an entire wall of a room, often require a special procedure because the V's of main lines are impossible to locate within the space available. One may always assume other lines, chosen at angles so that their V's will lie inside the picture, as the means of locating important points. Usually it is easier to find "fractional V's." With their aid a base line for each important series can be found, and the rest of the series can then be determined by interpolation.

In Illus. 6-7-C,

> *Given:* Point A (on the vertical axis through C).
>
> *Required:* Draw A-B so that it will vanish at V on HH without using any points outside the "border."
>
> *Solution:* Think back to the way in which V would be found in the plan by drawing a parallel to A-B through S. If the distance C-V is divided in half (or thirds or quarters), $V/2$ will fall on our board. The point $V/2$ may be found by drawing a parallel to A-B through $S/2$, the mid-point of C-S. Having laid off $V/2$ in perspective, join it to point $A/2$ which is the center of C-A. A parallel to $A/2$-$V/2$ through A will go to the inaccessible V. Note that the geometry holds good only for a starting point A on the vertical axis. Of course the line through A, once found, can be extended.

Similarly, a "fractional" M may be used in cases where a measurement on the horizontal line of measures falls off the board. If half (or one-third, etc.) of a dimension is laid off, and the measuring line is drawn to a point $M/2$ half way between V^R and M^R, the required point A on the vanishing line will be obtained.

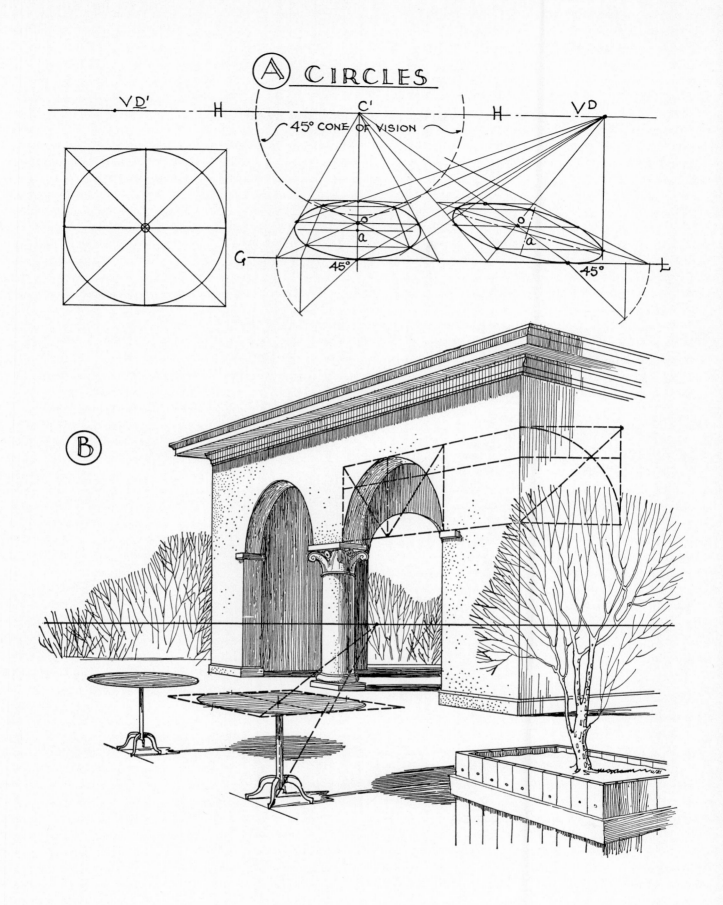

A CIRCLES

VD' H C' H VD

45° CONE OF VISION

45° 45°

G L

B

ILLUSTRATION 6-8

8. CIRCLES, CYLINDERS, CONES, ETC.

The problem of representing circles in linear perspective has fascinated the investigators of the mathematics of perspective for centuries. Many elaborate systems of finding "correctly" the points required have been published. It is easily demonstrated that the eye sees a circle as an ellipse unless it lies in a vertical plane with its center at C.[1] How to determine the curve accurately is an interesting problem, but not a very valuable procedure for the architectural draftsman to learn.

He should, however, know how to solve the most common cases—the horizontal circle (such as a column base, a floor pattern, or the spring of a dome) and the vertical circle (such as an arch, a clock face, or the end of a horizontal cylinder). Observation of such objects in actuality will clearly demonstrate two things. First we will be aware that the circular forms all appear to be flattened into ellipses, and second we will note the eye's instinctive tendency to center on the object when we try to decide on the exact shape of its curves. Try to see clearly what the circular top of a nearby stool looks like. Is it a true ellipse or only an approximation of one? Inevitably your eye will swing until $C.V.R.$ hits the center of the circle, which then can be accurately observed, and its truly elliptical appearance can be noted.

Before spending any time on wondering how to find such an ellipse geographically, remember how your own eye behaved and arrange your picture accordingly. **Always look directly at an object composed of circles** if its image will be an important part of your picture. **Never compose a perspective** with circular objects at the edges of the cone of correct vision. If this condition cannot be avoided (a colonnade will inevitably involve this difficulty), one is justified in "adjusting" (see Chap. 3, Sec. 10). Since the eye never sees accurately the visual change of curved shapes in perspective except when looking at them directly, it does not accept a geometrically exact drawing of things which are not as exactly fixed in our visual memories. We can recognize (even though it is not in the cone of correct vision) that the ellipse directly below C in Illus. 6-8-A represents a circle, but it is difficult to believe that the curve to the right is a correct view of the same circle.

Circles, like other curves, may be put into perspective by craticulation as already explained (Chap. 4, Sec. 8), or by finding significant points through which to draw a freehand line. If points of tangency to a superscribed polygon are selected, and the tangent sides are drawn, they will help greatly in guiding our eye and hand. A square is usually the minimum reference figure. It gives us four very important points and four tangents. These are often sufficient, but if more exactitude is necessary, the diagonals of the square can quickly be added, together with the 45° square through the intersections of the diagonals with the circumference (see Illus. 6-8-A).

Notice two peculiarities of the perspective of a circle: (1) a, the center of the image (which is an ellipse, considered merely as a mathematical figure) is not the same point as the o, image of the center of the circle; (2) the axes of the ellipse are not vertical and horizontal lines (on the paper), unless the center of the circle lies on $C.V.R.$

Many mistakes in representation arise from misunderstanding these unusual geometric relationships. Since the ellipses are often most important as determinants for the profiles of surfaces of revolution, which are drawn as the extreme tangents of the curves, it is essential that the draftsman have the "feel" of such projections and of the figures on which they are based. A cylinder (or column) for example, will actually be seen as a width slightly different from its diameter projected into perspective (see Illus. 3-7). The top and bottom curves should be drawn first, and then the sides as tangents to these ellipses.

---

[1] Another special case arises when the spectator is himself inside the circle (a circular room, for example). The visible curves will then be hyperbolic in relation to the horizon, or parabolic if the eye is located on the circle itself.

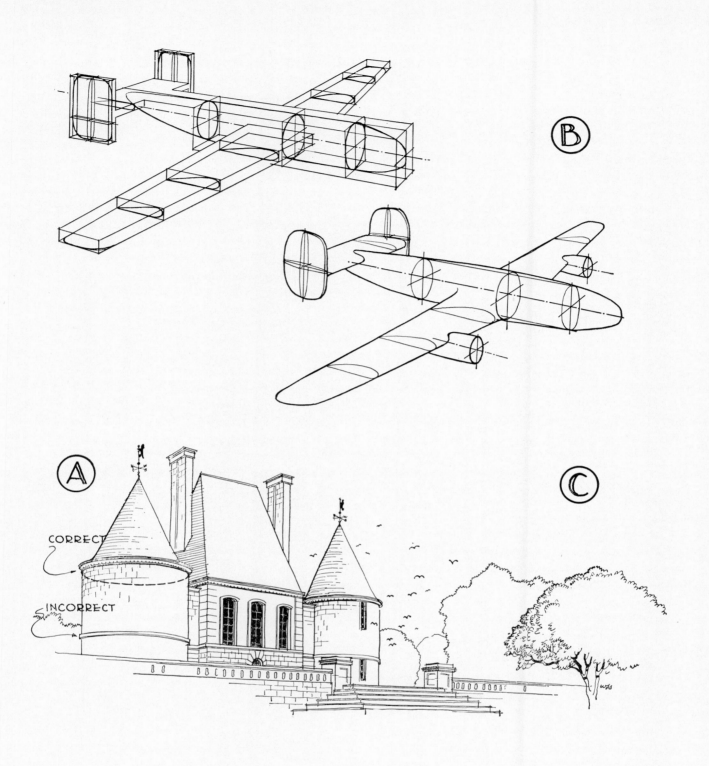

CORRECT

INCORRECT

Ⓐ Ⓑ Ⓒ

96

ILLUSTRATION 6-9

Intermediates, like stone courses in Illus. 6-9, can be interpolated if care is taken to see that they "go around," particularly at the profiles, and do not intersect the outlines. Watch that each ellipse becomes more open (round) as it lies farther above or below the horizon, where it will of course look like a straight line. Be careful also that where a cone terminates a cylinder of equal diameter, as at the roofs of the towers, the bounding lines of the two do not meet on the ellipse which represents their line of intersection. The sides of the cone are tangents to this line drawn from the apex, whereas the profiles of the cylindrical towers are verticals.

9. PLASTIC FORMS

Up to the twentieth century, architectural forms were traditionally based on materials such as stone, lumber, brick, concrete, etc., which were joined by cutting, bending, nailing, pouring into forms, etc. These processes resulted in volumes defined by the intersection of plane surfaces. Only in sculpture were found freely blending plastic shapes, such as today are becoming common through the quantity production of objects, ranging from automobile bodies to ladies' compacts, which are drawn, stamped, molded or die-cast. The resulting objects are not surfaces of revolution such as come from the potter's wheel or the lathe. They are not subject to exact mathematical analysis either of structure or shape. Yet they are already influencing our concepts of architectural design, especially for interiors, and we encounter them visually wherever we turn our eyes. Hence we must be able to draw them in perspective.

The best procedure is of course to "get the big things right, then add details." The principle of blocking-in, already explained in Chap. 4, Sec. 8, will be our best guide. Think of the sculptor "freeing" his statue from a block of marble, and first draw the block. Then make enough cross sections through each part to determine its volume at each critical change of form. Over this skeleton and within the block, draw the profiles which will express the object (Illus. 6-9-B).

Be careful to limit the amount of drawing in accordance with the distance of the object from the station point. Do not attempt to draw details unless they are nearby. The volume of an indefinite form, like a tree, may be quite large—100 to 150 ft. in height, or more—but the leaves are still only a few inches long. Hence they cannot be delineated individually without completely blackening the paper with lines. They must be treated as masses of foliage rather than as separate entities. The same restraint must be used in deciding how to represent airplanes, furniture, people, etc.

PEOPLE

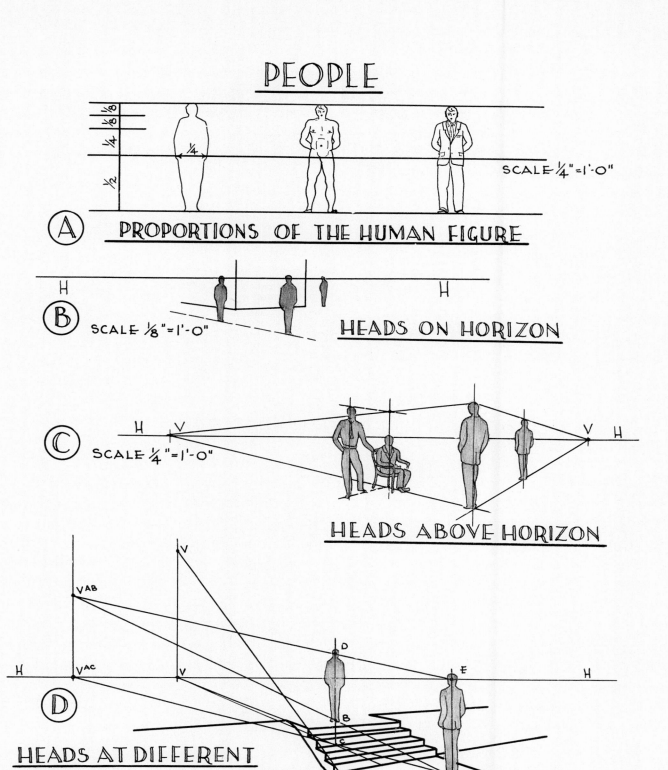

Ⓐ PROPORTIONS OF THE HUMAN FIGURE

SCALE ¼"=1'-0"

Ⓑ SCALE ⅛"=1'-0" **HEADS ON HORIZON**

Ⓒ SCALE ¼"=1'-0" **HEADS ABOVE HORIZON**

Ⓓ HEADS AT DIFFERENT LEVELS

10. PEOPLE

While architectural perspective is not primarily concerned with the representation of the human body (so-called *life drawing*), it is often called upon to add such elements to its primary subject matter, in order to increase interest, and especially in order to help give scale. "Man is the measure of all things," pictorial as well as philosophic, and his figure must be shown as well as implied by the design if we are to achieve an effect of reality.

Usually the people in an architectural drawing are small—at the scale of $\frac{1}{8}$ in. = 1 ft. an average man measures less than $\frac{3}{4}$ in. in height at the picture plane. Such a reduction means the elimination of detail. The height must be correct and the head proportioned to the rest of the figure. Occasionally arms and legs may be indicated, and if so, these parts should be subdivided from the over-all dimensions as shown in Illus. 6-10-A. More often, only a silhouette in block form will be necessary to serve the purpose intended. Greater precision would run the danger of making the people, who should serve only to enhance the architectural effect, become so interesting to the eye as to capture the attention which should be devoted to the building.

The drafting procedure involved when "putting people into perspective" is extremely simple. One simply has to decide where figures are needed, mark the spot where they are to stand, and then determine their heights (commonly taken as 5'-6") at the chosen points. Of course the measurement can only be made on the picture plane, and has to be referred back into perspective. If the people are assumed to be standing on level ground, and the horizon was taken at normal eye level (5'-3"), HH will pass through their eyes also, no matter where they are placed. The draftsman merely has to proportion correctly a figure whose height is established, by HH, as soon as the position of his feet is marked (Illus. 6-10-B).

When HH is taken lower than a normal man's eye level, or when the ground slopes down from the building toward the spectator, the positions of the heads of human figures are determined just as the tops of poles (or any other objects) would be—a true measurement on PP is carried back into perspective by means of the V's of parallel lines. It is often convenient to establish new V's for this purpose since thus one can avoid drawing construction lines across the picture. Illustration 6-10-C suggests that pairs of figures can be handled together easily in this way.

When a figure on a stair is required and also one in the foreground, the V of the sloping parallel lines connecting the feet and heads of the two men may conveniently be used (Illus. 6-10-D). Given the stair and points A and B, first find the point C, below B on the ground (*i.e.*, on the same horizontal plane as A). Draw A-C to establish its V on the HH. The V of A-B will lie on the vertical through the V of A-C, and can be found by drawing A-B to intersect this vertical. The line from E to V^{AB} will locate D on the prolongation of C-B. Other ways of locating C, in addition to that shown, will occur to the alert perspective draftsman.

Study for Holder Tower, Princeton, N.J.; Day & Klauder, architects; drawn by Charles Z. Klauder.

ILLUSTRATION 6-11

PROBLEMS

1. Find (approximately) the V's of the hips of a roof.

2. On a piece of tracing paper laid over Illus. 4-7, sketch in a coffee table in front of the sofa and at 45° to it. Use approximate V's.

3. On the left façade of the building block shown in Illus. 6-3-B, locate a door in the center, one-fifth as wide as the façade.

4. Draw a perspective of the skyscraper shown as Illus. 4-9 at an angle which shows the V of the wide side well beyond the board. Use the Hood method.

5. Check the accuracy of your perspective of the dormers and gables of Prob. 3, Chap. 5 by relation to their V's. (Locate the V's approximately if they fall off the board.)

6. Make a one-point interior perspective of the room shown in Illus. 4-7. Compare with the effect in the illustration. Which is preferable? Why?

7. Set up strips for the distant V in the perspective of a skyscraper which you made by the Hood method (see prob. 4 above). Draw picture and check results.

8. Three planes, mutually perpendicular, have a common point of intersection. With this point as a center, draw in perspective a circle on each plane. (The circle which will contain the resulting ellipses will be the perspective of a sphere with the same center and radius.)

9. Draw the perspective of an automobile by the method of Illus. 6-9-B, and about the same size. Use a photograph of a car that you like as a model for design.

10. Draw three human figures on each of the drawings that you have worked out in answer to Probs. 2, 4, 7, and 9.

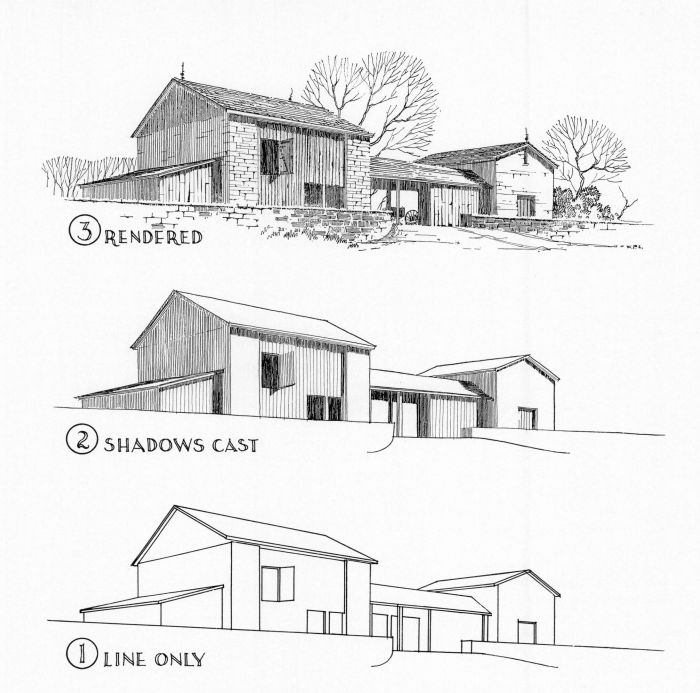

③ RENDERED

② SHADOWS CAST

① LINE ONLY

FROM LINE TO TONE

ILLUSTRATION 7-1

Chapter 7

LIGHT, SHADE, AND SHADOW

1. LIGHT

It has already been pointed out several times that linear perspective is at best a conventional method of representing real three-dimensional objects on the flat surface of paper or canvas. All line drawings are unnatural in the sense that no one has ever actually seen an object in space merely as a linear arrangement. There are no lines in the pictures which our eyes record on their retinas. Perhaps the nearest thing to a line which we ever see in nature is a wire silhouetted against the sky. Otherwise we see **surfaces**—differentiated by different tones and colors rather than bounded by thin dark lines.

Actual objects in space become visible by reflecting back to our eyes cones (or pyramids) of light rays which together identify **areas** of differing luminous intensities. The rays themselves are not visible. Air, like glass, is transparent to light. Only when moisture, dust, or smoke particles are suspended in the atmosphere can we perceive the rays themselves directly. At sunrise or sunset, when the sun's light is nearly parallel to the surface of the earth and hence travels through air carrying dust or smoke from the ground, we can often see the rays striking across the sky. A lamppost on a misty night will often seem to be giving out visible light, particularly if the effect is seen through the branches of trees, or is otherwise broken up. The concentrated beams from searchlights are so powerful that they pick up whatever particles of water, vapor, or solid matter are suspended in the air, and thus usually become visible. What we see is always the effect of light—its reflection back to the eye from some object—not the light itself. It would be more exact to speak of illumination in describing such lighted surfaces, but by long custom the illumined portions of an object are called the light areas on the drawing which represents it.

A photograph records all the forms before the camera by their relative values on a scale of tones ranging from black to white. Similarly a perspective can be rendered by shading the areas which represent the objects involved, rather than merely drawing their bounding lines. However, it is usually easier to make definite the shapes of these areas by finding their outlines first. The proper value of each surface can then be decided and the proper tone applied to it. The lines originally found by the process of linear perspective are used merely as guides for fixing the proper shape of each area, and should not be visible in the completed drawing. The final step is color, which is a subject in itself and beyond the scope of this text. In order, then, to obtain more natural effects than are possible by linear perspective alone, we must develop the principles by which we can determine the differing luminosities of all parts of an object, as well as merely finding its bounding edges. Nature presents us with an apparently overwhelming variation in the illumination of the things that we see. As the light changes with the progression of the sun from dawn to dusk, countless new and ever-changing patterns are formed. Since in any one drawing we can show only one of the many possible aspects of the exterior world about us, our first task is to decide on the exact position of the source of light under the particular conditions which we have selected. Some suggestions as to how to make our choice are given in Sec. 4. Once it has been made, the results are inevitable and can be worked out graphically.

We shall simplify our task if we use the term *light* (as applying to areas in our drawing) to describe only those portions of our object which the light rays strike directly when they come from the assumed direction. We are dealing now with the sun as our light source (see Sec. 9, for artificial light) and its power is so great that all the space which we are depicting is full of its rays, except where solid objects intervene. Not only are its rays innumerable but they come from so large and so distant a source that they can be considered to be parallel. Thus like all parallel lines they will seem in perspective to have a vanishing point, and we must find this point in order to draw them. The second step, then, is to locate V^{Ray}—the vanishing point of the light rays under the assumed conditions.

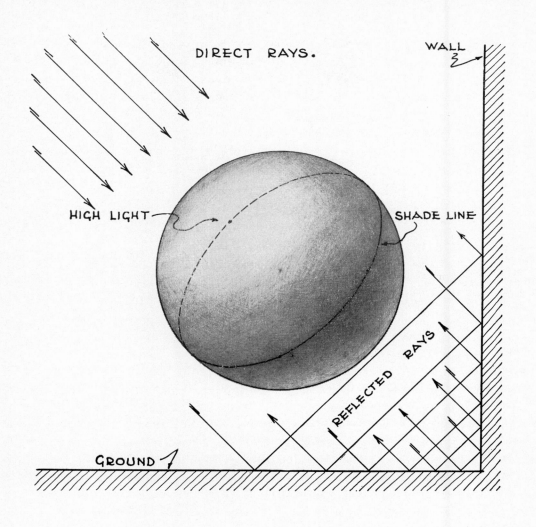

DIRECT RAYS.

WALL

HIGH LIGHT

SHADE LINE

REFLECTED RAYS

GROUND

SCALE OF VALUES

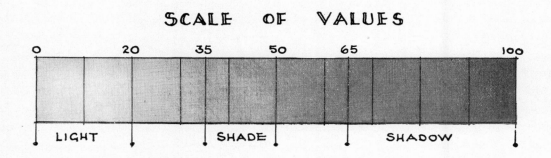

0   20   35   50   65   100

LIGHT   SHADE   SHADOW

ILLUSTRATION 7-2

Not all surfaces which the rays of the sun strike have the same brightness. The intensity of illumination depends on the angle between the surface and the rays. The brightest (whitest in our scale of light and dark which can vary only from white paper to black ink or pencil) portions of our picture will be reserved to depict areas at right angles to the light. These are called *high lights*, and are very considerably "whiter" than those portions turned nearly parallel to the rays.

A sphere, for example, will show us almost every possible relation between surface and light source. There will be one spot directly perpendicular to some one ray, and hence very bright indeed, while other portions will be less brilliant as they approach in their curvature the position of being parallel to the direction of light. They will all, however, be "in light," and as light areas they should be shaded (darkened) less than the other portions of the drawing.

If we chart the values at our command, calling the white of our paper (or our whitest pigment) 0, and our blackest ink (or pencil) 100, we should restrict our use of tones which are to express light surfaces to the range between 100 and 75. This is a somewhat arbitrary division, and should not be tested quantitatively but rather pictorially. The important thing is to make variations to express the different angular relations between surfaces and light rays and yet stay within a range which will be distinctly separate visually from the values used for unlighted surfaces.

2. *SHADE*

Most objects, especially rounded ones, present to us under natural illumination not only light areas which are directly exposed to the sun's rays, but also areas which are so situated that the rays cannot strike them. The undersides (soffits) of all planes lighted from above are common examples of this type of surface, which we call *shade*. A sphere will show a crescent of this character on the opposite side from the light, and a column (cylinder) will have a vertical band of shade on the left or right, unless the sun is directly in front of it.

Theoretically, since no light can strike such shade faces, they should be completely dark, and be rendered with our deepest black. Actually the fact that they are turned away from the direct light rays makes them all the more fully exposed to rays reflected from the ground or nearby objects. In nature only a part of the light is absorbed by the surface which the rays first encounter. Some of their intensity is reflected back at an *angle of reflection* equal to the *angle of incidence*.

The amount of light reflected depends on the color and texture of the surface as well as on the angle, and varies from 10 to 90 per cent of the intensity of direct rays, averaging about 35 to 40 per cent. Hence shade surfaces **are** illumined, although by reflection and never as intensely as light areas, but they do not show as wide variation in value. In our scale we may thus assign the range from 35 to 50 to shade areas. Notice that there is a gap of 15 points left below the darkest light area in order to differentiate between the two categories. Under particular artistic conditions, this distinction need not be followed punctiliously. For the sake of emphasis or contrast shade may sometimes be rendered lighter than light. Remember that for geniuses "rules are made to be broken," but for others they are a great help, especially at the beginning.

On rounded objects there is theoretically a definite line of tangency between the curving surface and the light rays, which marks off light from shade. This can occasionally be observed on highly polished materials as an exact line, but it usually seems to be blurred, because the eye cannot judge exactly the difference in value between the last points that receive light, and the first ones that fail to do so. This indistinct transition should be duplicated in a drawing, because it gives a clear means of showing the difference in character between round and angular objects. The latter have of course definite lines of demarcation between light and shade because of the sharp edges between their various faces.

However, every rounded object actually has a distinct line somewhere (although the eye may not distinguish it exactly) which separates its light from its shade surfaces and is called *the shade line* of the object. It may or may not be visible, in whole or in part, but it is extremely useful and important because it enables us to determine the limits of the third class of surfaces—those which are cut off from the light rays by an intervening object and which are therefore in shadow.

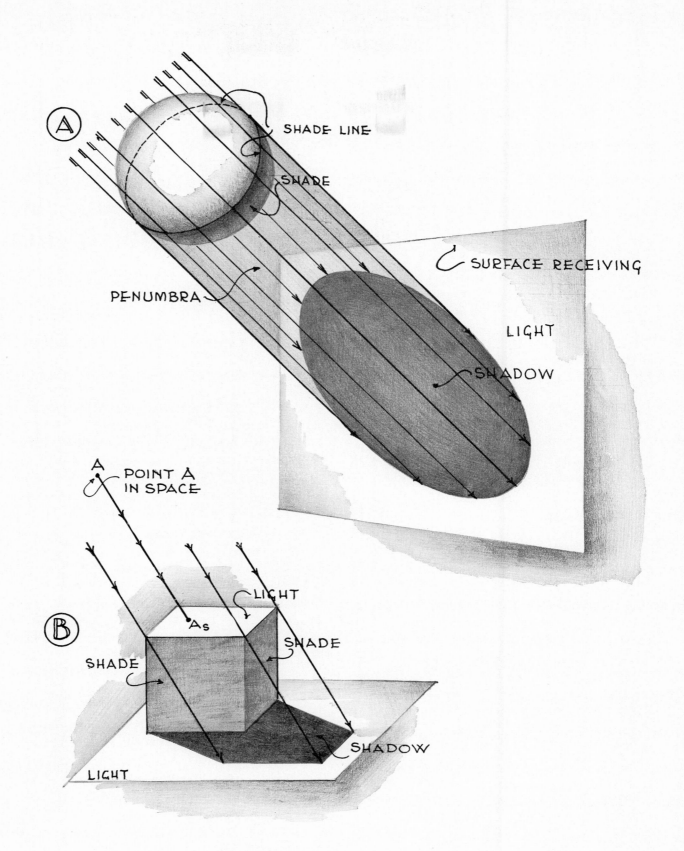

SHADE LINE

SHADE

SURFACE RECEIVING

PENUMBRA

LIGHT

SHADOW

A
POINT A
IN SPACE

LIGHT

As

SHADE

SHADE

SHADOW

LIGHT

ILLUSTRATION 7-3

3. SHADOW

Since we assume that all space is filled with light rays, any object which enters our field of vision must intercept a certain number of them. Some of its surfaces (the light areas) will thus become illumined, but the fact that certain rays have been intercepted will leave a part of the space beyond the object in darkness. Consequently, a sort of prism or cylinder without light rays, called the *penumbra*, is established which continues through space in the same direction as the rays until another object is affected by it. This second object would have been fully lighted if the first had not intervened, cutting off some of the rays that would otherwise have reached it, and preventing the illumination of the parts of its surface which would have been in light.

Such a darkened portion of a surface is called a *shadow*. Note that it requires two objects to cause this phenomena —one nearer the light source to intercept the rays, and one farther away whose lighted areas are thus partly (or wholly) obscured. The intercepting object **casts** the shadow and determines the form of the prism of darkness of which we become conscious only when it intercepts the surface of the receiving object.

Ordinarily our eyes cannot **see** the light rays as they travel through space because there is nothing to reflect them back and hence nothing to record on our retinas. Empty space looks black to us, although it is filled with light rays. Only when they strike some object and illume it, are the rays reflected back to our eyes, so that we can become conscious of their effect. Similarly we can rarely **see** the prism of shadow until it is interrupted by some object. The shadow becomes visible only as a darkened part of the otherwise illumined surface of another object.

Stormy skies sometimes send shafts of light through clouds in such a way as to cause visible streaks of light and dark through the air. Only the presence of water vapor in the otherwise transparent atmosphere permits such effects to be visible. The light striking through the openings between the clouds reflects from countless millions of minute water particles and becomes perceptible by our eyes, and the shadow voids between the shafts of light are observable by contrast. If conditions permit the eye to follow the rays to the earth, alternating darkened and illumined areas will be clearly distinguishable and can be traced back to the holes in the clouds which cause them. This is the reverse of the usual condition in that most of the light is cut off by the storm clouds, whereas we are more apt to think of open skies and unobstructed sunlight. In mountainous country one can often observe this abnormal condition, particularly near sunset (or sunrise). A cloud shadow is visible as a pattern of dark on an otherwise bright slope, and the eye can trace the prism of shadow back toward the sun, and mark the cloud that caused the phenomenon.

Three things are thus necessary to cause shadows—light, an intervening (casting) object, and a receiving surface. All three must be known exactly in order to determine what the outline of the shadow area will be. Its boundaries are the lines of intersection between a surface and a prism. The latter gets its form from the direction of the rays and from the shape of the **object casting.** The possibilities are endless, yet we can formulate some simple general laws which will enable us to work out most shadows accurately and easily. Two basic rules, more important than any others, grow out of the definition of a shadow as it has been explained above. Rule 1 is positive and starts us in the right direction in every case. Rule 2 is negative but eliminates a large class of possible errors.

Rule 1. The shadow of every point must lie on the ray through the point. Hence if we know how to draw the ray through each point involved in our picture, we have fixed for every point a line on which its shadow must somewhere be found. We have already defined a shadow as the absence of light from part of a surface because of the intervention of another object. The shadow of any point can thus be found exactly if we start with the point casting the shadow, and follow the ray through it until some other surface is encountered. To find just where the ray strikes is not always easy, but our rule greatly simplifies the problem, and in many important cases leads to a direct solution.

Rule 2. There can never be a shadow on a shade face. By our definition, shade faces are so turned that light rays cannot strike them. Hence they can never be the recipients of shadows, because these can occur only on surfaces which the light rays would strike, were they not cut off by the intervening object which casts the shadow.

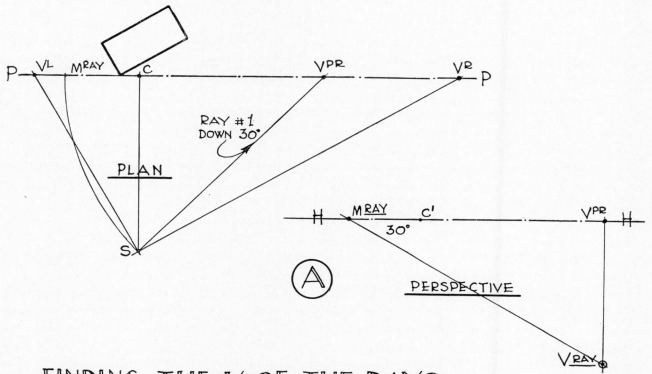

RAY #1
DOWN 30°

PLAN

30°

PERSPECTIVE

Ⓐ

FINDING THE V OF THE RAYS.

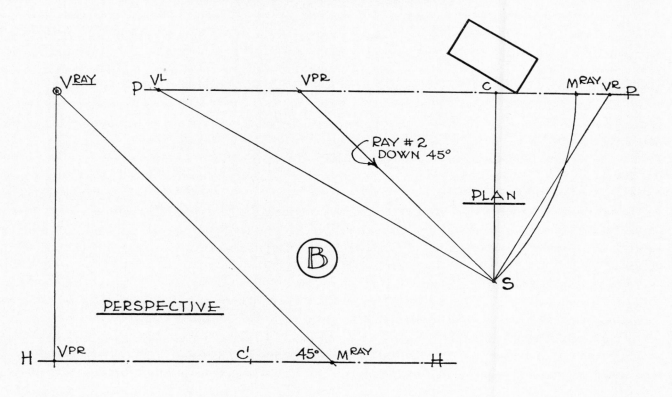

RAY #2
DOWN 45°

PLAN

Ⓑ

PERSPECTIVE

45°

ILLUSTRATION 7-4

4. THE VANISHING POINT OF THE RAYS

Since the problem of casting shadows depends on three factors—the direction of light, the shape of the object casting the shadow, and the type of surface on which the shadow falls—we must choose a definite angle for the light rays as the first step toward a solution. If the picture represents an outdoor view, lighted by the sun, the rays will be so nearly parallel that we can consider them actually to be so. Hence they will seem in perspective to converge at a vanishing point, like any other series of parallel lines. Once we have found this point we can easily draw rays wherever we need them in the perspective.

Such a vanishing point for light rays (symbol V^{Ray}) is found by the same process by which the vanishing point of any set of sloping parallel lines is determined (see Chap. 6, Sec. 1). The angle is usually shown by drawing the plan of a typical ray on the orthographic plan of the object, and then fixing the angle to the horizontal by a notation in degrees and an arrow indicating the inclination down or up. The necessary information may be given in various other ways, but the important thing is to record sufficient data so that the direction of the light rays is fixed exactly.

In Sec. 5 reasons are given for choosing a particular angle of light under particular conditions. Now we are concerned with translating the effect of our choice into a working point in our perspective drawing. The procedure is already familiar to us and is summed up in Proposition IX of Chap. 10.

Beginning in the orthographic plan, draw through S a parallel to the plan of the rays. Where this strikes the picture plane is the vanishing point of the plans of the rays (symbol V^{PR}). This will lie on the horizon in perspective, while all inclined lines whose plans lie in this same direction will vanish somewhere on the vertical through it.

In order to determine where the vanishing point of rays at our chosen angle will fall on this vertical, we must know the corresponding measuring point. This is found as usual by revolving S to PP in plan, using V^{PR} as a center. This M^{Ray} is then laid off on HH in perspective, and the true angle of the rays to the horizontal is drawn from it to intersect the vertical through V^{PR} at the point desired—which is V^{Ray} (the vanishing point of the rays).

At this stage students often get confused. Arguing that the sun is always above the earth when its light is striking objects which we can see, they want to draw the angle of the rays **above** the horizon, without thinking of the relation of the sun to the spectator. In most pictures it is assumed to be behind him. If that is the case, rays passing downward through his eye will hit the picture plane **below** the horizon, not above it. This should be obvious from Illus. 7-4-A.

It does seem rather queer to draw light rays in a perspective toward a point which is "under the ground." Yet that is exactly the direction in which the rays are going when the sun is behind us. Rays through the upper portions of the object are traveling down and away from us. When V^{Ray} is below the horizon and we draw rays to it in perspective, we are drawing the continuation of the rays **away** from their source and not toward it.

Whenever the sun is behind us, we use this infinite extension of the rays to their theoretical vanishing point as the means of drawing them in perspective. It will be farther to the right or left of C according to its angle in plan, and farther down from HH, according to its angle to the horizontal. Since we ordinarily have a free choice in deciding on the direction of light, many possibilities are presented. However, it is certainly a great convenience to keep V^{Ray} on the board. Usually satisfactory results can be obtained by limiting our selection to angles which produce that result.

If we want side lighting it is best to swing all the way around until the rays are parallel to the picture plane. Under these conditions there will be no V^{Ray}. When the rays are parallel to the picture plane they do not vanish, and can be drawn in perspective as geometrically parallel lines at the given angle to the horizon.

A third possible condition is that in which the rays are inclined **toward** the spectator. In this case V^{Ray} will be found by laying off at its true angle at M but this time **above** the horizon. Now the rays are coming toward us, and their vanishing point is the representation of their source, which is assumed to be infinitely distant and can therefore be represented in the same way as a vanishing point. The procedure in finding it is exactly similar to that in finding the vanishing point of the rays when the sun is behind the observer. The true angle of the rays to the horizontal is laid off at M^{Ray}, **above** HH, and prolonged to meet the vertical through V^{PR} at the desired V^{Ray} (Illus. 7-4-B).

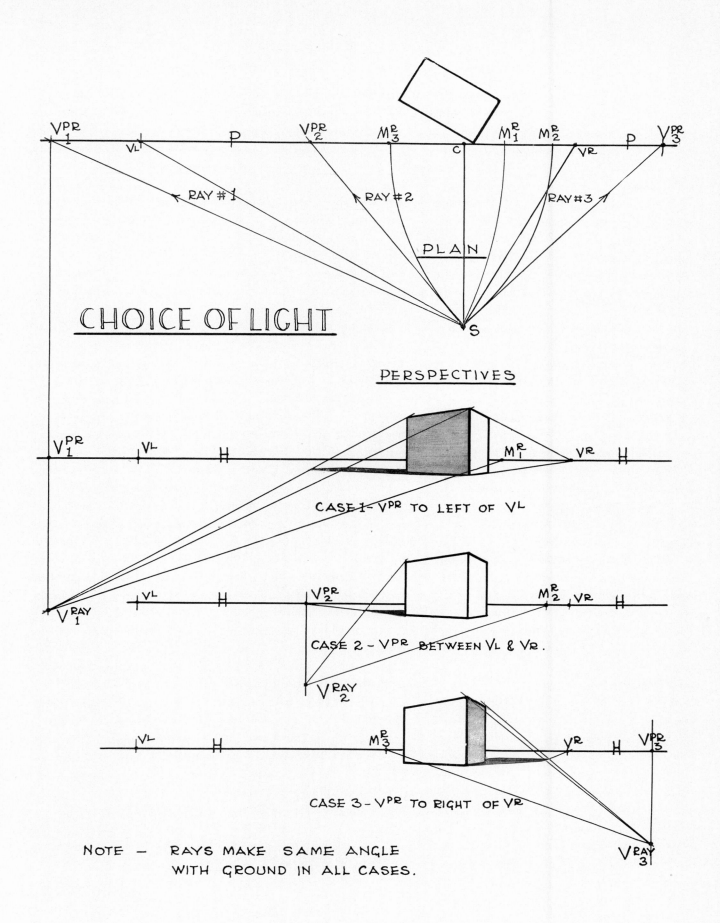

PLAN

CHOICE OF LIGHT

PERSPECTIVES

CASE 1 - V^PR TO LEFT OF V^L

CASE 2 - V^PR BETWEEN V^L & V^R.

CASE 3 - V^PR TO RIGHT OF V^R

NOTE — RAYS MAKE SAME ANGLE
WITH GROUND IN ALL CASES.

5. CHOOSING THE DIRECTION OF LIGHT

The distribution of light, shade, and shadow in a picture (called *chiaroscuro* by painters) is almost as important as the choice of a proper station point in producing the finest perspective effects. The possible variations are legion, and the mastery of such a subject is attained only through a lifetime of study and observation. Cross lights and reflections add endless opportunities for artistic composition and expression. In architectural drawing we are normally concerned not so much with such subtleties as with the exact determination of the effect of a given light source on a specific object.

The basic problem is to decide on the direction from which we want the light to come. The field of choice is so wide that even an expert architectural renderer must usually make several experimental sketches before he can determine the most effective decision for a given subject. However, there are a few simple guiding principles which will help us to work in the right direction. If they are kept in mind at the start we will be able to eliminate most of the undesirable possibilities. How much farther we will proceed along the road leading to the best possible distribution of light and dark masses in our picture will depend on our artistic ability, our experience, and our willingness to take pains.

If we are drawing from nature we will, of course, have to accept the conditions established by the actual relation of the sun to our object. In the Northern Hemisphere its southern sides will receive direct light at some time during each day. Its eastern faces will be in strong sunlight in the morning and its western faces during the afternoon. In summer the sun will rise farther to the northeast and will attain a high angle at noon before it passes to its setting in the northwest. In winter the angle with the surface of the earth will be less, even at midday. Morning light will begin south of east and afternoon light will end south of west. Buildings in the extreme north of this wide zone are never illumined by as high an angle of sunlight as are those in the extreme south, where the summer sun at noon stands almost vertically overhead.

In addition to geographical location we must consider the points of the compass on the actual site. The north side of a building in the North Temperate Zone never receives direct sunlight except for a few moments during the summer, and then only in the early morning or in the late afternoon. At such times the rays are nearly horizontal and strike the north portions of the object at a very flat angle. Of course the architectural design should give primary consideration to this condition, but in addition the lighting in a perspective representation of the object should accord with the natural possibilities.

This restriction is forgotten all too often. Many perspectives of buildings have been drawn showing a brilliant play of light and shade which could never exist in reality because the façade shown faced north. Such a drawing is of course deceitful and fails of its primary purpose, which is to show how the proposed building will look when actually built. The choice of light should be related to such limiting site conditions, just as the actual location should limit the choice of S in drawing an object which exists or which is intended to be erected in a particular place.

Having first noted approximately the angles of light possible under the given conditions, we have still a wide field of choice before we fix the rays exactly. Morning light may be chosen which will come from the right if we are facing north, or afternoon sun coming from the left. In either case, it is best generally to choose an angle oblique enough so that either the right- or left-hand faces (at right angles to each other in most buildings) will be in shade. Then our picture will contain the three basic kinds of surface—light, shade, and shadow—and will offer considerable opportunities for pictorial contrast. If we think first of the angle of the rays in plan (see Illus. 7-5) we will see that V^{PR} must lie to the left of V^L in order to put the left-hand faces in shade, when the light comes from the front. Conversely it must lie to the right of V^R if we wish to have shade on the right-hand faces.

If we locate V^{PR} between V^L and V^R both the principal faces of the object will be in light. While they will not be equally illuminated unless the rays bisect the angle between them, they will not offer as interesting a contrast as if one side or the other were in shade. Sometimes, however, it is required to show the whole object in light, and in that case we **must** place V^{PR} somewhere near the center of the picture, between the two principal V's.

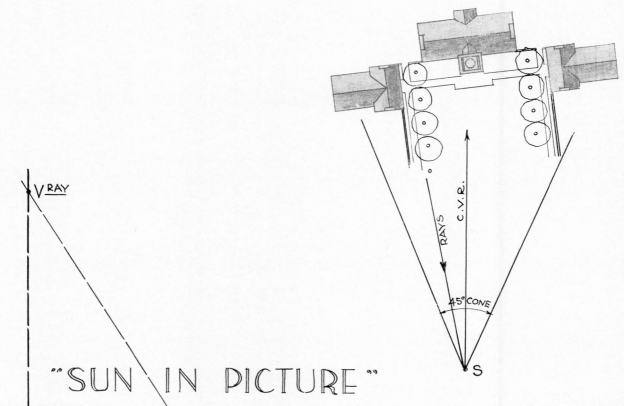

"SUN IN PICTURE"

Study for court, Westminster Choir College, Princeton, N.J.: Sherley W. Morgan, architect; drawn by Schell Lewis.

ILLUSTRATION 7-6

Having located V^{PR}, we draw the vertical through it on which V^{Ray} must be located. The farther we put it below the horizon, the steeper will be the angle of the rays to the horizontal. In practice it is rarely necessary to locate M^{Ray} exactly and draw a definite angle. Unless the conditions of the problem require such accuracy, it is sufficient to notice in the plan about where M must fall, and in the perspective to move V^{Ray} down from V^{PR} until approximately the desired angle would be formed by drawing to an M^{Ray} at about the proper location on HH. With a little practice V^{PR} and V^{Ray} may thus be located very quickly, yet so as to produce a play of light and shade in accordance with the site conditions and the pictorial results desired.

If we have chosen S to the north of the object for valid reasons, then we will be looking south, the sunlight will be coming toward us, and V^{Ray} will be above, instead of below the horizon. It will now represent the source of light rather than the eventual convergence of the rays when they are prolonged beyond the object to infinity. Such a direction of light is unusual enough to offer opportunities for producing striking effects, but these require skill in handling subtle differences of value and should be attempted only when the conditions justify them (Illus. 7-6).

In every case we must remember that our graphic procedure is designed to determine only the three principal conditions of illumination—light, shade, and shadow. Each will have wide variations within itself, depending on the angle of each part of the object to the direction of light that has been assumed. In order to interpret such differences with reasonable accuracy, we must always realize what approximate angle of light is involved in the choice we have made of V^{PR} and V^{Ray}. The experienced draftsman can assume these points and use them to determine shade and shadow, without first having decided on an exact direction of light, but he is always conscious of the approximate angle of illumination involved in his choice. It is excellent practice for the beginner to visualize about where the sun must have been to produce any location of V^{PR} and V^{Ray} which he has assumed.

Theoretically it is possible to determine by graphical methods the exact areas of light, shade, and shadow which will result from the selection of a particular direction of light. If the subject is composed largely of flat surfaces, meeting each other in definite edges, this process is not difficult and can be followed through geometrically. The infinite complexity of natural forms, such as vegetation, figures, etc., makes the process impossibly tedious to apply in such cases. Their illumination may, however, be approximated by using the "cubistic" method suggested for putting them into perspective, i.e., free plastic forms may be drawn by first determining the prismatic envelopes in which they might be enclosed. The shadows definitely determined on these envelopes will give the approximate shapes of the shadows on the "free" objects. The process is one of subdivision. The most important masses of light and dark are determined first, and then these larger areas are subdivided to approximate the different parts of the object no matter how complex they may be.

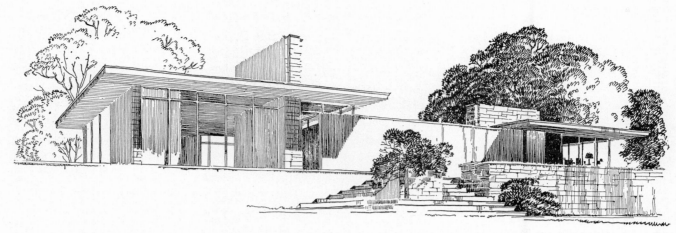

RIGHT

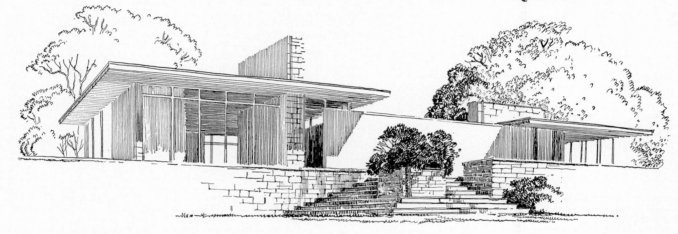

CENTER

LEFT

FOCUS·BY·CONTRAST

ILLUSTRATION 7-7

It has already been emphasized that light, shade, and shadow do not have fixed values in the scale from white paper to black ink. Considerable variations are possible within the range of tones suitable to each class of surface. Considering the picture as a whole, further variations should be made to simulate the focusing action of the eye. Because of focus and atmosphere the "brightest lights and deepest darks occur in the foreground." Thus contrast adds to form in creating the illusion of depth, which is the purpose of perspective drawing. However, the principal contrasts will not occur simply on the nearer portions of the object no matter how it is placed. Instead they will always center around C—the point toward which vision is directed.

Just as objects are seen less clearly as they are placed farther from the center of the cone of correct vision, and just as the focusing action of the eye limits the depth of field, so the tone contrasts of the picture must be most vivid around C, because it is the point toward which we have aimed the central visual ray in our perspective setup. Proper gradations of the tone values from the center out will greatly enhance the pictorial effect of our drawing. The direction of light should be selected with this in mind. The central portion of the picture should be emphasized by the pattern of light and dark as well as by the choice of station point. Near it should occur the sharpest contrasts, and any other pictorial relations, which will serve naturally to bring the eye of the person who sees the perspective to the point which was assumed as the center by the draftsman who laid out the drawing.

Since it is impossible to be certain, from looking at the finished perspective, exactly where C was located in the layout, it is often possible to shift the focus of values somewhat (without changing the outlines of the forms) in order to emphasize an important part of the object. Illustration 7-7 shows three different renderings of the same small building made over exactly the same perspective outline. By the use of changing values of light and dark the interest of the picture has been centered first to the right, then at the center, and then to the left. The effects produced are quite different even though the areas of light and shade are unchanged in shape.

This shifting of tone focus is a powerful tool which should be used with caution and not for the purpose of "faking." It is all too easy for the clever and unscrupulous draftsman to use pictorial manipulations which will produce a striking pattern on paper and divert attention from the actual form of the object. In architectural drawing, particularly when we are representing a building that has not yet been built, and are trying to show others how our design will appear if the building is actually erected, such "paper" manipulation is particularly to be avoided. Almost the worst thing that can happen because of it is for it to succeed in its deception, so that a faulty design is accepted and a building approved for construction which can never look like the perspective which was made of it in advance. But worst of all for the draftsman is to fool himself by his pictorial skill, and to believe that he has achieved a successful design, when he has made merely an effective picture.

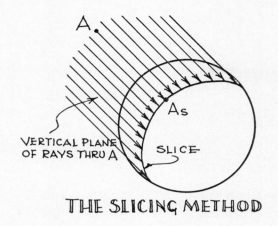

THE SLICING METHOD

CASE 1
SHADOW ON WALL

CASE 2
SHADOW ON GROUND

(PERSPECTIVES AT DOUBLE SCALE)

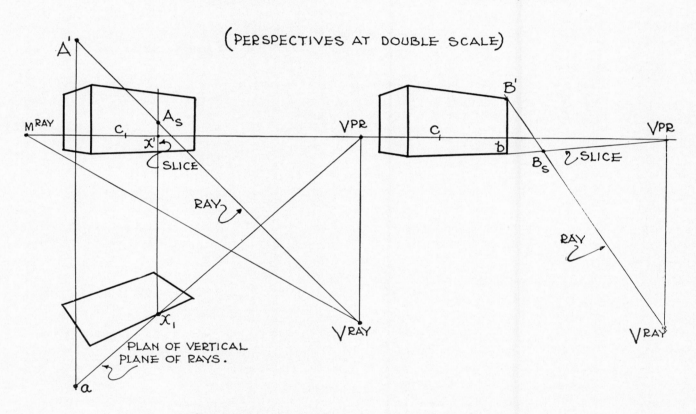

"DRAW THE RAY THRU THE POINT, AND THE
PLAN OF THE RAY THRU THE PLAN OF THE POINT"

ILLUSTRATION 7-8

6. THE SHADOW OF A POINT

From the definition of a shadow that we have already established, it is obvious that the graphical problem of determining the shadow of any point in a perspective drawing consists in finding where the ray through that point strikes some other surface. If we can solve this fundamental problem—how to find the shadow of a point—we can then find the shadow of **any line** by finding the shadows of enough of its points.

Since the visible objects we represent in perspective are defined by surfaces which are bounded by lines, we can find the shadows of solid objects if we can find the shadows of their shade lines, which determine the boundaries of the shadow areas. All shadows in even a complex drawing may thus be found if we have a simple and rapid method of finding the shadow of **any point.**

Such a procedure is provided by the so-called *slicing method*. It consists in finding the line of intersection between the surface receiving the shadow and a plane containing the light ray through the point casting the shadow. The line of intersection thus determined is the *slice* from which the method gets its name. The shadow of the given point must lie somewhere on this slice, because it is both part of the surface receiving the shadow and of a plane passing through the point and containing the ray, thus meeting our specification for a shadow. When the slice has been determined, we can then draw the ray through the point until it intersects the slice and thus determines the point of shadow that we are seeking.

The slicing method is universally valid provided that we can determine the slice. This is sometimes a lengthy and tedious process and seems scarcely worth the trouble necessary to locate only one point of the whole shadow. However, that one point may give us a start from which we can proceed rapidly by using other processes. A number of these are explained later. They expedite our work greatly but none of them can supplant the slicing method as a means of starting the solution.

If a vertical plane is selected as the slicing plane containing the ray, the problem of finding the slice will be greatly simplified, particularly for architectural subjects. In such drawings most of the surfaces are either vertical planes, such as walls; or horizontal planes, such as floors; or sloping planes, such as roofs. In each of these three cases the finding of the slice is quick and easy. Let us consider them separately.

Case 1. Shadows on vertical surfaces (*i.e.*, to locate A_s, the shadow of any point A, on any vertical surface such as W). Here the plane containing the ray, being vertical, must intersect the vertical surface receiving the shadow in a vertical line. The location of this slice can be determined quickly in plan, where the plane containing the ray will appear as a line having the same direction as that assumed for the rays.

If we make our perspective by using a perspective plan (Illus. 7-8-Case 1), we merely have to draw through the plan a of the point to V^{PR}. Where this line hits the plan of the vertical surface at x we can project vertically and thus find the slice. In the perspective drawing the ray can be drawn through point A' to V^{Ray}, and its intersection with the slice will be A_s.

If we have no perspective plan, the process may involve a little more work. We must go back to the orthographic plan and there draw through a (which is the plan of A) parallel to the direction of light. Where this line strikes the wall is the plan of the required slice. This point x can then be put into perspective, a vertical drawn through it, and the slice thus located. For complicated objects the advantages of a perspective plan are so great in simplifying the process of casting shadows that it is often worth while to make one as a timesaver even though the perspective may have been laid out by some other method.

Case 2. Shadows on horizontal surfaces (*i.e.*, to locate B_s, the shadow of any point B on any horizontal surface such as the ground). Finding such a shadow is even simpler than finding one on a vertical surface like a wall. In this case (Illus. 7-8-Case 2) a line through the plan of the point to V^{PR} will find the slice directly, since it is itself the line of intersection between the ground and a vertical plane whose direction is parallel to the rays. In perspective we have only to draw to V^{PR} through point b' (the plan of B') and find where the ray through B' intersects this slice.

The process can be summarized by saying **draw the ray through the point and the plan of the ray through the plan of the point.** Such a condensed and rhythmic statement is easy to remember and includes Case 1 if we consider that the plan of the ray will produce a vertical slice wherever it hits a vertical surface.

THE SLICING
(A) METHOD.

CASE III
SHADOW ON ROOF.

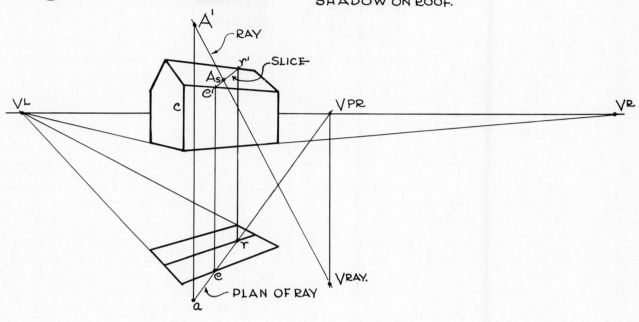

(B)

SHADOWS OF LINES
BY SHADOWS OF POINTS.

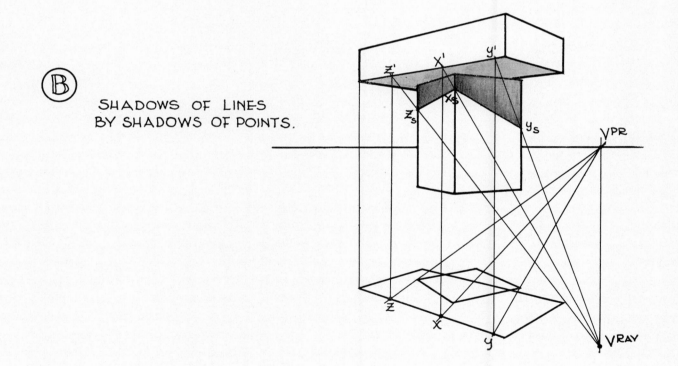

Case 3. Shadows on sloping planes (*i.e.*, to locate A_s on a sloping surface R like a roof). In this case the slice must be found by construction. However, we know that it will be a straight line, since it is the line of intersection of two planes. Two points will therefore suffice to determine it. If we consider that the roof and the front wall must meet in a straight line (eliminating the overhangs, etc.) the slice through the wall found by Case 1 will locate a point on the lower edge of the roof. We can easily imagine a second vertical wall under the ridge, which can be treated similarly and which will give a second point on the roof. Call the first point e and the second r. The slice is now determined as the line e-r, and we have only to draw the ray through A to intersect it at A_s (Illus. 7-9-A).

When the shadow of A falls on a curved surface, such as a dome, or a barrel vault, or a tree, the slice has to be worked out by appropriate geometrical methods. The slicing method is used as a control, and the shadows are determined by intelligent estimation rather than by mere guessing. It matters very little if there is a slight inaccuracy in a shadow on a natural form, since the spectator has no way of knowing the exact shape of the object.

The person looking at a picture gains his understanding of the forms that it portrays fully as much from the character of the shadows as from the outlines. Both must be correct in order to convey an exact impression. If the subject has definite form, like a building, the shadows must be as carefully and accurately drawn as are the profiles. If it is only a question of suggesting a type—like a tree or an automobile—meticulous accuracy is not as important as general character.

The slicing method can be used quickly and easily when applied to 95 per cent of the objects which are represented in architectural drawing. In the few remaining cases it can often be approximated with enough accuracy to give a reasonable answer without going through elaborate graphical constructions. The student should practice it until he is confident that he can apply it to any and all situations. Only then will he be ready to progress to other and shorter methods, which save much time but are not always applicable. When in doubt or difficulty, he will never be stumped if he has mastered the one method of casting shadows that never fails. There are no exceptions to the validity of the slicing method.

7. THE SHADOWS OF LINES

From our definition of a shadow, it follows that the shadow of any line will be caused by the rays through every point of the line. In the case of a straight line these rays will together form a plane whose intersection with any other plane surface must be a straight line. Hence the shadow of any straight line on any plane will be a straight line, and may be determined by knowing its two terminal points.

However, for determining shadows on complex objects there are usually simpler and quicker methods than proceeding point by point. In the first place time and effort can often be saved by selecting the proper point with which to begin. When the shadow of a line falls across two planes a broken shadow line will be caused, but we do not need to find four points as a consequence—provided that we begin with the point whose shadow falls on the line of the intersection of the two planes.

Instead of assuming points at random and finding their shadows, we must learn first to select the critical places for shadows on the object, then to work back to find the points which cast them. This procedure in applying the slicing method is a great timesaver, but is only possible of application when a perspective plan is available. Whenever shadows have to be cast it is always advantageous to lay out a perspective by the perspective plan method.

Take as an example the shadow of an overhanging object on two vertical surfaces at a salient angle to the spectator (Illus. 7-9-B). If we start in plan by drawing the plan of a ray **back** from the apex of the salient lower corner in order to find the plan of the point x whose shadow falls there, we can project up to find the actual point X' casting the shadow, and draw the ray through it down to hit the vertical edge between the two lower surfaces. We thus find a point of shadow which lies on both and will determine the shadows on each when only one other point has been found on each side.

In order to complete the determination of the shadows, these points are also selected in plan. Plans of rays are drawn back from V^{PR} to the outside corners of the façades in order to locate first the plans y and z and then the perspectives y' and z' of the points which cast shadows on these edges. All that we have to do is to draw the rays to V^{Ray} and mark the points where they intersect the edges and we have located the desired points y_s and z_s on the shadow lines.

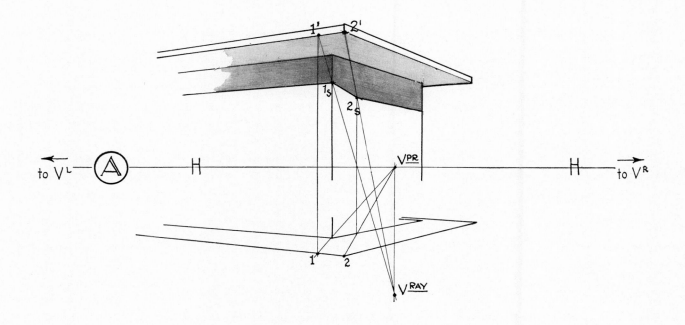

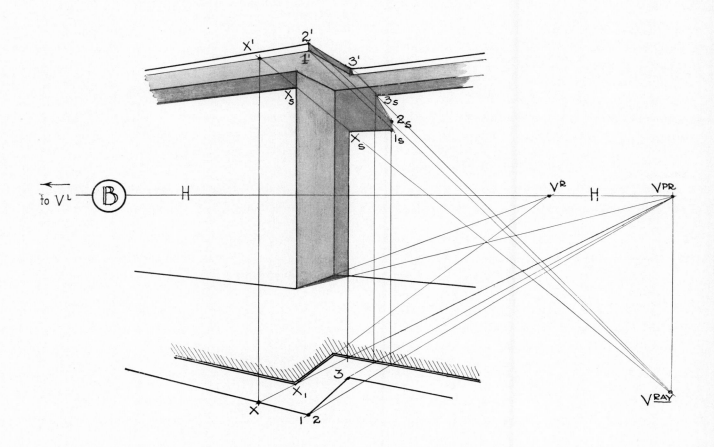

ILLUSTRATION 7-10

Very often this selective approach will solve a whole problem in shadows and require only one or two lines. Refer to Illus. 7-10-A—the very common case of an overhanging cornice carried around the salient intersection of two walls at the corner of a building. Here we need to find only two points by the slicing method, if we select first the point whose shadow will fall on the intersection of the walls, and then the corner point of the cornice.

The other two shadow boundaries will be those cast by lines on walls parallel to themselves. The rays through such lines must strike the receiving surfaces in lines parallel to those casting the shadows. In other words, the shadow is parallel to the line which causes it, and therefore will have the same vanishing point in perspective. In our figure, after 2_s and 1_s have been found from plan, the rest of the shadows may be fixed merely by drawing to V^R and V^L without using additional points.

Another very common case is shown at B. Here a projecting portion of a building causes a similar break in an overhanging member above. If we start in plan with the ray through the corner x_i of the nearer portion of the wall, we can work back to find point X' whose shadow falls on that corner in the perspective at X_s. We have just demonstrated that the shadow line to the left must go to V^L. Then if in plan we prolong the ray to hit the right-hand portion of the wall, it will determine a vertical slice, which can be cut by prolonging the ray through X_s giving another X_s on the wall. Point X' thus seems to have two shadows, one on the projecting corner and one on the recessed wall. As a matter of theory we can say that, in the first case, it is point X' whose shadow falls on the corner, and that it is X'', the next point to the right of X', whose shadow falls on the wall at X_s. As a matter of practical drafting the two points are identical and lie on the same ray.

From point X_s to the shadow of point 1 at 1_s the shadow must actually be parallel to X'-$1'$ (the line casting it), and therefore in perspective it will have the same vanishing point V^L as X'-$1'$. In other words we can now draw the shadow from X_s as far as its intersection with the ray through $1'$ by drawing through X_s a line from V^L. From X_s down the shadow will obviously be vertical until it meets the ground. Then it must close to the front corner. Note that the shadow on the ground, if prolonged, would lead to V^{PR}. We shall use this fact often. It is explained in Sec. 8.

The intersection of two known shadows will enable us to run back along the ray and find a third shadow on a higher part of the object. If the vertical shadow below X_s had been found first by drawing in the plan from the salient corner to V^{PR}, and 1_s had been located from plan, a line toward V^L through 1_s by its intersection at X_s with the vertical already found would have enabled us to run back along the ray from X_s and find the other X_s on the salient corner. A line to V^L would bound our shadow without having to find X' or its plan. This procedure can be stated as follows: **by running back along the ray from the point of intersection of two known shadows, the point may be found at which the shadow of the upper shade line crosses the lower shade line itself.**

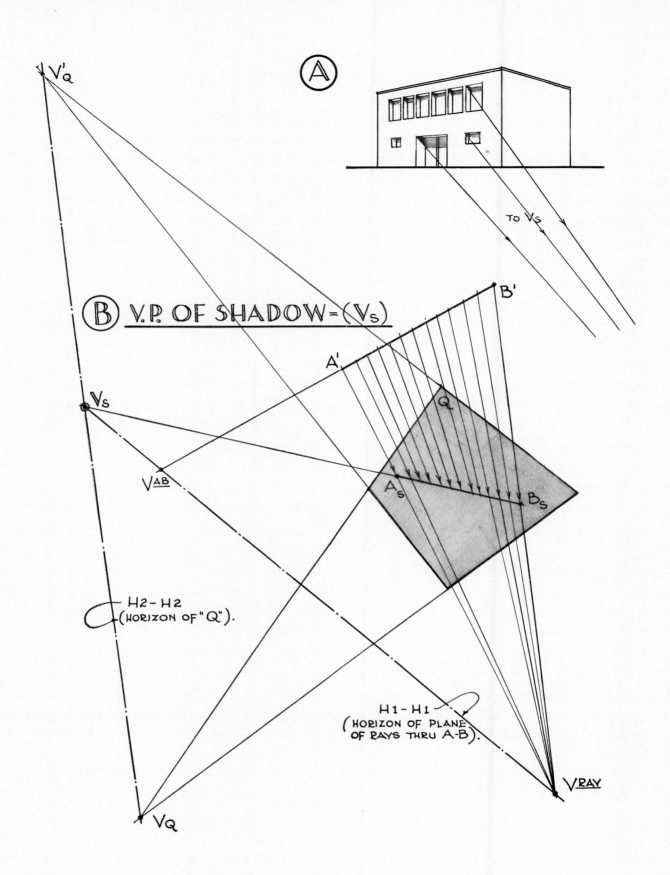

Ⓐ

Ⓑ V.P. OF SHADOW = (Vₛ)

V'_Q

V_S

V_{AB}

A'

B'

Q

A_S

B_S

TO Vₛ

H2 — H2
(HORIZON OF "Q").

H1 — H1
(HORIZON OF PLANE
OF RAYS THRU A-B).

V_{RAY}

V_Q

ILLUSTRATION 7-11

8. THE VANISHING POINTS OF SHADOW EDGES

When we are trying to find the shadow of the line A-B on the plane surface Q, we will often be in the situation of knowing A_s (the beginning point of the shadow) and the direction of the shadow (vertical, parallel to A-B, etc.).

This situation arises so often that it becomes worth while to ask ourselves, "How can the direction of the shadow of any line A-B on any surface Q be determined?" In perspective terminology this question may be changed to, "How can we find the vanishing point V_s of any shadow edge A_s-B_s?" This is the simplest way of stating the problem because, in perspective, lines, including shadow boundaries, are most easily found by drawing to their known vanishing points. Do not forget that verticals and other lines parallel to the picture plane are drawn in perspective parallel to their true position, and so are shadows of similar characteristics.

The vanishing points of shadows, when determined, become important timesavers in working out the light and shade on perspective drawings especially of architectural subjects. Most of the shadows on buildings are cast on vertical, horizontal, or sloping surfaces—such as walls, the ground, or roofs (see Sec. 6)—and are caused principally by vertical or horizontal lines. Thus, there are usually many parallel shadows in such pictures. If their vanishing points are known, they can be drawn very quickly. Notice the shadows cast by the window-heads in Illus. 7-11-A. In every case the point of beginning of the shadow is obviously the intersection of jamb and lintel. The shadow on the jamb of every window must be parallel to that in every other window, and hence must have the same vanishing point V_s. If we know this point and hence the direction of the shadows, we can draw them directly. Each shadow begins in the upper corner of its window and runs across the jamb toward V_s until it strikes the glass. On this new surface the shadow-edge will be parallel to the line casting, and hence will have a different V. This new V_s will be the same as the V of the line casting.

Wherever specific forms occur repeatedly and hence include many sets of parallel lines, much time and labor can be saved by knowing the V's of the various shadow lines. Even though such a V_s may fall off the paper, it is valuable to know its approximate location as a control.

Shadows are just as much a part of the perspective appearance of a building as are profiles and intersections. They too must be drawn under control if we are to produce correct representations. The time required to locate the vanishing points of shadows is nearly always saved many times over. In addition the control thus established insures the consistency of our work, even though it may not be meticulously accurate.

The process of finding the vanishing point of the shadow of any line A-B on any plane Q is not difficult if we understand the graphical concepts involved, and go through the steps of the solution methodically in each case until they are thoroughly rooted in our memory. By definition, a shadow is the line of intersection between Q (the surface receiving the shadow) and a plane of rays through A-B (the line casting the shadow). Since it belongs to both of these planes, its vanishing point V_s must lie on the horizon of each of them. Any point which must be on two different lines must lie at their intersection. Hence, we can find V_s as the intersection of two horizons—one, that of the plane Q, and the other, that of the plane of rays through A-B.

The horizon of any plane is determined by knowing the vanishing points of two sets of parallel lines which lie in that plane. Thus, in the case of the plane of rays through A-B (Illus. 7-11-B) its horizon can be determined by drawing a line from V^{Ray} to V^{AB}. The vanishing point that we are seeking must lie on this horizon, H_1H_1.

To find the horizon of plane Q we proceed in similar fashion. We first select the vanishing point of one set of lines lying in Q, and then that of another set. Having found the vanishing points of both of these series, we join these two V's to find H_2H_2. The intersection of H_1H_1 and H_2H_2 is V_s, the point which we are seeking.

In architectural drawing this procedure usually involves only a simple matter of observation and selection. The boundary lines of the plane Q usually have vanishing points which are already known. Very often one set of lines in Q will be vertical, which means that one vanishing point is at infinity and that H_2H_2 will therefore be a vertical through the other V. Q may be so placed as to have its horizon parallel to the principal horizon (e.g., a sloping bank of earth, or a roof with eaves and ridge parallel to PP). Then H_2H_2 will be a horizontal through the second V. In some cases it may be necessary to select or assume a set of lines lying in Q and go through the process of finding their vanishing point. By whatever means we determine the horizon of Q and locate H_2H_2, V_s **will lie at the intersection of H_1H_1 and H_2H_2.**

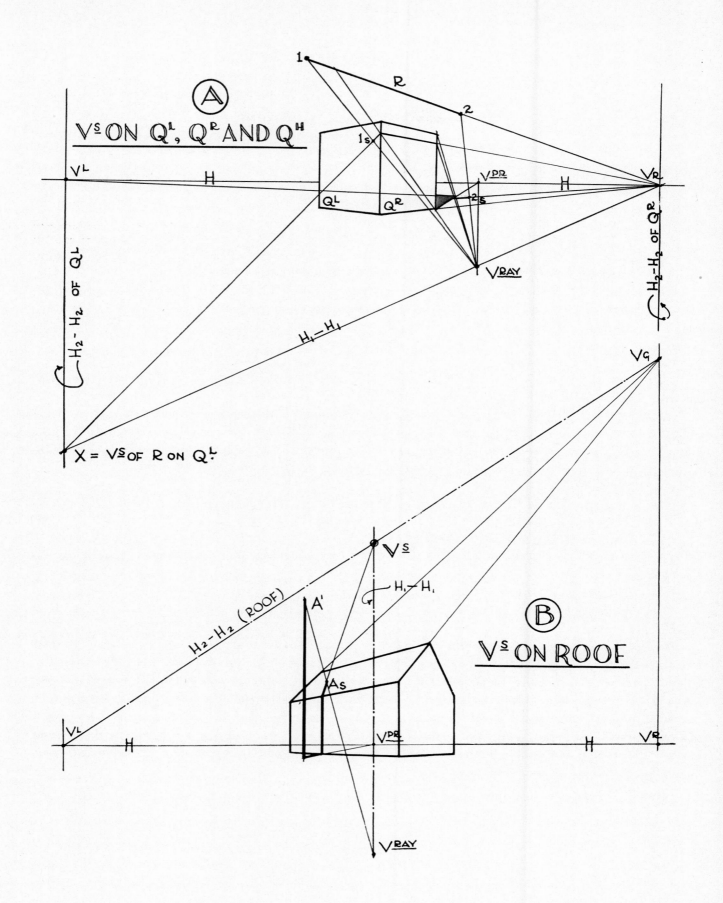

Ⓐ

<u>V^S ON Q^L, Q^R AND Q^H</u>

X = V^S OF R ON Q^L.

Ⓑ

<u>V^S ON ROOF</u>

ILLUSTRATION 7-12

To illustrate this procedure, let us work out step by step where V_s will fall in the case of the shadows cast by the various edges of a parallelepiped on the various surfaces of similar rectangular objects. The shadows of most of the objects in an architectural drawing will have their vanishing points either exactly or approximately where the V's of the shadows of such primary figures occur. If we know these V's we will be a long way toward the solution of any problem in shadows.

Taking a cube as our basic form, we see that its shadow-casting edges are either vertical, horizontals to the right, or horizontals to the left. Each one of these lines may cast its shadow on a left-hand or a right-hand vertical face, or on a horizontal face. Let us call these lines R, L, and V, and the surfaces Q^R, Q^L, and Q^H. Thus each principal line-casting may have three different directions of shadow, and there are nine possible combinations of line-casting and surface-receiving, each producing a V_s.

V_s in each case will be found by similar reasoning and procedure. Each step in determining V_s for line R on each plane is explained below. The student should work out in similar fashion where V_s will be for lines L and V on each of the surfaces so as to verify the conclusions which are given dogmatically for these cases.

Case 1. To find V_s of R on Q^R (Illus. 7-12-A).

H_1H_1 is found by joining V^{Ray} and V^R. H_2H_2 will be a vertical through V^R in this case. H_1H_1 and H_2H_2 intersect at V_s (which is coincident with V^R). Note that the shadow must be parallel to the line casting, since the latter is parallel to Q^R. Hence the shadow has the same vanishing point as R, *i.e.*, V^R.

Case 2. To find V_s of R on Q^L.

H_1H_1 is found by joining V^{Ray} and V^R as before. H_2H_2 is the vertical through V^L. The intersection of H_1H_1 and H_2H_2 locates this V_s at X.

Note that this is the very common case illustrated in the windows of the building of Illus. 7-11-A. While this V will often lie off the paper, it can be located approximately and the shadows controlled to converge toward it. A draftsman who attempts to work these little shadows out by points will inevitably produce enough inaccuracies so that many of them will diverge instead of converge, thus spoiling the consistency of the picture.

Case 3. To find the V_s of R on Q^H.

H_1H_1 is found by joining V^{Ray} to V^R. H_2H_2 is the principal HH. The intersection of H_1H_1 and H_2H_2 shows that V_s in this case coincides with V^R.

Cases 4, 5, and 6. To find V_s of L on Q^R, Q^L, and Q^H.

The V_s of L on Q^L is V^L. The V_s of L on Q^H is V^L. The V_s of L on Q^R is Y (must be found by construction like **Case 2** above).

Cases 7, 8, and 9. To find V_s of V on Q^R, Q^L, and Q^H.

The V_s of the shadow of V on Q^H is V^{PR}; the V_s of V on Q^R is at infinity (*i.e.*, the shadow is vertical); the V_s of V on Q^L is at infinity.

It is interesting to note that only two new points have to be located to determine the direction of all these important shadows. In seven out of the nine possible cases, V_s coincides with a point which is already known, *i.e.*, either V^L, V^R, or V^{PR}. However, the student must not attempt to remember the answer for each typical case, but rather should practice the general principle involved until he is sure that he can apply it under any circumstances.

As an example of the application of the general rule, Illus. 7-12-B shows how the vanishing point of the shadow of a line is found on a sloping plane such as a roof. The V_s involved lies conveniently on the paper, and is of great assistance in working out quickly and easily shadows, like those of chimneys, which must be drawn crisply and exactly in order to give character to the rendering.

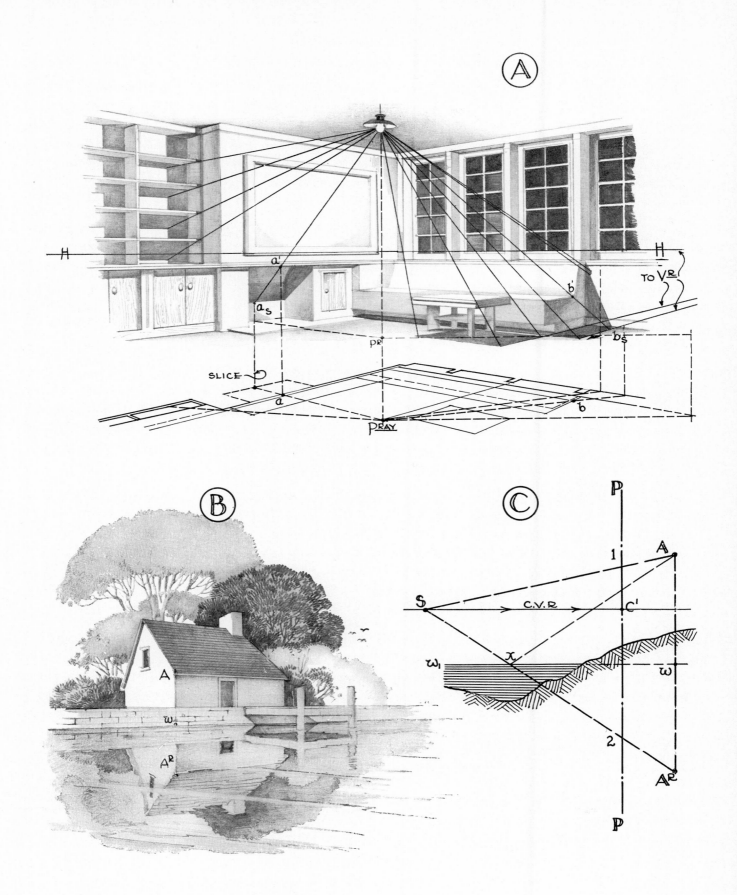

ILLUSTRATION 7-13

9. SHADOWS BY ARTIFICIAL LIGHT

Interior perspectives are often rendered to give the appearance of artificial lighting. If this illumination comes from several sources, the various effects due to direct and reflected rays are so complex as to defy graphical analysis. They can be studied best in a model or in a full-size "mock-up." It is almost impossible to work them out accurately on the drafting board.

If the light comes from a single source, the resulting pattern of shade and shadow can be determined in perspective by applying the principles that we have already established. The light source L appears in the picture, and rays can be drawn **from** it instead of **to** V^{Ray}. If we project the source onto the floor of the room at P^R, we can use our slogan—draw the ray through the point, and the plan of the ray through the plan of the point—thus applying the basic slicing method. A perspective plan is essential in order to obtain accurate intersections, to determine shade lines, etc. (see Illus. 7-13-A).

Our knowledge of the vanishing points of shadows will be useful in shortening the process. The shadow of a line on a plane parallel to it will be parallel to the line, and hence have the same vanishing point. Thus the horizontal edges of the seat, table, or fireplace will cast shadows on the floor that will have the same V's as the edges themselves, V^L or V^R, and the shelves of the bookcase will cast shadows on the back wall that will vanish at their own V. Verticals will have vertical shadows on vertical surfaces, and on horizontal planes will have shadows radiating from P^{Ray}.

10. REFLECTIONS

Since the natural setting of buildings often includes a body of water—a reflecting pool may even be part of the architectural composition—it is worth while to understand how to find the perspective of reflections (Illus. 7-13-B). The principle is very simple. It evolves from the optical phenomenon that light rays striking an object will rebound from its surface in a plane perpendicular to it and at the same angle as that at which they impinge upon it. In such cases, **the angle of reflection is always equal to the angle of incidence.**

Thus a point will have its reflection in perspective wherever a ray from it to the eye will strike the mirroring surface so as to establish such equal angles in a plane at right angles to the surface. If the surface is horizontal (like water) this point can easily be determined by the simple construction shown in Illus. 7-13-C.

Given: Point A and the water surface at level w_1-w.

Construction: Lay off A^R vertically below A so that A-$w = w$-A^R. The ray from S to A^R will strike the surface of the water at x, and the angles at the water from x to S and to A will be equal by geometry. (Triangles A-x-w and A^R-x-w are congruent. Their angles at x are equal. Angle S-x-w_1 = angle A^R-x-w = angle w-x-A.) So the perspective (2) of the reflection of A is found by drawing the ray to A^R.

The reflection of any other point can be found by the same process—drop a vertical to the water, and prolong to the same distance below the surface as the point is above it. Proceed from point to line to plane as in drawing a direct projection. Several special relationships may be observed which will shorten the process: (1) The reflections of horizontals have the same V's as their originals; (2) The reflections of verticals and other parallels to PP do not vanish, but vertical planes (like walls) have the same horizons as their originals; (3) The reflections of inclined lines have V's symmetrical (above or below HH) to those of the originals; (4) A hidden portion of an object may be visible in its reflection—and vice versa.

Mirrors on walls of interiors occasionally require the working out of reflections on vertical surfaces. The theory is identical to that for water, but turned ninety degrees, thus complicating the measurement of equal perpendiculars, because they must be diminished as well as drawn. The development of a method for finding reflections on inclined surfaces is explained in Prof. F. N. Willson's "Theoretical and Practical Graphics," and carried out fully in his special booklet on reflections.[1]

[1] Willson, Frederick Newton, "The Perspective of Reflections," New York, The Macmillan Company, 1900.

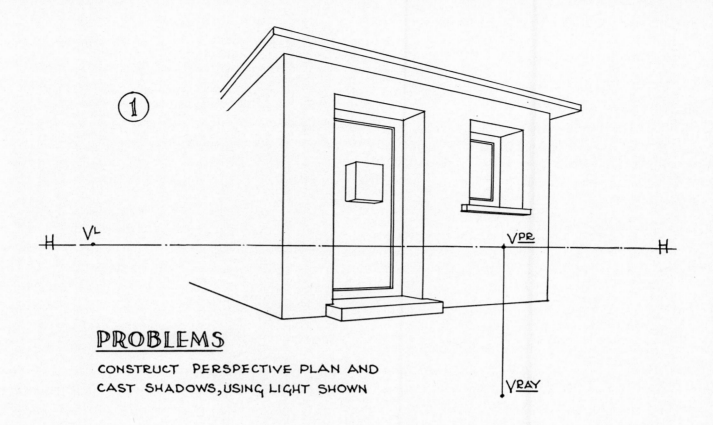

①

H   V^L   V^{PR}   H

V<u>RAY</u>

PROBLEMS

CONSTRUCT PERSPECTIVE PLAN AND
CAST SHADOWS, USING LIGHT SHOWN

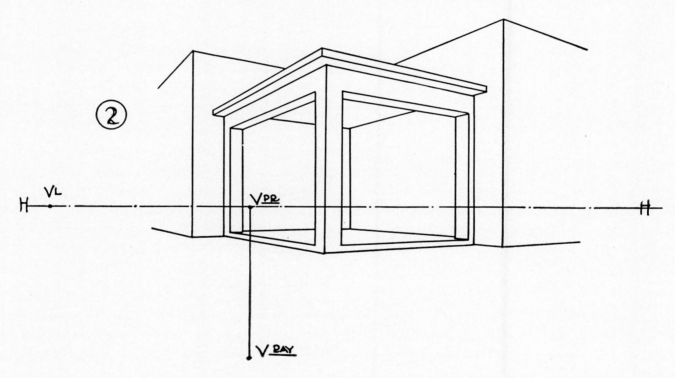

②

H   V^L   V^{PR}   H

V <u>RAY</u>

1. Find V^{Ray} when light is (*a*) 30° down over spectator's left shoulder; (*b*) 45° down over right shoulder.

2. Find V^{Ray} when (*a*) facing north at 3 P.M. in spring; (*b*) facing south at 10 A.M. in summer.

3. Find V_s for each of three flag poles projecting symmetrically from the wall of a building. All point up at 30° to the horizontal.

4. Demonstrate the slicing method in your own words and diagram.

5. Work out the shadows on Illus. 7-9-B with light 45° down from left and parallel to *PP*.

6. Check *V* of each shadow edge in Question 5.

7. Find a photo of a building taken so that the shadows of chimneys fall on a sloping roof. Check *V* of each shadow edge.

8. Mark light, shade, and shadow on an architectural photograph which you admire. Trace their outlines, decide on a value for each of them, and make your own rendering.

9. Render the house in Illus. 7-7 with light coming from behind it.

10. Add a stream in front of illustration in question 5, and work out the reflection of the object in it.

PROBLEMS

Construct perspective plan and cast shadows using light shown in Illus. 7-14, 7-15 and 7-16.

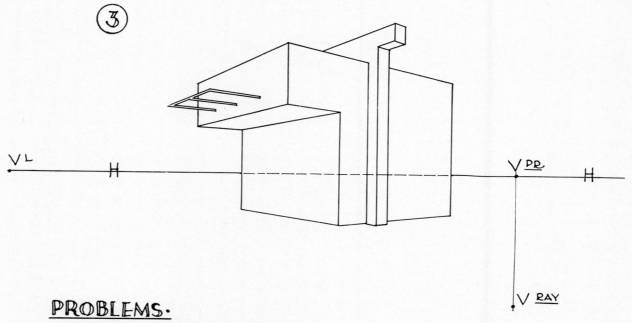

③

VL   H   V PR.   H

V RAY

PROBLEMS·

CONSTRUCT PERSPECTIVE PLAN &
CAST SHADOWS, USING LIGHT SHOWN

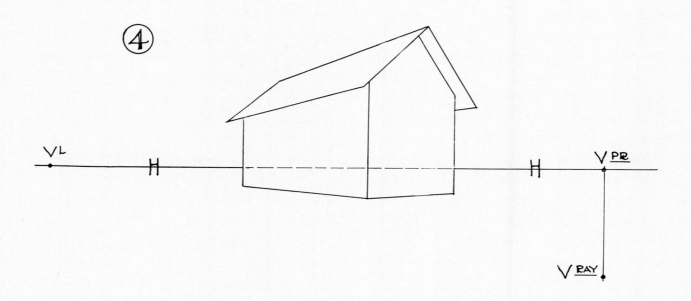

④

VL   H   H   V PR

V RAY

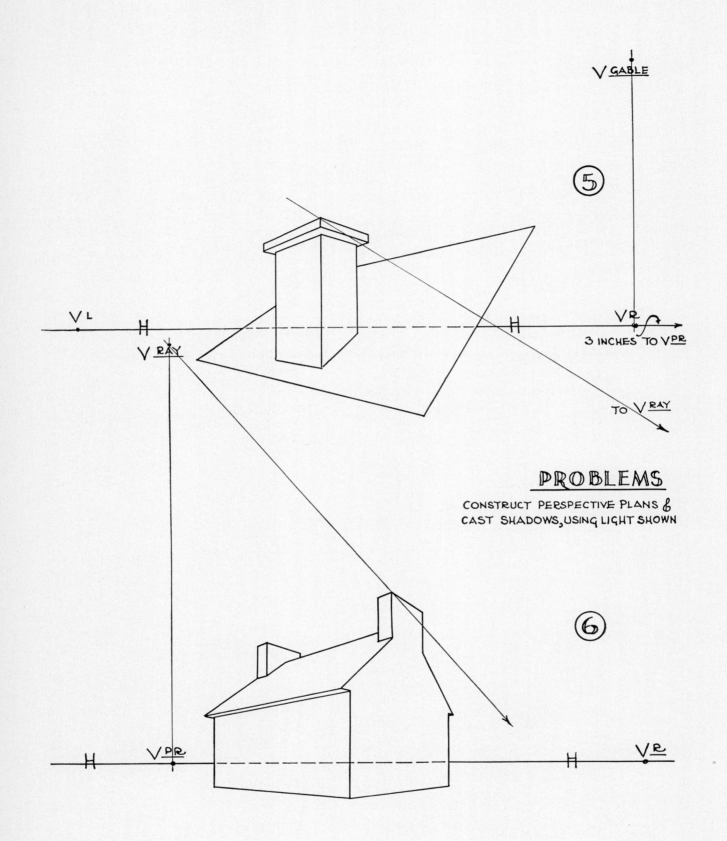

V GABLE

⑤

V R
3 INCHES TO V PR

TO V RAY

V L   H   H   V R

V RAY

PROBLEMS
CONSTRUCT PERSPECTIVE PLANS &
CAST SHADOWS, USING LIGHT SHOWN

⑥

H   V PR   H   V R

ILLUSTRATION 7-16   131

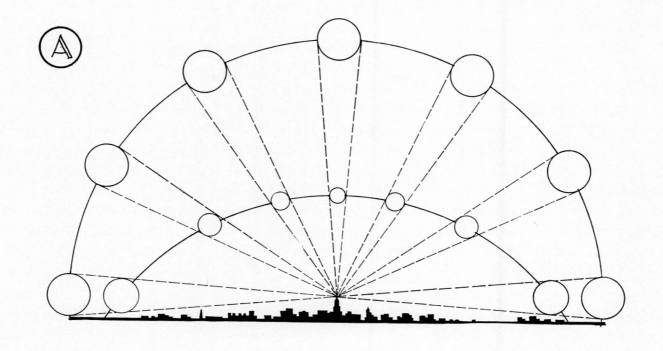

ILLUSTRATION 8-1

Chapter 8

AERIAL PERSPECTIVE (RENDERING)

1. THE REPRESENTATION OF SPACE

The problems of explaining external reality and the operation of the sense organs by which we perceive the outside world are the concern of philosophers rather than of artists, but some of the conclusions of the theorists[1] have a direct bearing on architectural drawing. The perception of depth as a third dimension requires a mental synthesis based on the impressions furnished to the brain by the eye. The flat retinal image must be interpreted.

The law of diminution provides the most obvious and valuable clue in judging depth relationships from visual appearances. The apparent size (in relation to their true dimensions) of known objects such as people and animals tells us at once how far away they are from us. Conversely we can estimate the size of any object if we can compare it to a known distance. When neither size nor location is fixed, there is no means of exact estimate, so we usually judge wrongly. Most people think that the moon looks larger as it rises, because they can then compare it to the greatly reduced size of objects near the horizon and known to be far away.[2] At the zenith, however, it rides along against space so great and so empty that we cannot conceive such immensity. Hence we imagine the moon to be nearer than it seems when seen in comparison with earthly distances and conclude that it must be smaller.

Next to size, perspective is of greatest importance as a means of realizing depth through the change in apparent shapes of known objects as they change position relative to us. Other valuable clues are provided by the varying contrast of light values and of color, clarity of focus, overlap, binocular vision, and movement of the observer. The last two are beyond the control of the draftsman but the others must all be taken into account when rendering a drawing. By expressing them, a linear perspective can be developed into an aerial perspective which will convey to the retina stimuli similar to those produced by actual three-dimensional space.

An aerial perspective is thus an optical illusion—but its purpose is to explain, not to mislead. Mere exact reproduction of nature is not its goal. The mechanical perfection of the camera has made such an achievement unnecessary today—if it was ever valid. We must use the means of representation to interpret our thought rather than to deceive the observer—to show him how a building will look and not to make him believe that he is seeing it.

2. CONTRAST AND COLOR

Since the intensity of the light reflected to our eyes from objects in space varies inversely as the square of their distance from us, it is obvious that the rays reflected from nearby objects will impinge more sharply on our retinas than those coming to us from more distant surfaces. Consequently the contrast between light, shade, and shadow is greater in the foreground of our field of vision and decreases rapidly for more distant objects.

"The darkest darks and the lightest lights are in the foreground." "Distance fades all contrasts to an even gray." "Colors are brightest and clearest near the observer." "Detail disappears as depth increases." "Textures count only on nearby objects." So run some of the rules of thumb by which artists have made practical this general law. Examination of any good picture (or photograph) will confirm their catchwords and suggest others of your own.

Pay particular attention to shadow-edges. On nearby objects they will be crisp, and will vary with the character of the surface of which they are a part. Smooth textures will be revealed by sharp clear edges; rough or broken surfaces by the serrations of the shadow-edge. In Illus. 8-1-B note the difference between the shadow-edges on the slate and on the glass, and compare the shadow of the chimney on the nearer building with that on the distant wing.

[1] Bailey, Samuel, "Berkeley's Theory of Sense Perception," London, 1853.
[2] Lukiesh, M., "Visual Illusions and Their Applications," New York, D. Van Nostrand Company, Inc., 1922.

VIEW THRU ARCH

VIEW OF ARCH

ILLUSTRATION 8-2

3. FOCUS AND OVERLAP

The focusing action of the lenses in our eyes provides another source of information by which to judge distance on the basis of the flat patterns of which our visual impressions consist. Whether the brain is attempting to interpret the image on the retina made by real three-dimensional forms, or merely judging the spatial effect conveyed by a drawing, the clarity of the sensation (or drawing) is a clue to the distance from the observer that it represents. We have already considered (Chap. 2, Sec. 7) how to take focus into account when we lay out a perspective. Now we must apply it so as to improve the rendering of our picture and increase the impression of space that it conveys.

For nearby objects, the eye has a very limited depth of field. In such perspectives only the center of interest should be clearly delineated. All other profiles, shadows, etc., should be blurred and all colors dulled, in addition to the decrease in contrast already noted in Sec. 2. When the principal object is over 100 ft. from the observer, no change of focus will be needed for more distant forms, but any foreground will rapidly get fuzzy. Pictures looking through arches or from under trees should therefore be rendered without clear detail on the framing shapes, or they will detract from the interest of the true subject.

The experiments of Prof. Ames[1] of the Dartmouth Eye Institute have demonstrated that we use the visual overlap of nearer and farther objects to assist our judgment of their positions in space. The tests of size, shape, contrast, and focus are applied to each object but are modified and checked by the fact that an object which masks another must be the nearer. However, if the forms are previously unknown, and are of irregular mass placed so as to suggest shapes different from the true ones, the eye may easily be deceived, and the brain may misinterpret the visual message.

Since a perspective presupposes a fixed point of view, we must be especially careful not to select one which will cause confusing overlaps. This is another reason for the care in the choice of S that has already been emphasized.

4. BINOCULAR VISION

In real life our perception of space (particularly within a few feet of our eyes) is greatly aided by the fact that the brain has constantly before it two slightly different images on which to base its judgment of depth. With two eyes, even though they are only a few inches apart, we can see simultaneously both sides as well as the fronts of nearby objects. Increasing distance reduces the difference between the two retinal images, and thus tells the mind that the objects are farther away. (See Illus. 1-3-B).

Since one eye cannot record two impressions simultaneously, the assumptions which make linear perspective possible preclude the use of this means of judging depth in a drawing, but the possibilities of binocular vision in photography were explored as soon as the camera made accurate perspectives quickly and easily available. We are all familiar with the extraordinary effects of space achieved by stereopticon views. When two photographs taken at the same time, from the same position as two human eyes, are mounted and viewed so that each eye sees only the proper image, the brain will interpret the message it records from the two retinas exactly as it has learned to understand similar sensations caused by looking at actual space organizations. Consequently a completely convincing sensation of three-dimensional depth is conveyed to the observer by the flat surface of two pictures on paper.[2]

The stereoscopic photographs at the bottom of Illus. 8-2 seem identical when seen individually, but the slight differences between them are sufficient to give an impression of full relief, when one sees them simultaneously through a viewing device which limits each eye to seeing the picture corresponding to its normal visual image.

While the stereoscopic illusion is most effective for objects within 200 ft. of the observer, it may be applied to more distant scenes by increasing the distance between the points of exposure of the photographs. Airplane pictures taken several hundred yards apart will reveal the relative heights of structures on the ground. In war this process has been used to detect camouflage nets over enemy installations, and in peace, to obtain contour maps of unexplored terrain.

[1] Ames, Adelbert, "Some Demonstrations Concerned with the Origin and Nature of our Sensations," Hanover, N.H., Hanover Institute, 1946.

[2] Hardy, A.C., and F.H. Perrin, "The Principles of Optics," New York, McGraw-Hill Book Company, Inc., 1922.

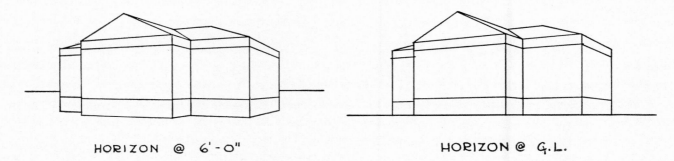

HORIZON @ 6'-0"   HORIZON @ G.L.

JUSTIFIED

EXAGGERATIONS

EXCESSIVE

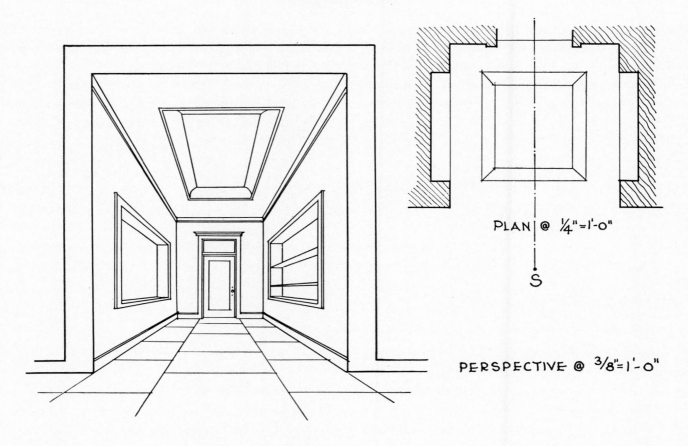

PLAN @ ¼"=1'-0"

S

PERSPECTIVE @ 3/8"=1'-0"

5. EXAGGERATION

Perspective effects may be emphasized, or even forced, by disregard of our ordinary rules for laying out the drawing. Such tricks are outside the scope of the ordinary architectural rendering, but they may be used in modified form to obtain more dramatic effects than the normal perspective. A common example is the practice of assuming the horizon at the ground level instead of 5'-6" above it. This has the advantage of emphasizing the visual slope of horizontal lines, particularly in the case of flat-roofed buildings. Their form is much more clearly brought out if *HH* is kept low. Rural structures thus drawn have the further advantage of seeming to stand on rising ground. Since they are usually so located, the pictorial gain is in accord with normal field conditions as well as giving a more striking effect.

The building shown twice in Illus. 8-3 seems much more impressive in the right-hand drawing than in the view at the left, yet both perspectives are identical except for the level of *HH*. This gain in scale or monumentality (call it what you will) is so often achieved by the simple device of a low horizon that we might almost make it a rule to have *HH* coincide with the ground line when drawing exterior views of buildings.

Care must be exercised not to produce overemphasized effects at the expense of true interpretation. It is all too easy, especially with interiors, to make perspectives that look much more impressive than the actual construction. The contemporary interest in nonrepresentational art has led many draftsmen, in their excitement over unusual pictorial qualities, to forget their fundamental obligation to present fact. Bitter disappointments have been caused when construction has been authorized on the basis of exaggerated perspectives, and then later the dissatisfied owners have found the resulting buildings to be entirely different from those that they had dreamed of when shown the architect's preliminary drawings.

Through disregard of our rules for choosing *S* and *HH*, the small vestibule shown in plan at the right of Illus. 8-3 has been projected into a perspective at the left which gives an entirely false impression of its size and proportions. Further rendering of such a layout will only further falsify the effect of such a drawing.

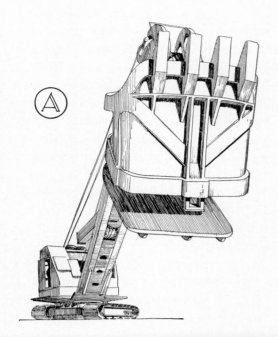

Life, New York City, July 19, 1943. Reproduced by permission.

ILLUSTRATION 8-4

6. *INTENTIONAL DISTORTION*

Many of the means of conveying the effect of depth in a perspective drawing may be consciously emphasized for the purpose of increasing pictorial impact. Advertisements, posters, etc., are often intentionally drawn with a depth of field impossible for the human eye, in order to make a more striking demand on the attention of the beholder. The power shovel in Illus. 8-4-A is shown as it might appear if one looked at it from a point a few feet from its "head." In nature, the operating cab would consequently be completely out of focus, and its retinal image merely a blur. By drawing it as clearly as the nearer portion, the mental effect is that which would be produced if the head was suddenly swung in front of a person whose eyes were directed toward the cab. Full attention would instantly be compelled. The intentionally distorted perspective has somewhat the same psychological power.

The high horizon, and inclined picture plane, of Illus. 8-4-B add to its exaggerated depth of field the impression that one is soaring down in an airplane directly toward the resort hotel which might use such a sketch to call attention to its announcement. Under such conditions, one would look hard at the building below, and that is exactly what the advertiser wants you to do. His problem is to catch your eye, and he succeeds through conscious distortion gained by exceeding normal visual limitations.

In the movies the camera is intentionally made to transgress our ordinary considerations as to the choice of a station point. It is often placed in positions that could only be achieved by the eye at the risk of life or limb. Audiences can actually be made to duck when the screen shows a fist swinging straight toward their faces, or to cower before the onrush of an express train, seen from track level as though one were lying on the rails.

The distortion resulting from too large a cone of vision can also be used to produce arresting effects. The development of cameras with wide-angle lenses (90° and more) has accustomed the contemporary observer to the acceptance of perspectives which would have been condemned a generation ago. The magazine *Life* published a photograph of the interior of St. Patrick's Cathedral (New York City) taken with a lens of 210°. It actually includes in one view parts of the building **behind** the station-point! It is interesting to note the curvature of horizontal lines above and below the horizon, and that the verticals also bend symmetrically around the central axis of the picture.

ILLUSIONS.

Ⓐ ARE ANGLES 1-2-3 AND
1-4-5 RIGHT ANGLES?
HOW MANY DEGREES IS 1-3-2?

Ⓑ IS HAT TALLER THAN WIDE
OR WIDER THAN TALL?

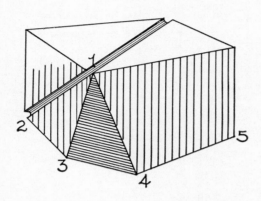

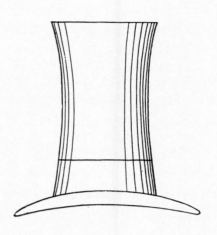

Ⓒ WHICH END OF TUBE IS NEARER?

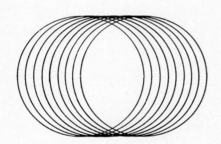

Ⓓ WHICH
CIRCLE IS
LARGER?

7. OPTICAL ILLUSIONS

Any perspective drawing is an optical illusion in that it seeks to convey to the eye the sensation of depth by the pattern of lines and tones arranged on its two-dimensional surface. Hence it is well for the draftsman, although his intent should never be to deceive, to be aware of some of the common means by which the eye can be confused and the brain led to wrong conclusions. Several of these are shown in Illus. 8-5.

The principles of such optical deceptions are the reverse of those which we have reviewed in this chapter as the means of enhancing the effect of depth. Shading especially (notably absent in all primitive art) can be used to convey a false visual impression (Illus. 8-5-A). Contrast and juxtaposition will cause mistaken judgments as to length (and hence size). Can you tell without measurement whether the hat is wider or taller (Illus. 8-5-B)?

An ellipse suggests a circle seen in perspective. Several of them will seem to form a hollow cylinder or tube—but which end is nearer? Only further drawing would make Illus. 8-5-C clear. Equal diffused lighting from all angles will make a sphere indistinguishable from a circular disc. Reversal of color values and hues will make size reverse (Illus. 8-5-D) or destroy distance. Broken patterns can destroy form.

Endless examples can be given, and a whole system of deception has been worked out for use in military concealment. Under the name of *camouflage*, the science and art of **denying** the appearance of form in space has been developed, and many texts have been published on its practice and principles.

8. TROMPE-L'ŒIL

It is possible to use all the means of conveying the impression of depth to such an extent that an actual illusion of three-dimensional reality is achieved by a flat surface. If the object is shown full size—a still life for example, or moldings on a wall—and the pictorial lighting agrees with that really existing (as can be controlled in an interior) the observer may be completely deceived and will believe that he is seeing reality rather than representation. "Reach out and feel the frame around the mural," says the guide—and one touches a smooth plaster wall! Such effects have earned themselves the name of *trompe-l'œil* (eye-deceiver). They were greatly admired in the nineteenth century but are rated today, perhaps more justly, as trickery rather than art.

Since architectural drawings are nearly always made at greatly reduced scale as compared to the objects depicted, there is little temptation to use such literal realism in our work. *Trompe-l'œil* should be mentioned, however, as proving the importance of artistic selection and restraint. There is no more true artistic achievement in using every known means to deceive the eye than there is in playing every known musical instrument at once so as to imitate a steam whistle. The result may be a perfect reproduction but it is not music.

MAKING A RENDERING

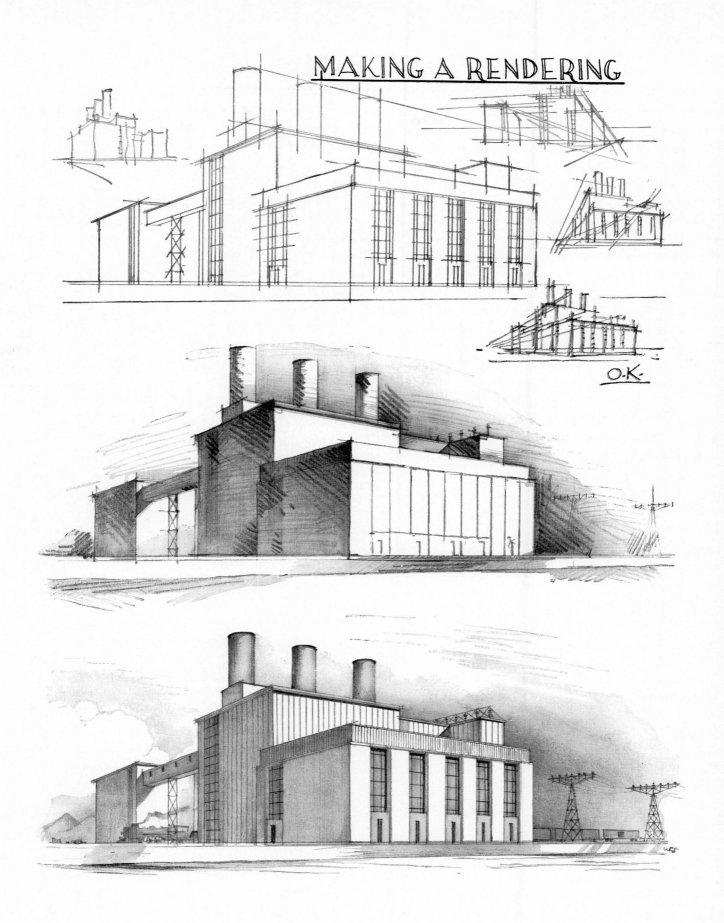

O·K·

ILLUSTRATION 8-6

9. PLANNING AN ARCHITECTURAL RENDERING

The final aim of most architectural perspectives is a picture rendered to convey an impression of spatial reality. The procedure in making them is a definite sequence of steps, as has already been explained in detail: (1) try several thumbnail compositions; (2) select one, choose S, $C.V.R.$, and HH, and project a linear perspective; (3) choose V^{Ray}; (4) cast shadows; (5) render in value, and/or color. The first four steps require judgment and knowledge, but can be controlled by exact graphical processes. The last involves artistic feeling and cannot be reduced to rules, although its general principles can be stated.

Many books have been written about the technique and problems of architectural rendering. No matter how much one reads about rendering, his ability to **do it** will depend on his native talent, and on continued practice. Each draftsman must learn for himself through the labor of repeated effort. However, the principles which have been presented in this chapter should be of help in getting started in the right direction. Test them against the best examples; reappraise or rephrase them if you will; add others in your own words; but do not transgress them until you can prove by your own work that you no longer need their guidance.

In Sec. 10 of Chap. 11 ten rules for rendering are listed. They apply as fully to perspective drawings as to orthographic projections—in fact their application is perhaps more obvious and direct in the former type because of its less conventional basis. These rules are merely a codification of the principles developed in this chapter and are repeated in Chap. 11 for the benefit of students concerned with rendering elevations and plans. Refer to them now and answer at this time the questions of Chap. 11 as well as those following Chap. 8.

A final word of advice is important at this stage. Before you start to render, decide on the kind of impression you wish to make on those who will look at your work. Choose your medium accordingly and keep steadily in mind the chosen objective as you proceed. Good results are rarely achieved by accident—in art, as in most human affairs. The experienced draftsman may seem to the beginner to be throwing values or colors around in a fine haphazard frenzy—actually he is carrying out (whether consciously or through long training) a careful plan of campaign. There will be unexpected minor failures or successes which will modify the results slightly because they occur, but the general effect desired will always control the procedure.

Such decisions as choosing between a rough sketch or a careful presentation should be made before the drawing is begun and, if made in advance, will probably save much wasted effort.

Even more important is the choice of type (style) of artistic expression. A wrong decision on this basic matter will make worthless all subsequent effort. Drawings must appeal to the people for whom they are made. Only in school work, perhaps, can an architect afford to be an "artist's artist," whose renderings are admired by a chosen few but are "caviar to the general."

During the late nineteenth and early twentieth centuries, while impressionism ruled the world of painting, most architectural drawings were rendered in transparent water color to show the building as it might look to an artist sketching it on a fine summer day. An impression was produced—localized in time, space, and light. Today we prefer a more enduring type of presentation which will suggest the permanence and solidity of architecture and make the beholder remember that a building must face changing seasons, storm as well as sunshine, dusk as well as noon. Our objective is to convey the idea of a continuing form rather than an evanescent shape. We put our stress on the solidity of stone or concrete, the transparency of glass, the qualities of texture and color in all materials. We emphasize the architecture and minimize its surroundings unless they also are permanent. Hence we choose less delicate media, prefer solid tones, and eliminate naturalistic additions which tend to make the picture a street scene, or a landscape with figures, rather than an architectural drawing.

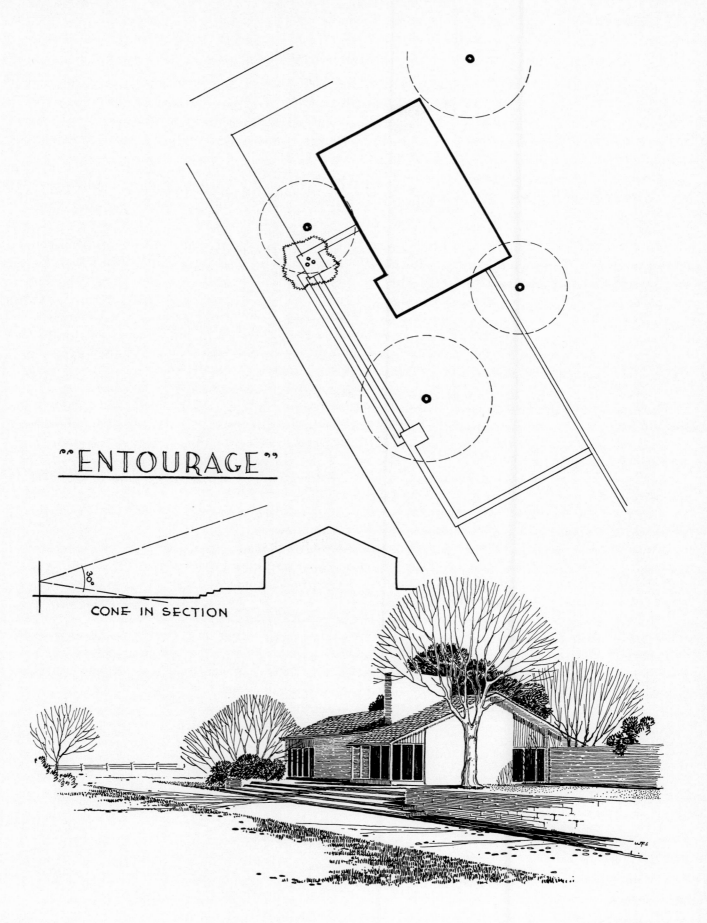

"ENTOURAGE"

30°

CONE IN SECTION

ILLUSTRATION 8-7

10. ENTOURAGE

Since architecture is created by and for man, who reorganizes nature for his special purposes, an architectural drawing is incomplete unless it meets the problem of the relation between a building and its surroundings. The people, streets, trees, lawns, hills, pools, etc., which are involved, are most easily referred to by the French word *entourage*. (We have no such inclusive but exact term in English.) How much *entourage* to include, and how to draw it, are questions that must always be answered.

Trees are probably the commonest difficulty. How often does the beginner, with his building already drawn, wonder helplessly what to put around it! Usually he asks his senior friend just "to draw a tree for me." The best reply is to quote Joyce Kilmer: "Only God can make a tree"—but that does not finish the picture! Let us be practical and suggest definite ways of meeting the situation.

1. Lay out nearby walks, trees, etc., in plan and project their locations as accurately as you did the building. Be particularly careful to get heights correct. Most natural objects grow (or are constructed) to fairly uniform sizes. Consequently they play a big part in conveying the scale of the drawing. Full-grown elms for example, are nearly twice as tall as two-story houses, and should be drawn that tall.

2. Be careful of general forms, and eliminate all detail in order to show correct masses. A leaf 3 in. long is scarcely visible at the far end of a building, but the shape of a whole tree there is very significant. All living things have a characteristic form, especially for adult members of a species, and this form should be brought out by the drawing. Observation of real specimens, plus reference to books on drawing in various media[1] will help in attaining speed and skill.

3. Keep the expression simple. Do not compete for interest with the true subject. We are trying to draw a **building** set in nature, not a **landscape** with a building in it. Simplify the surroundings, or they will steal the show.

4. Watch your values. Keep the individual parts of the entourage within the general range established for the whole, so as to gain contrast with both building and sky.

5. Reduce the foreground. Keep the horizon low for drives, walks, hedges, etc., between building and spectator. Otherwise the ground will seem to slope down unnaturally, and the nearby objects will gain too much in importance. Try a cone of vision in section, and see how little vertical space on the perspective must include everything on the ground in front of the building. Most beginners go way wrong on this point.

6. Make the people less solid than the architecture. Since people outdoors are usually in motion, rather than stationary like a building, I have often felt that the attempt should be made to suggest their mobility by means other than posture. Efforts to photograph speeding trains or automobiles with ordinary cameras have made us all familiar with the blurring that results from an object which moves too fast for the shutter. Why not use this distortion purposely to contrast traffic and structure? I have seen a few quick sketches in which the swirling crowd around urban architecture was shown by horizontally continuous streaks, rather than by the normal "balls on sticks." Some clever draftsman should develop this idea further. It offers the possibility of more effective contrast than the usual instantaneous snapshot technique now so universally used which tends to make the passing crowd look as motionless as the building.

[1] e. g. Kautzky, Theodore, "Pencil Broadsides," New York, Reinhold Publishing Corporation, 1940.

Possible development of the New York City Hall area for the Regional Plan Association.
Designed and drawn by Chester B. Price under direction of Thomas Adams, 1931.

146   ILLUSTRATION 8-8

PROBLEMS

1. Give sketch examples of the four principal means by which the impression of depth is conveyed in the drawing of a cube.

2. Analyze the use of contrast to show distance in an architectural rendering which you admire.

3. Compare the limitation of focus in order to add depth in two photographs selected by you as "good" and "bad."

4. Report on one of Prof. Ames's experiments in the perception of depth, and on the possible use of his conclusion in architectural drawing.

5. Cut out from a current magazine (or advertisement) a successful pictorial example of exaggeration. Justify it as a rendering.

6. Discuss the validity of a distorted perspective in an architectural composition. (Look up an actual example.)

7. Find in the library an illustration of an optical illusion based on light.

8. Trace the linear perspective of Illus. 8-6; place the lighting behind the building and render in three values only (light, shade, and shadow).

9. Read Hugh Ferris' article on Architectural Rendering in the *Encyclopaedia Britannica*, and report on it to the class.

10. Draw an adult elm (maple, pine, etc.), 10 in. high, 6 in. high, and 3 in. high. (*Note:* Each student should take a different species, and the sketches should be exhibited together. Other natural forms, such as hedges, lawns, pools, etc., may be used so that each student has a different subject.)

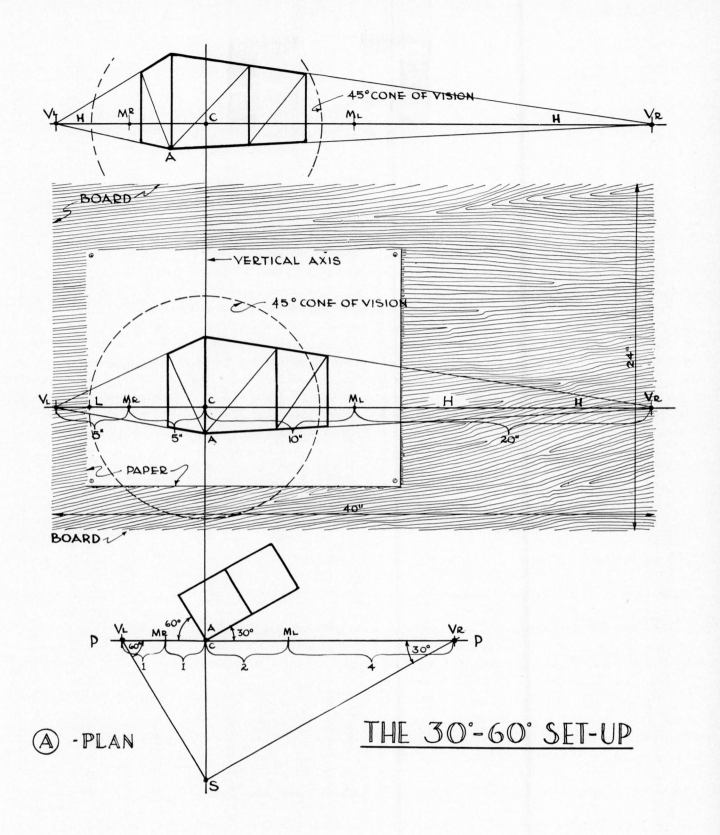

45° CONE OF VISION

BOARD

VERTICAL AXIS

45° CONE OF VISION

24"

V_L H M_R C M_L H V_R

A

V_L L M_R C M_L H   H V_R

5"   5"   A   10"   20"

PAPER

40"

BOARD

P V_L M_R 60°   A   30° M_L V_R P

60°   C   30°

1   1   2   4

S

Ⓐ - PLAN

THE 30°-60° SET-UP

Chapter 9

SPECIAL PROCEDURES

1. SHORT CUTS BY PREDETERMINED ANGLES

When even an untrained person is asked to make a sketch he will usually begin by trying to fit his picture to the size of the available paper. This is a sensible and straightforward attack on the problem which ignores complications such as station points, vanishing points, and sometimes even the horizon. The result is often crude but it is big enough to be seen, whereas the outcome of correct (but ill-applied) perspective procedure is often either disconcertingly small, or else involves working with points far outside the drawing. We should not ask, "How big a perspective can I make on this board?" This question would involve the forbidden practice of choosing S to fit the equipment. We can ask, "What can we show properly within the limitations of available apparatus?"

The size of our paper will determine the distance at which a normal observer will prefer to hold our picture in order to see it comfortably all at once. Since we want his eye to correspond to the position of S that we shall assume, we can thus fix an approximate dimension for S-C. For a 12- by 18-in. drawing it might vary from 20 to 30 in. If we draw to scale instead of full size, the observer will mentally adjust the pictorial value of this fixed dimension but he will not change its actual length if he can help it. So we can most agreeably (to him) assume that at $\frac{1}{4}$ in. = 1 ft., S-C will measure between 80 and 120 ft., which is far enough away to focus a house of moderate size. At $\frac{1}{8}$ in. = 1 ft., we can show larger buildings, at $\frac{1}{16}$ in. still larger, etc.

If we have a 24- by 40-in. drawing board on which to put our 12- by 18-in. sheet, how can we find our working points so as to be reasonably correct, and still keep them within the limits set by our equipment? Turning the board lengthwise, it is obvious that our principal V's can be no more than 40 in. apart. We can assume them to be at the edges of the board, and draw HH through them, but what then? C could be anywhere between, depending on the angles that our object makes with PP and the choice of S and $C.V.R.$ To proceed we must assume these angles. Have we anything to guide our choice? Yes—remember that normally it is wise to "make big things look big." That means a flat angle to PP for the long sides and a sharp angle for the short faces perpendicular to them.

If now we decide on 30° and 60° (our object's main surfaces being perpendicular to each other) as the angles with PP, we can find all our other working points without drawing a plan, and by a rule so simple that it can be memorized easily, *i.e.*, **keep dividing in half.** Thus, if we wish to find two M's and C between our V's and keep C to the left, we make V^L-$M^L = \frac{1}{2}V^L$-V^R; V^L-$C = \frac{1}{2}V^L$-M^L; V^L-$M^R = \frac{1}{2}V^L$-C; and V^L-$L = \frac{1}{2}V^L$-M^R.

The proof of this rule for assuming working points depends on the relations of the sides of a 30°–60° right triangle. If the short side is 1, then the hypotenuse will be 2 and the long side will be $\sqrt{3}$. Calling the latter 1.75 (or $1\frac{3}{4}$) instead of 1.732+ is the only mathematical inaccuracy and this is usually negligible graphically.

If we make a plan layout of a perspective in which the sides of the object make 30° and 60° with PP, the parallels through S by which the V's are found will determine two other triangles (V^L-C-S and V^R-C-S) as marked in Illus. 9-1-A. Each is similar to V^L-V^R-S. In the triangle V^L-V^R-S, let us say that V^L-$V^R = 8$ units. Then V^L-S will equal $\frac{1}{2}$ of 8 = 4, and S-$V^R = 4\sqrt{3} = 4 \times 1\frac{3}{4} = 7$. In triangle V^L-C-S, V^L-$C = \frac{1}{2} V^L$-$S = 2$. Now if we revolve to find the M's, then V^L-$M^R = V^L$-$V^R - V^R$-$S = 8 - 7 = 1$; and C-$M^L = V^L$-$S - V^L$-$C = 4 - 2 = 2$; and M^L-$V^R = V^L$-$V^R - V^L$-$M^L = 8 - 4 = 4$.

Point L fixes a circle, with C as its center, which will represent the limits of a cone of vision of approximately 45°. This relation is the basis for the old rule of thumb—the picture should not cover more than one-third the distance between the V's (here three-eighths).

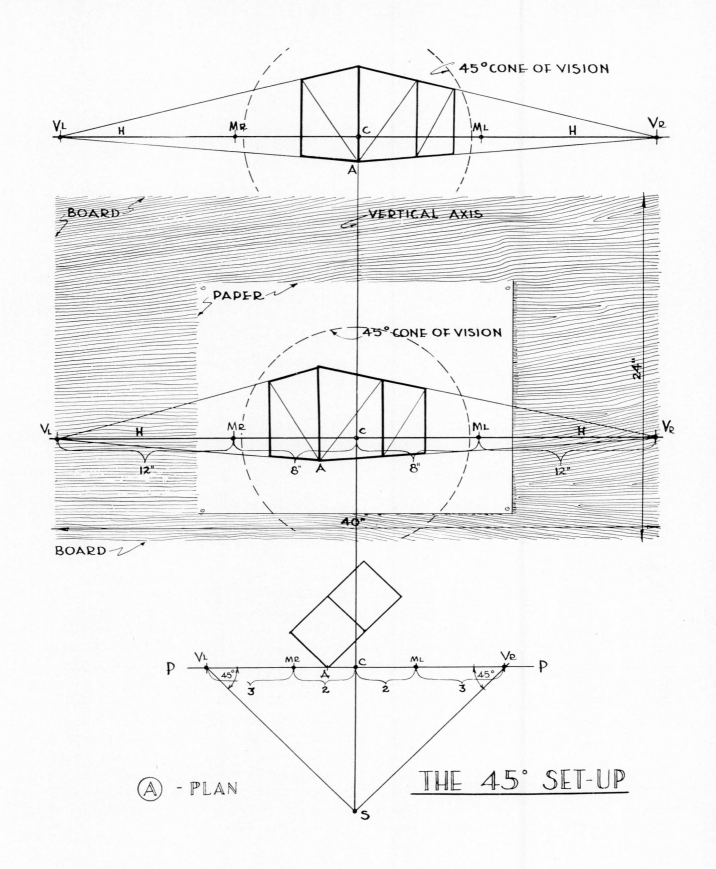

45° CONE OF VISION

BOARD

VERTICAL AXIS

PAPER

45° CONE OF VISION

24"

V_L H M_R C M_L H V_R

12"   8"   A   8"   12"

40"

BOARD

P V_L 45° M_R A   C M_L V_R 45°   P

3   2   2   3

S

Ⓐ - PLAN

THE 45° SET-UP

L is put at the center of V^L-M^R to continue the system, since the cone of vision is not an exactly definable quantity. C-$S = 2\sqrt{3} = 2 \times 1\frac{3}{4} = 3\frac{1}{2} = L - M^L$. This should be kept in mind to help realize the allowable depth of field.

Instead of the 30°–60° relationship just discussed, excellent results may be obtained by placing the PP so that the sides of the object (provided that they are at 90° to each other) both make 45° angles with PP. This setup permits even easier and quicker utilization of the existing facilities. If we put V^L and V^R at the extremities of our board (*i.e.*, 40 in. apart) C will be at the center, and the two M's will each be almost exactly two-fifths—in this case 8 in.—of the distance from C to either V (Illus. 9-2-A).

C will also be the V of the bisectors of the angles of the object, and a circle drawn through the M's with C as center, will mark a limiting cone of vision of a little less than 45°.

C-S will be equal to C-V, or 20 in., and will thus be the maximum possible when the given board limits the distance between the V's.

Prof. Ware strongly advocated the selection of this angular relationship for all perspective drawings not limited by some special condition.[1] He compensated for the pictorial loss which would result from foreshortening both sides of the object equally, by placing it to one side of the center. He could thus emphasize either face and regain the artistic clarity which would otherwise be lost through monotonous regularity.

In the case of large objects like buildings the fact that the spectator is looking **beside** rather than **at** his subject is not noticeable in the final picture, unless it is too greatly overdone. In fact, there is often some point of interest like a door or a gable which would naturally draw the eye away from the nearest corner.

It is interesting to compare (Illus. 9-2) the appearance of a double cube under the above conditions, with the perspective of the same object drawn at 30° to 60° at the same scale, and with V's the same distance apart (Illus. 9-1). Also consider the changed effect produced by pointing $C.V.R.$ at the nearest corner or to one side of it. Which outline seems to you most significant? Which best tells its story and best expresses the real character of the object? All four are true records of its appearance under different choices of S and $C.V.R.$ The artist must select the one which best fits the purpose of his drawing.

[1] Ware, William Robert, "Modern Perspective," rev. ed. New York, The Macmillan Company, 1914.

ALBERTI'S "CONSTRUZIONE LEGITTIMA" A.D. 1436

PROBLEM
TO FIND THE PERSPECTIVE OF A
HORIZONTAL SQUARE WITH BASE A-B

SOLUTION
LAY OFF D-E EQUAL TO S-C.
DRAW HORIZONTAL THRU M TO P

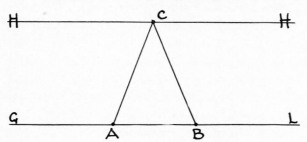

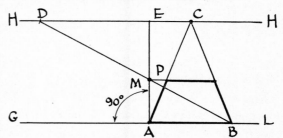

VIATOR'S CONSTRUCTION A.D. 1505.

SOLUTION
LAY OFF C-D EQUAL TO S-C
DRAW B-D TO FIND P ON A-C

PROOF
IN PLAN FIND "V" OF DIAGONAL
OF SQUARE. C-D = S-C.

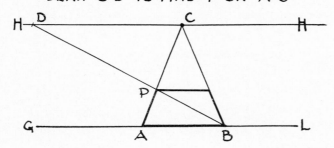

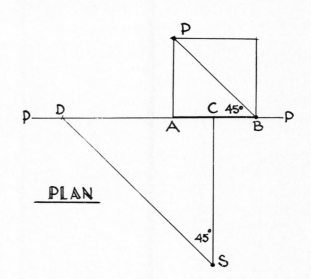

PERSPECTIVE

PLAN

ILLUSTRATION 9-3

2. ONE-POINT PERSPECTIVE AND PERSPECTIVE GRIDS

In the first chapter attention was called to the efforts made by the investigators of perspective in the fifteenth and sixteenth centuries, to find an exact method for determining the **amount** of diminution which would occur under given conditions. The phenomenon itself had long been observed. It is a commonplace of our daily visual experience that things look smaller as they become more distant from the eye. The problem is **how much** smaller in a particular case?

Alberti and his successors realized that the endless variations possible in nature could be approximated accurately if three-dimensional space was subdivided into a system of regular cubes by a *grid* of equally spaced lines, consisting of one set of verticals and two sets of horizontals (one parallel to the picture and one perpendicular to it). Any object of known position could then be drawn in its proper "space cube." The fondness of these artists for painting tessellated floors made up of alternating black-and-white squares was perhaps due to their realization that such a checkerboard, once accurately drawn, would permit the exact placement of any object standing on it. Heights could similarly be related to a wall divided into equal squares, if the wall could first be put accurately into perspective.

They thus reduced the general problem of diminution into the specific question of how to draw exactly the perspective of a square lying on the ground with its front parallel to the picture plane. From observation of a model, Alberti[1] discovered that the diagonals of square floor tiles seemed to converge at a point on the horizon. His rather clumsy construction for finding this point of convergence (vanishing point as we call it today) was demonstrated to be geometrically exact by Leonardo, and was known as the "costruzione legittima" (Illus. 9-3-A). It was used for centuries by painters, especially Italians, even after Jean Pélérin (under the nom de plume Viator) published in 1505 the simplified version which is commonly employed today.

Viator demonstrated that X could be found by drawing from B to a point D, whose distance from the perspective center C was equal to the distance from the station point to the picture plane. No proof of his construction was included in Viator's book but its correctness is obvious to us who know how to lay out a perspective in plan. D is of course simply the vanishing point of the diagonals of squares which have their fronts in or parallel to PP. It is found (like the V of any other horizontal line) by drawing a parallel to S through PP. Hence a 45° right triangle S-C-D is formed, whose sides S-C and C-D must be equal.

Simple as this seems to us now, the discovery was a tremendous one in its day. Let us not forget that descriptive geometry was then unknown. Alberti and Viator knew nothing of a plan as a mathematical concept controlled by definite geometrical laws. In fact the study of perspective **led to,** rather than **evolved from,** the development of today's exact graphical science.

The artist using such a method began with a perspective setup in which two of the principal systems of lines would not vanish while the third system would vanish at C. Hence only one vanishing point was necessary, and the name of *one-point* or *parallel* perspective was given to this type of representation. It produces quite satisfactory results for interiors, street scenes, and other conditions in which more or less similar objects are placed on either side of the center of interest. (See Illus. 6-4-A.)

The distance point D required for constructing the squares of reference is merely another vanishing point, although called by a different name, and the basic theory of one-point perspective is the same as that of *two-point* (or angular) perspective. There is no essential difference involved because of the number of V's employed—the interest for us in the method lies in its subdivision of space by equally placed lines.

[1] For an account of Alberti's experiments and conclusion, see Ivins, William Mills, "On the Rationalization of Sight. . . ," New York, Metropolitan Museum of Art, 1938.

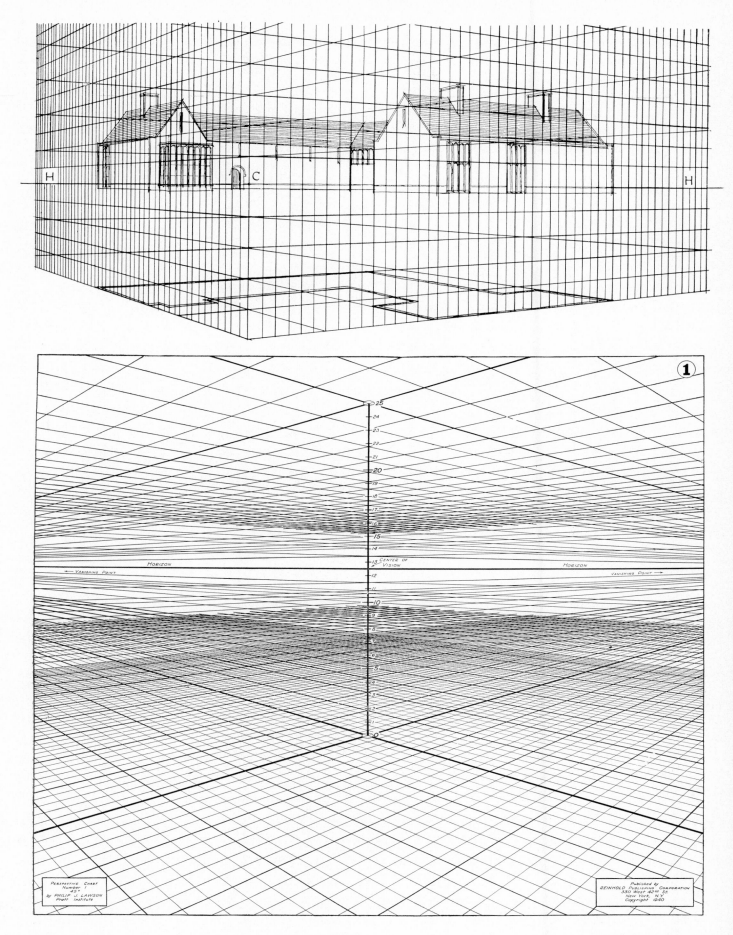

ILLUSTRATION 9-4

The idea of drawing perspectives on such grids is particularly applicable to contemporary drafting-room practice. Today most drawings, particularly studies and preliminary sketches, are made on tracing paper. Draftsmen are accustomed to working on such a surface, and know how to get the best effects on it quickly with pencil or crayon. If a perspective is desired, why not make it also on transparent material, over a previously developed grid? The latter can be prepared carefully in ink, and the picture drawn over it freehand, quickly and dashingly, but under control. The draftsman can give his full attention to his design and its presentation, instead of worrying about the rules of perspective (which in most cases he uses only occasionally, and may have trouble in remembering). When drawing over an accurate framework, he cannot make technical mistakes and thus spoil the pictorial effect of ideas that may really be good spatial concepts.

There is only one flaw in what would otherwise be an obviously sound procedure—the time, knowledge, and care needed to make the grid. These would not be grudged if only **one** had to be made. Unfortunately, as our study of perspective has shown, a new S should be chosen for each new drawing. Hence a new grid must be made for each perspective if we wish to get the best results. It is usually easier to lay out the main masses of the object to be drawn than to go through such a tedious preliminary for each new picture.

However, as Sec. 1 of this chapter has attempted to demonstrate, most rectilinear objects can be successfully represented using 30°–60° or 45° perspective setups. If we have grids for such conditions and, in addition, a number of grids based on varying distances from S to C, we shall command a considerable choice of angles and distances of view. Since each can be used at several different scales, the focus can also be varied, and the number of possible choices thus increased.

In order to provide such a series of grids as perspective tools which will save drafting time, several types of printed graphs have been placed on the market. When used with understanding they are legitimate timesavers and produce excellent results. Every draftsman who uses perspective primarily for its general illustrative value, and is not concerned with trying for the utmost in pictorial expression, will find them serviceable.

As an illustration, the Reinhold Publishing Corporation, New York, has given permission to publish one of their Lawson Charts. Full directions for use accompany each chart. Several other sets of charts are available commercially, including those published by the Probox Perspective Chart Company of Los Angeles.

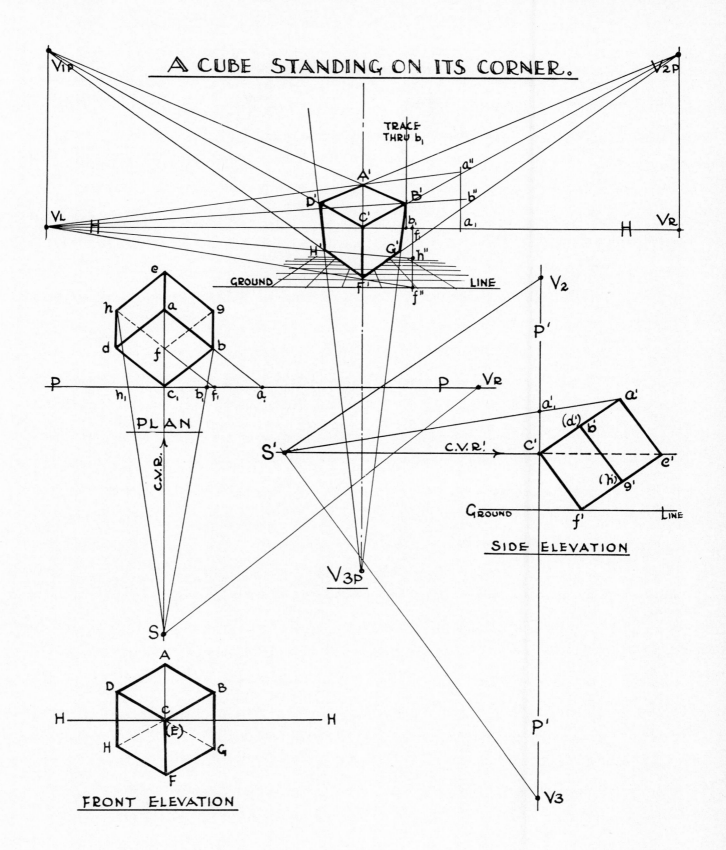

A CUBE STANDING ON ITS CORNER.

PLAN

FRONT ELEVATION

SIDE ELEVATION

ILLUSTRATION 9-5

3. THREE-POINT PERSPECTIVE

It has already been emphasized in other sections of this book that our basic method of perspective procedure will provide the solution to all possible problems. Many special variations of this method may be developed for meeting particular requirements, but these are advantageous only if the draftsman has occasion to meet such conditions so often that it becomes worth his while to master individual techniques for them. As long as we assume a vertical picture plane and a horizontal central visual ray, the perspective of any point can be found as the intersection of two lines which are put in perspective by our basic method. Names such as *parallel perspective, two-point perspective*, etc., simply tend to confuse the beginner and actually introduce no new problems.

Illustration 9-5 shows how to find the perspective of a cube standing on one corner in such a position that the three visible faces make equal angles with the picture plane. Perhaps the most difficult part of this problem is to draw the elevations and plan of a cube in this unusual position—another example of it being more difficult to catch the rabbit than to make the pie! The shortest procedure is to begin with the side elevation—determining the plan and front elevation from it.

We then locate the perspective of each point (like B or H) as usual by finding where the trace on PP containing its visual ray intersects a horizontal assumed through the point (a''-A'-V^L or h''-H'-V^L). Note that while these assumed lines have the same direction in plan as the edges of the cube, they are not really parallel to these edges, but are **horizontal** construction lines added for the purpose.

The edges of the cube being sloping lines, their V's could have been found by our regular procedure (erecting the true angle with the horizontal at the proper M). However, an easier means of locating them is available because of the side elevation which we have had to prepare. In that drawing a parallel to c'-b' through S' to $P'P'$ will give us point V_2, which in perspective must lie on the vertical through V^R, because the plan of C-b vanishes at V^R. The distance from C' to V_2 in side elevation is accordingly laid off above V^R in perspective, thus locating the required vanishing point V_{2P}.

The only unusual part of the construction is concerned with the edges C-F, D-H, and B-G—those which we would normally expect to be vertical but which are actually sloping away from the beholder in this special case. Their vanishing point V_{3P} may also be determined by a parallel through S' in side elevation. Since the parallel to them in plan strikes the picture plane at C, the perspective of point V_3 must lie directly below C in perspective by a distance equal to C' and V_3. This point is V_{3P}, and is used in Illus. 9-5 to draw B'-G' and D'-H'. Now that V's have been located for all principal lines of the cube, they may be employed to shorten and control the drawing of the perspective.

It is evident that visual rays drawn from S' in side elevation to the various corner points of the cube will determine on $P'P'$ the height above or below C' for the perspective of each point. If these distances had been laid off from HH in the perspective, the assumption of horizontals through the points would have been unnecessary and our work would have been simplified. The horizontal trace for any point as established by rays in side elevation will locate its perspective position by intersection with the vertical trace obtained from rays in plan (a'-c' laid off above C' gives A').

Such a use of rays in side elevation as well as in plan has been generalized and fully explored as a perspective method by E. I. Freese.[1] The procedure is direct and easy to understand, but depends on perfect draftsmanship to secure proper results. Since no vanishing points are used, there is no control for systems of parallel lines. Slight mistakes in measurement or drawing may thus produce unfortunately exaggerated effects. Before beginning the perspective one must project an elevation perpendicular to the picture plane, or have such a drawing available. Since the latter is rarely prepared except for this purpose, the extra labor involved in making such a special projection is usually greater than that required to construct a perspective by our normal theory. In addition it is apt to involve a further possibility of inaccuracies, or actual errors, in drafting.

[1] Freese, Ernest Irving, "Perspective Projection," New York, Pencil Points Press, Inc., 1930.

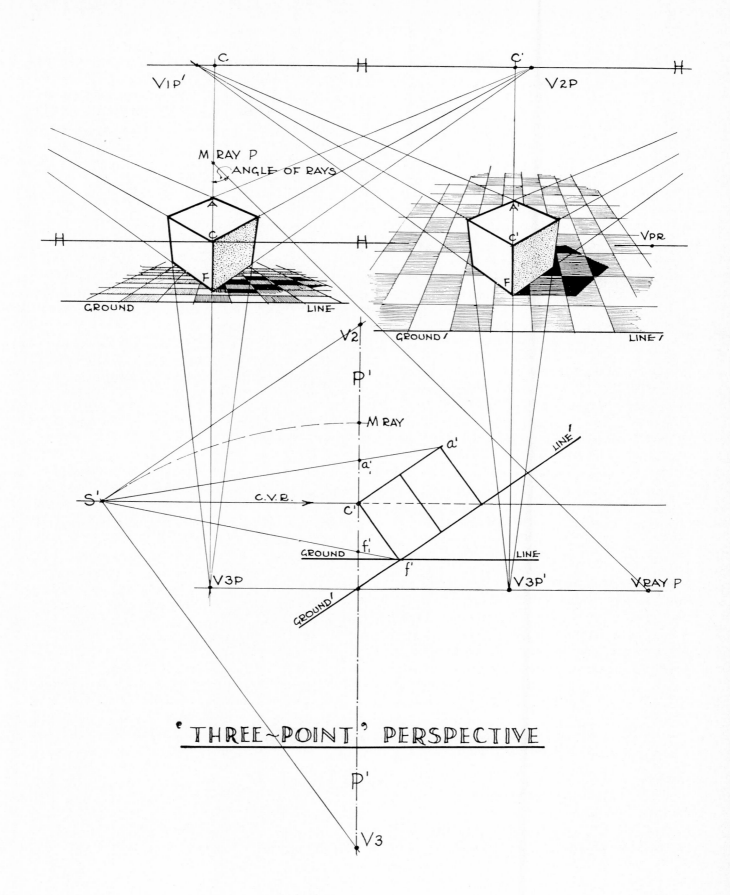

'THREE-POINT' PERSPECTIVE

ILLUSTRATION 9-6

There are, however, a number of situations in which the use of a side elevation (or section) projected parallel to the picture plane is the simplest way of meeting the perspective problems involved. These are the cases where the picture plane is inclined instead of vertical. A better way of stating the problem would be to say that these are cases in which the best choice of $C.V.R.$ is no longer a horizontal, and hence the picture plane can no longer be vertical. (Remember that PP must always be perpendicular to $C.V.R.$ because that is the way our eyes are constructed by nature.)

For centuries perspectives were always and unquestioningly made on vertical picture planes. Projection onto inclined picture planes was recognized as geometrically possible, but was considered artistically undesirable because the objective was to make a picture which could be hung on a wall, and would be looked at by a standing observer whose $C.V.R.$ would normally be perpendicular to the wall and hence horizontal. Any other relationship seemed unnatural, and the results hard to understand, besides being difficult to work out in perspective.

Then, with the advent of the camera, photography made it easy to achieve inclined views, and gradually the public became accustomed to them. The development of the multistory building undoubtedly also contributed, by providing us with daily memories of how a tall building looks when we throw back our head to see the top of it. More recently the popularity of air travel is making people conscious of how objects on the earth look when seen from far above by an observer looking down at an angle to the ground.

A demand for such views has developed which cannot be satisfied by the ordinary bird's-eye or worm's-eye view. When we are up in a plane we do not look out horizontally (*i.e.*, perpendicular to gravity) if we wish to see something on the earth below us. Instead, we turn our eyes downward and thus produce the condition that is involved graphically by an inclined picture plane.

A similar condition arises when we wish to represent nearby objects which are normally below the level of our eye, such as things on a table, etc. Painters have long used an inclined picture plane for still life groups which normally would be viewed from above.

Actually no new theory is needed to meet this situation by the rules of linear perspective. Illustration 9-6 compares the tilted cube of Illus. 9-5 with a cube of the same size placed in a normal position on a horizontal plane so that its edges are either verticals or horizontals. If S is taken the same distance away as in the earlier illustration, and $C.V.R.$, so chosen that PP makes the same angle with the cube as before, the geometry of finding the perspective and the resultant outline of the object will be exactly the same in both cases.

Illustration 9-6 involves what is often called *three-point* perspective, and considered a very difficult special problem. The term *three-point* is in itself confusing. It derives from the fact that most architectural objects are delimited by three sets of parallel lines, two horizontal and one vertical. For a vertical picture plane each of the two horizontal sets has its vanishing point, while the verticals remain parallel. With an inclined picture plane all three sets will vanish. Hence the name. But it is a rather meaningless title, since many objects (like our tilted cube) have three vanishing points although the picture plane is vertical, and others might have only two vanishing points even though the picture plane were inclined.

The perspective procedure and the resultant picture are the same, whether we consider $G'.L'.$ to be the ground line which represents the normal horizontality of the earth's surface (so that the cube has vertical sides, and $C.V.R.$ and PP are inclined); or whether we assume that the latter two are in their normal horizontal and vertical relationship to $G.L.$, so that our cube is standing on one corner. The horizontal surface of the earth (as indicated by the squares of flooring and by the shadows) will have a different appearance in each case, and the relation of the horizon to the cube varies, but the perspective of the cube is the same.

V^{Ray}, which of course is necessary in order to cast the shadows, is also determined from the side elevation in which the rays are assumed as parallel to S'-V_3. Their true angle with the vertical can be seen by revolving the triangle S'-V_3-V^{Ray} into PP, S will then fall at M^{Ray} which in turn can be located in perspective at M^{RayP}. At this point then, we lay off the desired vertical angle of light and prolong to intersect a horizontal through V_{3P} at V^{RayP}. The shadows are then worked out by our normal procedure.

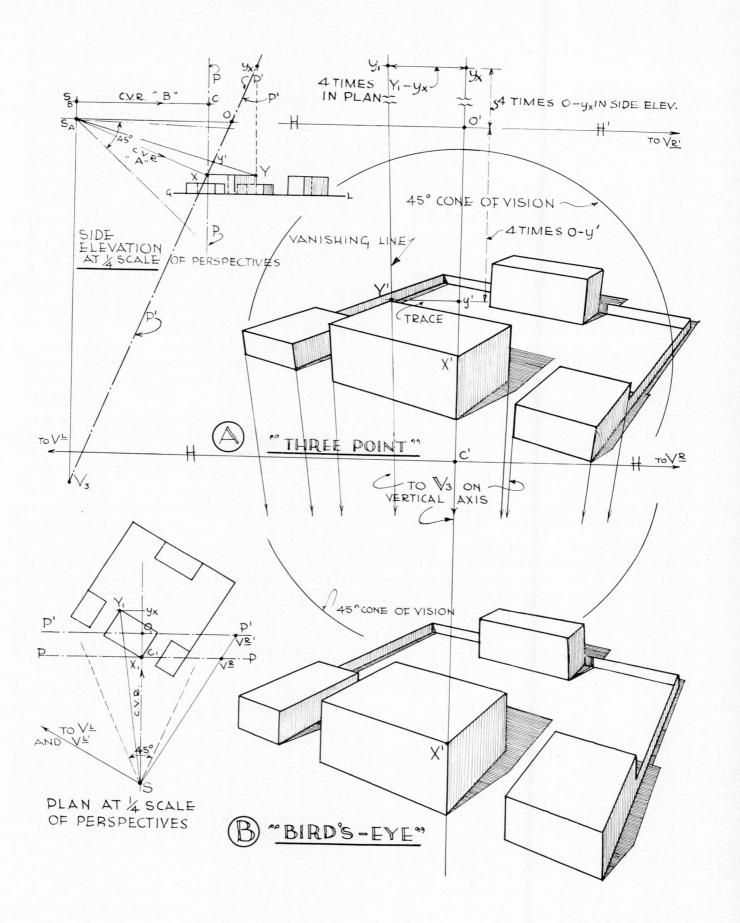

SIDE ELEVATION AT ¼ SCALE OF PERSPECTIVES

C.V.R. "B"

C.V.R. "A"

45°

4 TIMES Y₁-yₓ IN PLAN

4 TIMES O-yₓ IN SIDE ELEV.

TO Vᴿ'

45° CONE OF VISION

4 TIMES O-y'

VANISHING LINE

TRACE

TO Vᴸ

Ⓐ "THREE POINT"

TO V₃ ON VERTICAL AXIS

TO Vᴿ

V₃

45° CONE OF VISION

PLAN AT ¼ SCALE OF PERSPECTIVES

C.V.R.

TO Vᴸ AND Vᴸ'

45°

Ⓑ "BIRD'S-EYE"

4. DIRECT PROJECTION

Occasionally the architectural draftsman is called on to make perspective drawings of furniture as well as of buildings. In such cases the best solution is usually a view made from above with $C.V.R.$ directed downward toward the chair, table, etc., from the level at which a standing observer would ordinarily see it.

Such a problem requires an inclined picture plane since PP must always remain at right angles to $C.V.R.$ Often the object has few if any systems of horizontals and most of its parallels are inclined lines. Our normal procedure would involve the determination of a large number of vanishing points, most of which would be located far off the drawing board, because of the relatively small cone of vision needed to include such objects, and the relatively large distances between them and S, for normal views.

Under these conditions it is often quicker to establish by direct projection the main points needed to make the drawing, as is shown in Illus. 9-8. If the plan is arranged above an elevation projected at right angles to $C.V.R.$, the perspective can be developed without the use of vanishing points by determining the location of each point in relation to C. In elevation a ray from S to the point will establish its height, and a ray in plan will determine its distance from the vertical axis, at the level thus fixed.

After S, $C.V.R.$, and PP have been decided, the perspective A', of any point such as A, is found as follows: In side elevation, draw the ray from S' to a', piercing PP at a''. Mark off the distance of a'' above (or below) C', from the center C selected for the perspective. Then in plan draw the ray to a, and project a'' to $C.V.R.$ at A_2. Measure the distance from this point to A_1 on the ray through a, and lay off this dimension to the left (or right) of the center line in perspective, giving A' on the horizontal through a_2.

Accurate drafting is required to establish each point exactly by this process. Besides the necessity of projecting a special elevation at the proper angle, a further difficulty arises from the necessity of working with many points which are hidden in the elevation, since the perspective will show faces of the object different from those revealed by the elevation. However, there is no reason why satisfactory results should not be obtained if care is taken in making all the projections involved.

If a larger picture is desired, PP may be moved behind the object, as has already been explained in Chap. 2, Sec. 4. The procedure for all points will then be illustrated by point B. It is the same as for A, except that the rays have to be extended beyond the plan and elevation of the point in order to intersect both PP, and the line projected from the level thus determined.

This method has been developed to include vanishing points, measuring points, and perspective plans by Prof. Beal of the University of Kansas,[1] who has worked out fully the graphic problems involved in making perspectives on inclined picture planes, based on the process of direct projection.

[1] Beal, George Malcolm, "Perspective, a Practical Development of Basic Principles," 3d. ed., Ann Arbor, Mich., Edwards Bros. Inc., 1947.

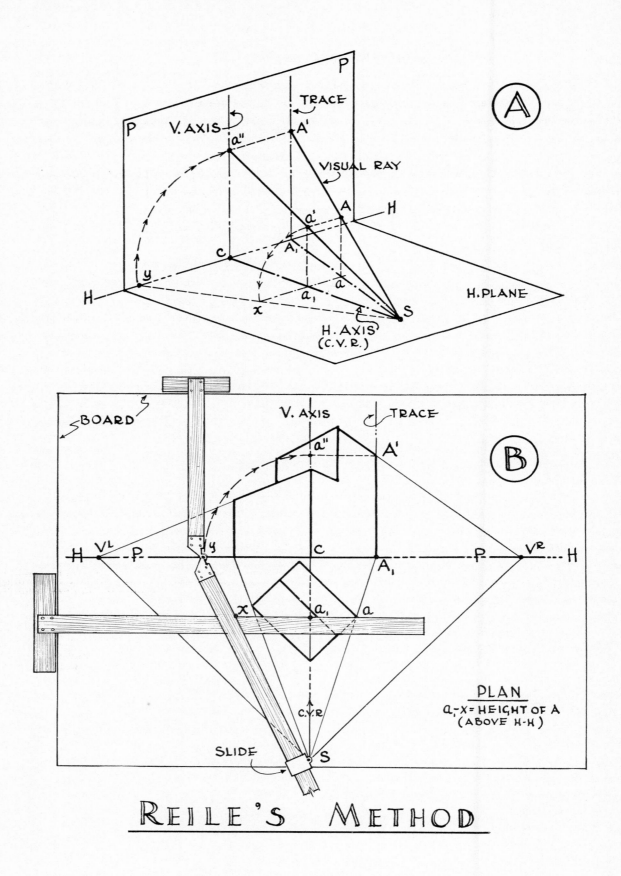

PLAN
a_1-x = HEIGHT OF A
(ABOVE H-H)

REILE'S METHOD

ILLUSTRATION 9-9

5. REILE'S METHOD

In 1927 Alfred Metscher of Los Angeles first published in English[1] the method of perspective projection developed by Prof. Adolf Reile of Stuttgart, Germany. The draftsman who learns this procedure can eliminate, by the use of a special T square and a pair of dividers, many of the construction lines which are required to find points by intersection. A perspective can be blocked in very rapidly, and the success of the chosen station point quickly tested.

An even greater advantage (which the author either did not fully realize or at least failed to emphasize) is that this method produces **large** perspectives from **small** orthographic drawings—thus eliminating completely a difficulty inherent in all other commonly used perspective processes. Reile's method makes it easier to project onto a picture plane **behind** the object than onto one **in front of it.** He thus obtains a picture bigger than the plans and elevations with which he starts.

Of course the basic phenomena of perspective still apply even with this different technique. Vanishing points are used, although they often fall off the board and interpolation is usually necessary. Proportional division is employed to subdivide the principal forms, and only the most important points are determined by Reile's special construction. After a little practice there is no doubt that one can block in large perspectives more quickly by this method than by any other yet developed—provided one has the special T square available. Unfortunately these are no longer on the market as far as can now be determined.

Reile's procedure is based on the fundamental concept of all perspective drawing, *i.e.*, that the image of any point will be found where the visual ray through that point pierces the picture plane. Thus the perspective of A is A', where the ray S-A meets PP (Illus. 9-9-A). The position of A' to the right or left of the vertical axis can be readily determined in plan, as in the office method by the ray through a, which locates point A_1 and thus the vertical trace containing A'. Its height above HH is more difficult to establish.

Reile's idea (Illus. 9-9-A) is to project A horizontally and parallel to PP until it lies at a', on the vertical plane through S perpendicular to PP, and then revolve it parallel to PP into the H plane at X. We now have its true height on a parallel to $G.L.$, through its plan a, and laid off to the left of S-C. Next a ray may be passed through x from S, to strike PP at y. The distance y-C will be equal to the perspective height of A above HH, and may be laid off vertically above A_1 to determine A'—the point desired. Or y may be revolved to the vertical axis at a'', and projected horizontally to the vertical through A_1.

This procedure may seem complicated and slow in explanation, but it is not so in practice. An ordinary T square set on a in plan (Illus. 9-9-B) gives the horizontal line on which X may be laid off very quickly, by picking up with dividers its distance above (or below) HH on the elevation. The special T square easily projects X to HH, so that y-C may be picked up with the dividers. Then the special T square is moved to pass through a to A_1, and the dividers mark off y-C above A_1. After enough points have thus been determined to block in the principal masses, the picture is completed by the use of all the auxiliary means explained in Chap. 6, including vanishing points where needed and accessible.

This method offers such real advantages that it deserves to be more widely known. The special jointed T square, with its sliding collar fitting around a pin through S, is very simple to use and requires no new skill. Since it operates from the top of the drawing board, it does not interfere with the normal T square, which is always at hand to make the horizontal projection on which X is laid off.

Even if no special T square can be purchased (or made up) the method still can be applied by using any straight edge to project the rays through S, just as is done in the office method. After a very little practice, one can find any required point (such as A' in Illus. 9-9-B) more quickly by Reile's method than by any other. It takes no longer to project x to y on HH, pick up y-C with dividers and lay it off on the trace, than it does to lay off the true height on a $V.L.M.$ and draw to a V by a new setting of the T square.

Note that PP in Reile's plan coincides with HH and, being **behind** the object, produces a large image. The student should check the location of A' by the office method, timing himself to see the relative lengths of each operation, and counting the number of movements involved in each.

[1] Reile, Adolf, "The New Perspective for the Architect," translated by Alfred Metscher, copyright 1927.

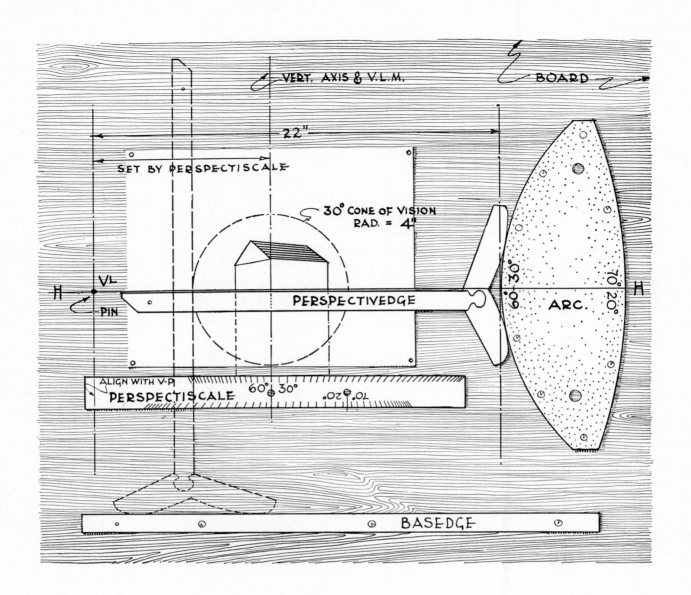

PRICE'S

'PERSPECTIGRAF.'

ILLUSTRATION 9-10

6. PERSPECTIGRAF

Another perspective aid designed to eliminate the necessity of laying out, drawing to V's, and using visual rays to find traces, has been developed under the name of *Perspectigraf*.[1]

The outfit consists of a special T square (called the *Perspectivedge*), two *Vanishing Arcs* (allowing four different angles of view), a *Basedge* for drawing verticals with the Perspectivedge, and a *Perspectiscale*. The latter is calibrated in numbered units of feet and inches, foreshortened according to the four angles established by the arcs.

In all cases the arcs are set up at the right of the drawing board, tangent to a vertical line drawn 22 in. to the right of a pin which has been placed as the left-hand V. (*HH* of course runs horizontally through this point). C is located by the zero point of the Perspectiscale, which is marked for a definite relation to V^L or to the arc intersection.

With the special equipment we are able to draw mechanically the three sets of lines most important in linear perspective, and to measure distances along them. The blade of the Perspectivedge when held against the pin at the left automatically gives us the apparent slope, in relation to *HH*, of lines actually horizontal and running in that direction. Distances on these parallels are marked off according to the divisions of the Perspectiscale. Horizontals to the right are established by sliding the branching head of the Perspectivedge against the vanishing arc. Points along these lines can be located by reading their true lengths on the gradations of the Perspectiscale to the right of its zero point. Verticals are drawn by sliding the Perspectivedge against the Basedge, and their subdivisions are found by using a regular architect's scale of the same proportion as the Perspectiscale, on V.L.M.

This process is direct and simple. The special implements required are similar to ordinary drafting equipment and involve no special skills. The four settings available with the same outfit give the draftsman considerable latitude in choice of angular relation between his subject and his station point. After the picture has been blocked in by scaled dimensions, details may be developed by any (or all) the methods explained in Chap. 6. A perspective plan is often drawn in order to obtain sharper intersections for projecting points. At this stage in the process of making a drawing, one profits greatly from being able to draw so many vanishing lines automatically, instead of having to join points which have been laboriously established. The draftsman can think more about **what** to draw, since he does not have to worry about **how** to draw it.

It is to be noted that the Vanishing Arcs and Perspectiscale are worked out on the basis of a fixed distance of 15 in. from S to C. While this is a good average assumption, especially for architectural subjects, it will not fit all conditions. However, since the Perspectiscale units can be equated to any proportion desired in relation to full size, the scale value of S-C will vary accordingly, giving a large number of variations, each of which has four angular possibilities. Mr. Price recommends trying a number of the available combinations before deciding definitely which one to "work-up." Let me add the caution to keep inside a 30° cone of correct vision (whose radius on the drawing will be about 4 in., centered at C, in all cases) and not to exceed the depth of field suggested by the marked divisions of the Perspectiscale.

[1] Invented, patented, and sold by Llewelyn Price, Architect, through the Letterite Company of Fort Washington, Pa. (1948). Reproduced by permission.

COMPARISON OF PERSPECTIVE METHODS

METHOD	DATA·REQUIRED	SPECIAL·EQUIPMENT	REMARKS	REFER TO
OFFICE	ORTHOGRAPHIC DRAWINGS - PLAN AT LARGER SCALE	NONE	MOST COMMONLY USED BECAUSE DATA AVAILABLE	III - SEC. 6 IV - SEC. 10
MEASURING POINTS	ORTHOGRAPHIC DRAWINGS AT ANY SCALE	NONE	BEST UNDER MOST CONDITIONS ESPECIALLY FOR RENDERING	V - SEC. 2 SEC. 10
DIRECT PROJECTION	ORTHOGRAPHIC DRAWINGS PLUS ELEVATION ⊥ TO P-P AT CHOSEN ANGLE.	NONE	BEST FOR "3-POINTS", DEPENDS ON EXACT DRAFTING- NO "CONTROL"	IX - SEC. 4
REILE	ORTHOGRAPHIC DRAWINGS	SPECIAL T-SQUARE (NOT NOW ON MARKET)	BEST FOR REENTRANT OBJECTS- LARGE PERSPECTIVE FROM SMALL PLAN	IX - SEC. 5
PERSPEC-TIGRAPH	DIMENSIONS OF OBJECT	SPECIAL T-SQUARE ARCS. SCALE ETC. (AVAILABLE & INEXPENSIVE)	SIMPLE TO USE-PERMITS DESIGNING DIRECTLY IN PERSPECTIVE	IX - SEC. 6
CHARTS	DIMENSIONS OF OBJECT	SPECIAL CHART (SEVERAL ON MARKET)	LIMITS CHOICE OF S TO CHART AVAILABLE	IX - SEC. 2 SEC. 7
CALIBRON MACHINE	ORTHOGRAPHIC PLAN AND KNOWN HEIGHTS	SPECIAL MACHINE (EXPENSIVE AND UNAVAILABLE)	DISTANCE S-C LIMITED TO FIXED RATIO.	IX - SEC. 7
PHOTO-GRAPHY	EXISTING OBJECT IN SPACE	(CAMERA, FILM, DEVELOPING & PRINTING	CANNOT BE USED TO DESIGN-ONLY RECORD	I

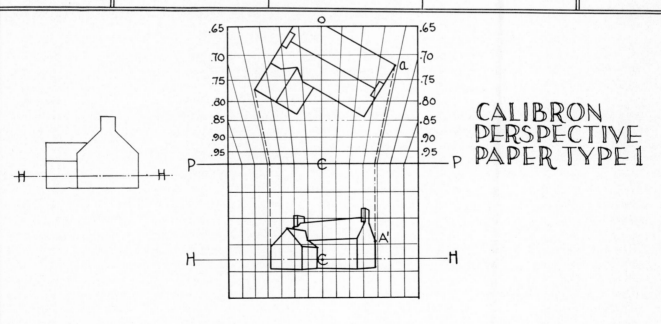

CALIBRON PERSPECTIVE PAPER TYPE 1

ILLUSTRATION 9-11

7. CALIBRON DEVICES

In May, 1936, the Calibron Products, Inc., issued No. 3 of their Notebook series, devoted to the subject of "Perspective and Optical Illusions of Depth."[1] This pamphlet of only 44 pages gives an excellent summary of the graphical problems involved, and of the many methods and devices which have been worked out for their solution.

The Calibron perspective-machine (patented) has never been produced in quantity sufficient to make it widely available, and to bring its cost within reach of the ordinary draftsman. However, Calibron Perspective Paper Type I has been put on the market. Its principle is simple, and it permits complete flexibility in the relation between the subject and the observer, instead of the rigid assumptions on which most grid papers are based.

The upper part of each sheet is ruled with converging lines, leading to a station point 20 in. below, but stopping at a horizontal marked PP. This portion is, therefore, a plan layout with a regular mesh of visual rays, across which are shown a series of parallels to PP, each marked with decimals (0.95, 0.90, 0.85, 0.80, etc.). These values have been worked out to express the diminution of vertical lines under the given conditions, and at the marked distance behind PP.

Each ray is continued as a vertical across the lower portion of the paper, thus giving the traces on PP for any point in the plan portion, either directly or by interpolation. Horizontals are also provided at regular intervals as a guide for choosing HH, and for measuring heights.

To make a perspective, a plan of the chosen object is drawn (or traced) on the upper part of the perspective paper, at the desired angle to PP, and far enough **behind** it to give a large enough image, as shown by the bounding rays. (Obviously the entire object must be **in back of** PP.) The lateral location of any point can be quickly found by following the nearest ray through to PP and onto the proper vertical trace.

Heights are determined by multiplying the true distance of the point from HH (above or below) by the index decimal marked for its distance behind PP in plan. The resultant value is scaled off from HH in perspective on the trace already determined. Enough key points are found by this procedure to fix the main outlines of the object, and details are added by relation to the principal masses. Calibron adds:

It is well to remember that each set of parallel lines has a vanishing point toward which all the lines in the set converge. This fact will be found of great convenience in determining the correct slope of a line where points are very close together, in checking the accuracy of lines already drawn, and in adding lines freehand.

Calibron perspective paper is thus a special mathematical application of what we have called the office method. It offers a ready-made layout with enough rays already drawn and projected as traces to save considerable drafting. For heights it relies on calculation and the scaling off of rather minute dimensions. Each draftsman must decide whether there is more or less error likely, in view of his own graphical skill and habit of mind, in making such calculations, or in finding heights from a vertical line of measure, according to our regular procedure. Even if he decides on the latter course, Calibron paper will gain some time for him, and help him to check rapidly how he wishes to place the object in relation to S.

[1] Published by Calibron Products, Inc., West Orange, N.J. See especially page 43. Illustration 9-11 is based largely on their conclusions and is reproduced with their permission. It puts the principal perspective methods in comparison and provides a clear tabular presentation of the well-nigh endless claims and counterclaims as to the best and easiest way to produce linear perspectives.

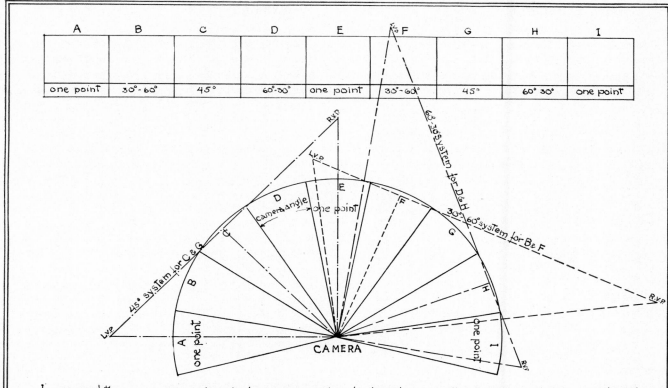

A	B	C	D	E	F	G	H	I
one point	30°-60°	45°	60°-30°	one point	30°-60°	45°	60° 30°	one point

In general the panorama is treated as nine individual pictures with a common station point and common horizon. The panel is painted flat then bent into the arc of a circle with the Camera at the common station point. The station point is determined by the Camera angle which varies according to the lens.

Chesley Bonestell

April 21-1946

ILLUSTRATION 9-12

8. CYLINDRICAL PERSPECTIVE

In Chap. 1 (page 11) it was explained that the painter who wishes to draw a wide landscape records on his picture an overlapping series of perspectives in which each object is shown as it looks when he turns his eyes directly toward it. The equivalent of this *freehand* process, based on observation of existing objects, can be achieved in the exact projection of orthographic drawings, by making the picture plane a vertical cylinder instead of a flat plane.

The perspective picture is then the *roll-out* of a cylindrical surface, and if the spectator stands at the assumed S and sweeps his eye across the scene, a very natural effect is produced. On a large scale the process may even be extended to 360°, like the well-known panorama of the Battle of Gettysburg which is observed from the center of a large circular hall.

Cameras with revolving lenses have been manufactured to obtain such extended fields of view and most of us are familiar with the "panoramic" photographs thus taken. Drawings which are worked out on this principle are less successful, because the curvature of horizontal lines (above and below HH) becomes noticeable and disturbing if the object is parallel to the assumed PP, while it looks curiously flattened if it is placed so as to present a salient corner to the observer (see also Chap. 8, Sec. 6).

In recent years the motion picture industry has demonstrated how the perspective draftsman may help out the camera by a somewhat similar procedure. The expense of constructing elaborate settings, or of transporting actors to the actual spot which is the scene of a story, may be avoided by using a perspective drawing instead of the real locality. Only the part of the scene where the actors move need be built—above that a photograph of a perspective may be introduced by a clever production department. At first such drawings were crudely done; the transition was obvious and was greeted by the audience with cries of "Fake!" Now, when the perspective is carefully worked out and artistically rendered, it is almost impossible to detect the trick.

Mr. Chesley Bonestell of Warner Brothers Pictures Incorporated has obtained their consent to publishing the material which he has generously supplied for Illus. 9-12. This shows how a perspective background may be used for a movie set. In explanation he writes:

Each painting is twenty-one feet long, and for general purposes, the four different perspective systems, with a common Horizon and Station Point, cover the situation. Variations such as would exist are included in the painting but always from the same common Station Point and, of course, the same Horizon.

In this case, the action takes place at the beginning and extreme end of the panorama. By cutting a small card of screen proportions (3 x 4), and sliding it along the picture from left to right, you can get the effect on the screen.

Multistory buildings confront the delineator with a dilemma. If he moves S far enough away to include their full height in a 30° cone of vision, he will be, in reality, too far away to see clearly the detail desired. A very small image would result and very distant V's. If this tiny picture is enlarged sufficiently to permit drawing its smaller parts, the effect is apt to be that produced when photographs taken with a telephoto lens are enlarged. The relation of the masses does not agree with the completeness of the detail. We have produced an effect mechanically which is impossible to the human eye, and hence is rejected by our visual memories.

On the other hand, if we stand near enough to see the detail, the upper portions will be out of the cone of correct vision and so unpleasantly distorted as to ruin the desired effect. Most draftsmen, under these circumstances, resort to corrections made by "eye" (*i.e.*, by guess). They use a series of horizons and V's, raising them as the building rises.

An equivalent effect can be achieved accurately by projecting onto the surface of a horizontal cylinder as a picture plane. Only a few principal points need to be worked out; the rest can be interpolated without difficulty. Those interested in learning the method of producing this special type of perspective should consult Ware's "Modern Perspective."[1]

Another method which involves projection onto a spherical surface, so as to include a larger angle of vision than our regular cone of correct vision permits, and yet avoid distortion, has been developed by the Italian architect Francesco la Grassa, under the name of "Prospettottica".[2] Unfortunately his work is not yet available in English.

[1] *Op. cit.*, Chap. XIII.
[2] *Giornale del Genio Civile*, Luglio-Agosto 1947, and *Rivista del Catasto e dei Servizi Tecnici Erariali*, No. 2, 1948, published by the Istituto Poligrafico dello Stato, Rome.

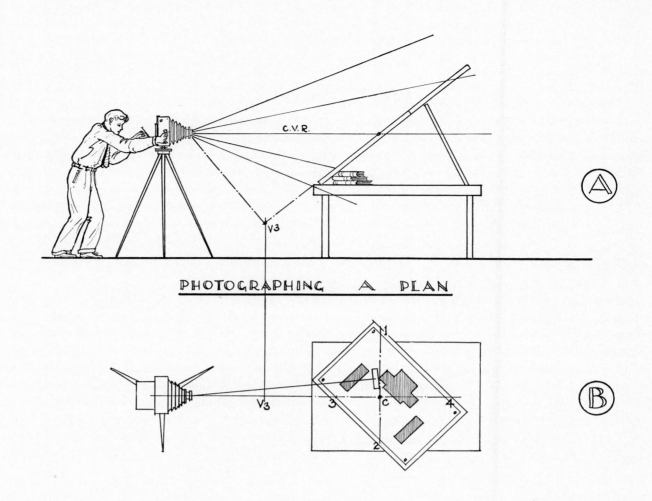

PHOTOGRAPHING A PLAN

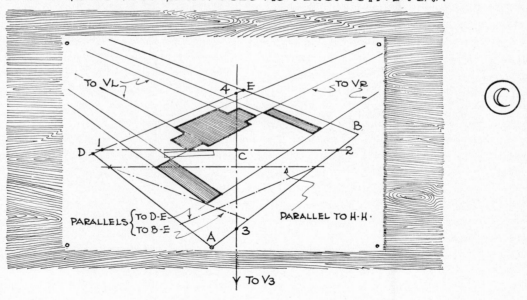

ENLARGED PHOTOGRAPH USED AS PERSPECTIVE PLAN

ILLUSTRATION 9-13

9. PERSPECTIVE PLANS BY PHOTOGRAPHY

The camera is not only an accurate instrument for making perspectives of existing objects, but may also be employed in the delineation and representation of projects still to be executed. A photograph of an architectural plan is the quickest and easiest way of producing a perspective plan, provided the necessary apparatus is available. Today nearly everyone has a camera or can borrow one. Films can be developed quickly almost anywhere, and most communities are served by companies that will enlarge the prints to any desired size. By planning in advance for cooperation, it is usually possible to have a photographic perspective plan made and ready for use, almost as quickly as one could be drawn up—and of course with considerably less drafting effort.

Illustration 9-13 shows in diagrammatic form the simple process of photographing an architectural plan while it is still on the drawing board. Be sure to make a graphic scale and place it on the drawing to be photographed. It will be invaluable in working up the perspective picture. Also be sure to make note of the position of the camera in relation to the board, and especially of the point C to which the $C.V.R.$ of the camera is directed in taking the photograph. If possible use one with an open back and a ground glass on which the pictorial composition may be studied. If such a camera is not at hand, test out the position of S and $C.V.R.$ by eye.

A wise choice of these two basic determinants is just as important in a camera perspective as it is in one worked out graphically. An improvised cone of vision made out of a rolled-up piece of paper will be of great assistance in deciding on the best location for S. Mr. Parker[1] recommends the use of a special instrument called the *Aldrich Viewer* for studying the composition before making a decision. If we are going to make a lot of three-point perspectives, a permanent viewer will be very useful. If we make only an occasional air-view, it will scarcely earn its salt.

The beginner may be puzzled to determine how to place the enlarged photo-plan on his drawing board. If the lines 1-C-2 and 3-C-4 are added to the orthographic plan before the exposure is made, there will be no trouble. The photo must be tacked down so that 1-C-2 is horizontal (thus establishing the direction of HH). Accordingly 4-C-3 will be our vertical axis, and V_3 will be located on it.

Sometimes, however, this precaution has not been taken in advance, and we have no direct way of relating our perspective plan to our drawing board. HH (or a parallel to it) is needed.

Divide A-B and A-D each into any number of equal parts. From the division points nearest to A, draw parallels to B-E and D-E. Where these parallels intersect A-B and A-D are points which, when joined, will give us a parallel to HH.

The development of the perspective picture over the perspective plan presents few difficulties. In most cases the V's of the principal sets of horizontal lines will fall off the board, but strips or arcs can easily be set up to take care of them. A series of height lines should be worked out at C to allow for the foreshortening of vertical lines. This may be done exactly from an accurate diagram, as in Illus. 9-6, or can be approximated by relation to the scale put on the drawing for that purpose.

Do not forget that the horizontal line 1-2 through C is the only line in which the object and the picture plane coincide, and therefore the only line on which true scale dimensions can be laid off. If a number of small graphic scales ($\frac{1}{2}$ by 2 in.) are placed at strategic points on the orthographic plan and so turned as to be perpendicular to the visual rays to those points, they will automatically photograph into perspective scales.

Occasionally a practical problem arises in the drafting room which the camera will solve. A large bird's-eye view has been made and found unsatisfactory. There is no time for another layout. What to do? Photograph the perspective! If the camera is placed carefully at the assumed S, and the bird's-eye is revolved around HH, a photo can be taken of the **rendered drawing** as seen from above (or below) at any desired angle. The result is equivalent to an original three-point perspective of the object. In fact, it has been advocated that results often justify adopting this procedure intentionally, first making a normal perspective, and then photographing it to get an aerial effect.[2]

[1] Parker, *op. cit.*, pp. 3 and 4.
[2] Hall, H. G., "Aerial Drafting," *Architectural Forum*, February, 1929, pp. 287–289.

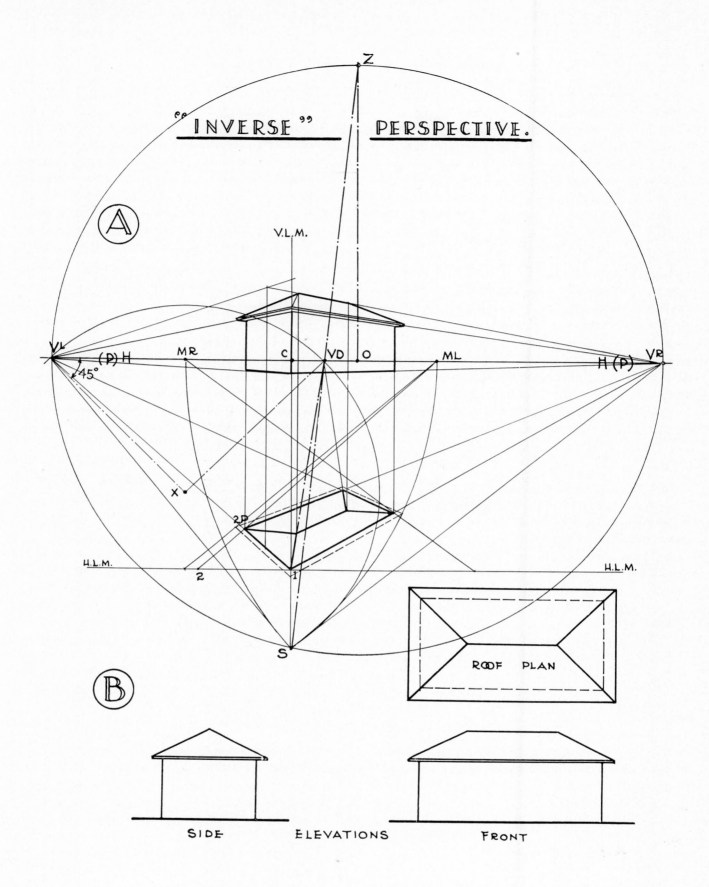

"INVERSE" PERSPECTIVE.

ROOF PLAN

SIDE   ELEVATIONS   FRONT

ILLUSTRATION 9-14

10. INVERSE PERSPECTIVE

An airplane photograph of an existing geographical area will of course produce an accurate three-point perspective of the landscape. Such pictures are, however, incommensurate. It used to be impossible to determine directly from them the true size of the objects shown. During the First World War, when the combination of airplane and camera first made possible the photographic reconnaissance of enemy terrain, it became vitally important to find out how such perspectives could be worked back into scale maps on which distances could be measured accurately so as to control artillery fire, etc. The Staff of the Allied Armies worked for several years on this problem without finding a satisfactory answer.

It was not until 1922 that John William Gordon[1] published an exact solution. It is interesting to note his acknowledgment that after making his own study he discovered that the true answer had remained unnoticed for over two centuries in one of the forgotten theorems in Part II of Brook Taylor's "Linear Perspective."[2] The eighteenth-century mathematician had foreseen and solved all the possible geometrical relationships between an object and its perspective image, although the invention of the camera still lay over a hundred years in the future. Taylor did not even dream that a simple and accurate machine would be perfected in the nineteenth century which would make perspectives (in the form of photographs) a commonplace part of our everyday lives, but as a scientist he wished to explore all the implications of his subject and thus included *inverse perspective* in his study.

The practical importance of this process soon became as evident in peace as in war. By it, unexplored country can be mapped, highways laid out, bridges located, contour surveys provided, etc., with a slight fraction of the time and effort which would be required to make the usual surveys on the ground. So the relations of overlapping views were worked out, stereoptical effects were coordinated, even the color spectrum was made to contribute, and a new science had been born, called *photogrammetry*. It is a fascinating subject and a whole study in itself, far beyond the scope of this book.

Occasionally, however, one needs to work back from a perspective drawing (or a photograph) to actual dimensions by graphical methods. The geometry of the process is fairly simple, but its accuracy depends on very careful drafting, and the results are usually more of theoretical than of practical interest.[3] However, as in most other problems, the ability to "do it backwards" is an excellent test of one's knowledge of basic principles, and hence a valuable mental exercise, if nothing more.

Suppose that we are given the linear perspective (or photograph) of a small building (Illus. 9-14-A) and asked to find its true (scaled) dimensions—*i.e.*, to reconstruct the plans and elevations of the building which the picture represents. Obviously we must find the working-points by which the drawing was made before we can get back to actual lengths or heights.

By prolonging enough horizontals we can easily find the two principal V's, and a line joining them will give us HH. Somewhere on a semicircle, centered on HH and containing the V's, will lie S in plan (if we consider PP coincident with HH). When the exact location of S is known we can revolve the V's to find our M's. By using them we can change perspective dimensions into true lengths. (1-2 is obviously the true length of 1-2P.)

However, before we can determine where S lies on the semicircle, we must know V^D (the vanishing point of the bisectors of the angle V^L-S-V^R, and hence of lines at 45° to the sides of the building). In this case, the perspective of such a line is given us by the forward hip of the roof, and we need only to know its plan and prolong it to PP in order to find V^D. Often some ingenuity is required to find a line which will give us V^D, but there is nearly always an obvious square (or a circle around which a square can be drawn) in the perspective of any architectural object, and the diagonal of a square will give V^D at once.

First, we must construct a perspective plan, in order to have the horizontal equivalent of the hip which we can prolong to HH, and thus find V^D. Then S can be located by completing the circle through the V's, projecting its center vertically to Z, and drawing Z-V^D until it strikes the semicircle at S. Or 45° lines from V^L and V^D may be drawn which will intersect at X, the center of a circle which will determine S by cutting the semicircle through the V's.

---

[1] Gordon, John William, "Generalized Linear Perspective," Constable & Co., Ltd., London, 1922.
[2] Taylor, Brook, "Linear Perspective," London, 1715 (many later editions).
[3] For a full exposition of this problem, see Deneux, H. L., "La Métrophotographie," Paris, Catin, 1930.

Study for chapel of the University of Maryland, Baltimore, Md.; Henry P. Hopkins, architect; drawn by Schell Lewis.

ILLUSTRATION 10-1

Chapter 10

THE TEN BASIC RULES OF PERSPECTIVE

THE TEN basic operations upon which the science of linear perspective are based are summarized here in short form for easy memorizing. Demonstrations of the reasons for the procedures and proofs of their graphical correctness are given in the chapters and sections to which reference is made.

Until the student is perfectly sure of these propositions and has practiced applying them until they are instinctive, he has not mastered the fundamentals of perspective drafting and is likely to become confused whenever an unusual problem presents itself. As soon as he knows them as thoroughly as he knows the multiplication table, he is ready to go on with confidence and to undertake any perspective problem whatever. There are no exceptions to these rules. They are always valid and will always provide a solution. Every other method is a special case, worth learning if in constant enough demand, but otherwise apt to be a source of confusion.

Proposition I. How to choose S, $C.V.R.$, **and** HH. Considering actual site conditions, locate S in order to get object in cone of correct vision, and so turned as to emphasize its most important side. Direct $C.V.R.$ at its most interesting point. Limit depth of field and choose HH to bring out its best features, (Chap. 2, Sec. 3, and Chap. 4, Sec. 1).

Proposition II. How to find the vanishing point of any series of horizontal lines. In plan, draw a parallel to them through S to PP at V. In perspective lay off V on HH by its relation to C. (Chap. 3, Sec. 8.)

Proposition III. How to find the perspective of any horizontal line (of infinite length). Find where it pierces PP (by measurement) and join to its V (found by Proposition II). (Chap. 3, Sec. 8.)

Proposition IV. How to find the perspective A' **of any point** A. Draw the perspective of any two horizontal lines which go through A (by Proposition III). Their intersection in perspective is A'. Assume the lines if necessary. (Chap. 3, Sec. 6.)

Proposition V. How to find the perspective of any line A-B. Find A' and B' (the perspectives of A and B respectively) by Proposition IV. Join A' and B'. (Chap. 3, Sec. 6.)

Proposition VI. How to find the M **(measuring point) for any series of horizontal lines.** In plan, revolve S into PP with V as center. In perspective, lay off this point M on HH by its relation to C. (Chap. 5, Sec. 5.)

Proposition VII. How to find the V **of any series of lines.** In plan, find V and M for the **plans** of the series. In perspective, lay off their true angle to the horizontal at M, and prolong to meet a vertical through V at the V required. Draw the angle down from HH if the line of the series through S goes down toward PP, and conversely. (Chap. 6, Sec. 1.)

Proposition VIII. How to choose the direction of light for rendering. If the object has (or will have if built) a definite location, use the angle appropriate to the season and time of day at that place. If the location is indefinite, consider the best pictorial possibilities. Express the rays as a series of parallel lines with a definite (drawn or noted) angle to PP in plan, and to HH in elevation (Chap. 7, Sec. 5).

Proposition IX. How to find the V **of the light rays.** Having drawn a typical ray, find the V^{Ray} by Proposition VII. Note that: (1) if V^{PR} lies to the right of V^R, the righthand faces of the object will be in shade (and similarly to the left); (2) the further V^{Ray} is from HH, the steeper the angle of light is to the horizontal (Chap. 7, Sec. 4).

Proposition X. How to find the V **of a shadow-edge** V_s. V_s lies at the intersection of two horizons H_1H_1 and H_2H_2. Find H_1H_1 by joining V^{Ray} and the V of the line casting the shadow. Find H_2H_2 (the horizon of the plane containing the shadow) by joining the V's of any two sets of lines in it. Assume them if necessary. (Chap. 7, Sec. 8.)

ILLUSTRATION 11-1

Chapter 11

RENDERING ORTHOGRAPHIC DRAWINGS

1. LINE VS. TONE REPRESENTATION

Since prehistoric times man has used line drawing as a means of depicting the objects in the world around him. From the representations of animals which adorned the walls of caves in the childhood of our race to the naïve profiles that the child of today produces in kindergarten, the use of linear boundaries in order to indicate the shape of things is so universal that we accept it without question.

Yet it is a convention, not a realistic reproduction of what we actually see. Our eyes never report to our minds images that are composed of **lines.** It remained for the Industrial Age, the telegraph and the wire-making machine, to show any human eye anything in nature even approximating what we have always drawn. Wires against the sky are the closest thing to lines that have ever actually been **seen,** but the use of lines to represent objects pictorially is so ancient that we never question its validity.

Undoubtedly the technique of drawing has influenced the establishment and acceptance of the line convention. Whether we scratch a rock with the corner of a flint, or mark a dried skin with a charred stick, or write on paper with a pen or pencil, the process depends on a pointed tool which will leave its mark in the form of a line. Our method of production thus results inevitably in the use of lines, as the basic visual material out of which our pictures will be developed. The draftsman, the lithographer, the engraver, and especially the etcher, have explored the possibilities of graphic expression based on line, and carried the medium into the realm of a very fine art. They have learned how to build up tones and textures out of **lines** so that they can suggest to our eyes the **values**[1] of the **areas** of light and dark and color, which our light-sensitive retinas perceive. At this point line ceases to be a convention for depicting objects by their profiles and becomes one of the many ways of representing **surfaces.**

In order to reproduce the true appearance of objects, we must have a technique for recording the **areas** of light and dark which the eye would register in actually looking at three-dimensional forms. (Like a black-and-white photograph, a drawing can record even color in terms of its value or equivalent brightness.) Many pictorial media are available for this purpose, from pencil, charcoal, brush, and wash, to the "blow-gun." In all of them the demand for skill of hand and eye is so great, merely to cover each area and keep its edges accurately, that only the greatest masters are capable of working without guide lines. The whole procedure demands that the artist simplify his technical difficulties by dividing his task. It is not only easier, but also quicker, for him to **draw** first, and then build up **values** within the boundaries established by **lines.**

[1] A pictorial "value" may be defined as the position of a shaded area on a scale of tones graded from white to black. See Illus. 7-2.

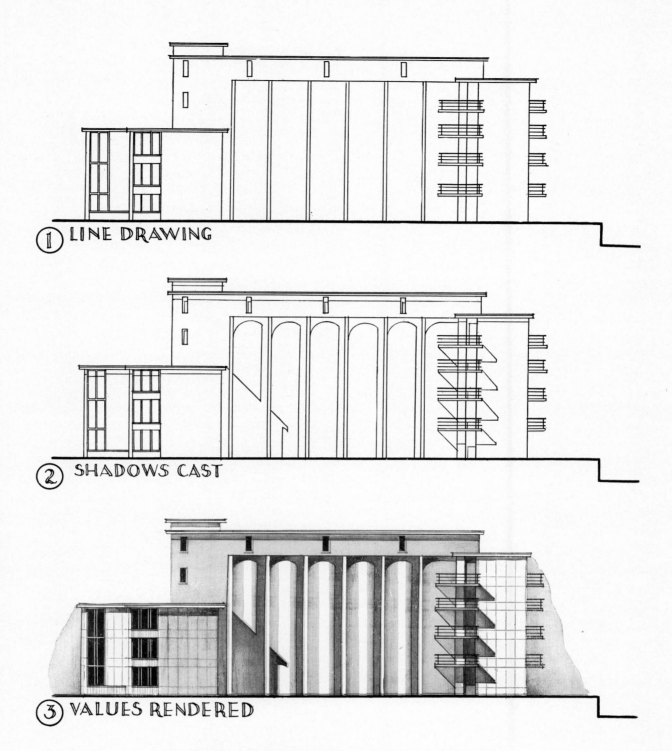

① LINE DRAWING

② SHADOWS CAST

③ VALUES RENDERED

STEPS IN RENDERING

ILLUSTRATION 11-2

The process of developing an outline drawing into a tone drawing is called *rendering*. Its purpose is to make as realistic a representation of the object as possible. By adding light and dark to line, it seeks to tell the observer more about the true form of the thing represented than he could grasp from a linear representation of it. A rendered drawing brings into the picture the third dimension which is missing on paper or canvas. Of course the effect is most realistic when the object is represented in perspective, as the eye would perceive it, but orthographic projections may also be rendered.

The play of light and shade which reveals form is due to the true shape of the object represented. It exists because of the actual surfaces involved, and is more truly the expression of three-dimensional qualities, than is any outline. Of course values change as the direction and intensity of light is varied, while contour remains fixed. In this sense, the form shown by a line drawing is capable of unnumbered variations in rendering.

When we cast shadows on a line drawing, it is important to remember that we are recording tonal qualities due to the actual shape of the object in space. The shadows are **on the object** and due to its form; they are **not** something merely **on the drawing.** They should be determined on the three-dimensional object, and **projected** onto the paper, in exactly the same way in which we determine outlines and record them on a drawing. Only by visualizing a real form in space can we understand the play of light upon it, and thus accurately determine the areas of various tones by which it may best be represented.

Because our technical process directs us first to draw outlines and then to put in tones, we must not think of shading as something that is **added** after a true representation has been established. On the contrary, we must realize that a line drawing is but a step on the way to a fuller expression, a convention which is far short of the whole story.

Architects use rendered drawings for two purposes—both as part of the process of studying their designs, and as a means of expressing their ideas to others. In either case exact and truthful representation is important. The designer must know how to cast shadows accurately, and how to render faithfully. The drawing must show exactly how the object will really look—graphic representation must express actual form without compromise.

The pictorial qualities of the rendering must not be allowed to govern. Architectural composition is concerned with the three dimensions of space, not with the two-dimensional surface of paper. It is the building behind the drawing that must be expressed. Its form is the important thing. We must never let our interest in the drawing, as a drawing, control our design. Otherwise "paper" architecture results. Faking is bad enough when done intentionally to fool others—it is unpardonable when it fools its author. Like the man who does not play fair in solitaire, he is cheating himself.

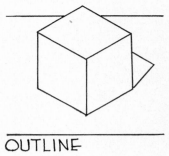
OUTLINE

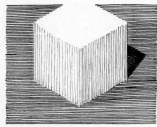
VALUES

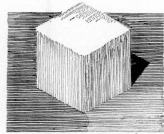
GRADED TONES

"LIGHT" FACES
AND COLORED MATERIALS

SHADE

SHADE

RAYS

LIGHT

HIGH LIGHT

WHITE SQUARE AT 45°

COLORED CYLINDER

2. *LIGHT, SHADE, AND SHADOW*

In Secs. 1, 2, and 3 of Chap. 7 the distinctions between surfaces in light, surfaces in shade, and surfaces in shadow have already been explained. Be careful not to confuse the use of the word light as applied to those surfaces of an object on which the rays from the light source fall directly, with the use of the same word to refer to the flux of light rays by which the object is illuminated. For the sake of clarity we shall hereafter italicize the word when we intend the former definition. Thus *light* will always mean an illuminated surface. The beams which radiate from a light source we shall call the *rays*.

Nearly all architectural drawings (even the interiors seen in sections) represent natural conditions—that is, they assume illumination by the sun (very rarely the moon). Hence the rays come from such a distance that they are considered to be parallel, and to be completely filling a clear sky. Such conditions will actually produce a very wide range of intensities of illumination. Direct sunlight falling on a white surface will cause it to be many times brighter than a black object in shadow. In a drawing our scale of values is limited to the modest difference between white paper and black pencil or ink—a total variation very much less than nature's. Consequently we must be most careful to keep clear the distinctions between *light*, shade, and shadow, and to save our white paper for the brightest parts of our object. The scale of values shown on Illus. 7-2 must be carefully followed—except by the expert who knows that "rules were made to be broken"—and when to break them!

3. *LIGHT FACES*

For any given direction of rays—corresponding to any given time of day and year at any particular point on the earth's surface—the *light* faces of an object may be quickly determined by comparison with the angle of the rays. Vertical surfaces are most easily checked in plan where the horizontal projection of the rays shows clearly which faces will be lighted, and how intensely. Those most nearly perpendicular to the rays will be the brightest.

Sloping surfaces, like roofs, may cause some difficulty as they approach the angle of the rays. An oblique projection diagram will quickly show whether or not they are "in light"; or the shadows of both ridge and eaves may be cast on the ground as a check. Because of their slope, roofs are apt to be more nearly perpendicular (or parallel) to the rays than are walls. Consequently they are usually either more (or less) intensely illuminated.

Since the angle of reflection when light rays strike a reflecting surface is equal to the angle of incidence, the brightest possible position for any given plane surface is that in which the reflected rays will come directly toward the spectator—*i.e.*, at 90° to the vertical plane of projection (in an elevation drawing). This situation rarely arises with roofs (and never with walls) in sunlight, but is of common occurrence on rounded objects where one point or even a considerable area may be turned so as to meet the conditions. In this case a high light is produced and should be located and rendered, as the painter does on an apple or a jar in a still life. The cylindrical shaft of a columnar support approaches this condition and its streak of approximate high light is as important a part of rendering it as is its shade area.

While the difference in value in rendering between the darkest and the brightest *light* faces is not great, it is extremely important. To neglect to differentiate the various *light* surfaces will produce a harsh garish effect. All tones should be graded, rather than uniform, throughout a given area in order to bring out form.

The hues of colored materials must also be taken into account. A dark substance, like a roof, may have a darker value when in *light*, than the shade faces of a light-colored surface, like the white-painted wall of a house. The brightly illumined upper faces of horizontal planes should be suggested by bounding their front sides by **light** lines, rather than dark—*e.g.* the top of the plinth under the shaft of Illus. 11-3.

A

 B

ILLUSTRATION 11-4

4. SHADE FACES

The rays may strike the surface of an object making it *light*, or be cut off from all (or part) of it by an intervening object, thus throwing it into shadow. If other parts of the object are completely turned away from the rays, they are thus in shade. Somewhere between *light* and shade lies the dividing line, which we call the *shade line*. The rays on one side of it strike the object; those on the other miss it and continue through space, eventually illuminating some other surface.

Thus the shade line not only differentiates *light* from shade in our rendering of an object, it is even more important because it determines the boundary between *light* and shadow on whatever other surface receives the shadow. If we know the shade line, we have only to find its shadow in order to complete our representation.

On rectangular objects, the shade line is an intersection of two planes, and hence is a sharp and definite line of demarcation between areas of the drawing having different values. Curved surfaces, on the other hand, have their shade lines blurred in rendering because the line of tangency to the light rays is not visually exact. The part of the object **almost** in light is optically very nearly as dark as the part just beyond, which is turned **just** enough to be in shade. The eye cannot distinguish.

Illustration 11-4-A shows a sphere and shaft, with shadows on a wall. Note that there is no definite hard line of separation between *light* and shade, but that the sharp outline of the shadow proves the existence of an exact shade line, nonetheless.

Since by definition a shade face is one so situated that the rays can never strike it, the corollary follows that **there can never be a shadow on a shade face.**

Since shade faces are those which are turned **away** from the rays under our chosen conditions, they must be turned **toward** any reflected light, as it comes back from surrounding objects. In nature, there are always numerous reflections, and hence shade faces are always more or less illumined. That is why they lie between *light* and shadow in our scale of values. Their tone will vary, within our limits, in accord with their angle to the rays—the more they are turned away from direct illumination, the more they will receive reflected light and hence the brighter they will appear. The nearer they are to the reflecting surface the more light will come back to them. Thus the shade on a column will be darker at the top than at the bottom, where it is diluted by reflected light from the ground.

The human eye is a most wonderful optical instrument but it does not work by only mathematical laws. The impressions that it records are interpreted by the brain according to psychological standards as well. One of these is commonly called *contrast*. It explains why a certain value will **seem** darker to us if it is juxtaposed to a very bright area, or will seem lighter than it really is, if we superimpose it on a very dark value. In the two figures of Illus. 11-4-B the chevrons have exactly the same value, but the one with a light background seems to be a much darker gray than the one with a background almost black.

5. SHADOW AREAS

Shadows are by our definition portions of *light* faces from which the rays are excluded by some intervening object. Hence no reflected light can reach them except on the second or third rebound when its intensity is very much reduced. In addition shadows **look** darker because of contrast with the *light* surface of which they are part.

(A) SHADOWS REVEAL TEXTURE

(B) SHADOWS REVEAL FORM OF OBJECTS

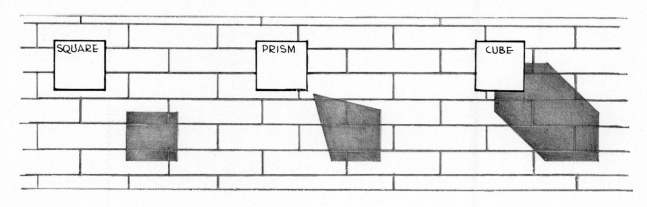

(C) SHADOWS REVEAL SHAPE OF SURFACE

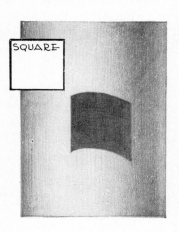

ILLUSTRATION 11-5

Shadow edges are especially important. Their character tells us a great deal about the objects which cause them, and also about the surfaces of which they are a part. They are our most significant means of expressing both form and texture. Nothing tells us so exactly the shape of an object as its shadow, because the shadow explains portions of the object that may be concealed in an unrendered elevation (Illus. 11-5-B).

Furthermore, the shadow edge reveals the character of the "surface receiving." It follows irregularities, brings out texture, and even suggests qualities such as smoothness or shininess. In practice the general shape of the shadow is first determined as though it fell on a theoretical plane equivalent to the average surface of the actual material, then the edges are broken up to emphasize the special conditions. Indication of texture is carried over all the shadow area after the edges have been crisply drawn. Full exposure to light tends to wash out particular surface peculiarities. The brighter the light, the more texture is eliminated, whereas shadow (and shade) should reveal it, as shown in Illus. 11-5-A.

6. PROCEDURE IN SHADOW CASTING

The shadow A_s of any point A is by definition the point in which the ray through A strikes some surface Q. Hence the shadow A_s-B_s of any line A-B will be the line of intersection with Q of the plane made up by all the rays through all the points which together form the line A-B. In other words the shadow of a straight line on a plane is the line of intersection of two planes and therefore is itself a straight line.

If the plane receiving the shadow is a curved surface, the shadow will also curve. The *surface receiving* (as we shall call it from now on) has as important an effect on the shape of the shadow as has the object casting. The latter will determine the form of the plane of rays which will cut the shadow, but the resulting pattern will also reflect the form of the surface thus intercepted.

We have already demonstrated that the shadow of an **object** is determined by the shadows of its shade lines. The light rays intercepted by the object leave a portion of space unlighted—a sort of prism of dark which is called the *penumbra* (see Illus. 7-3-A)—but this is invisible to us. Our eyes can perceive only the dark area (shadow) that is marked on some surface which would otherwise be fully illumined. This shadow area is bounded by the shadows of the shade lines of the object casting it, and these boundaries or edges are made up of the shadows of the points of which each shade line is composed.

Hence our graphical problem can be reduced to finding the shadows of points. Enough of these will give us the shadows of lines, and by the shadows of lines we can bound the shadows of objects. All that we have to do, in short, is to find where any given ray strikes some known surface.

Obviously then, we must know (1) the direction of the rays; (2) the position of the point whose shadow we are casting; and (3) the form and location of the surface receiving. Unless all three are fully known there is no problem, yet most difficulties in shadow casting are due to inadequate information about one or another of these three basic factors. In all cases the shadow must by definition lie on the ray through the point. In order to draw this ray, we must know the angle of the rays, and this angle will further govern our choice of points since it determines the shade line on the object casting.

In summary,

1. Fix the direction of the rays.
2. Find the resulting shade lines.
3. Cast the shadows of the shade lines on the surfaces receiving.

THE SLICING METHOD

GIVEN —
{
ANGLE OF RAYS IN PLAN & ELEVATION

LINES CASTING & SURFACES RECEIVING
}

ELEVATIONS

Ⓐ WALL   Ⓑ ROOF   Ⓒ TREE

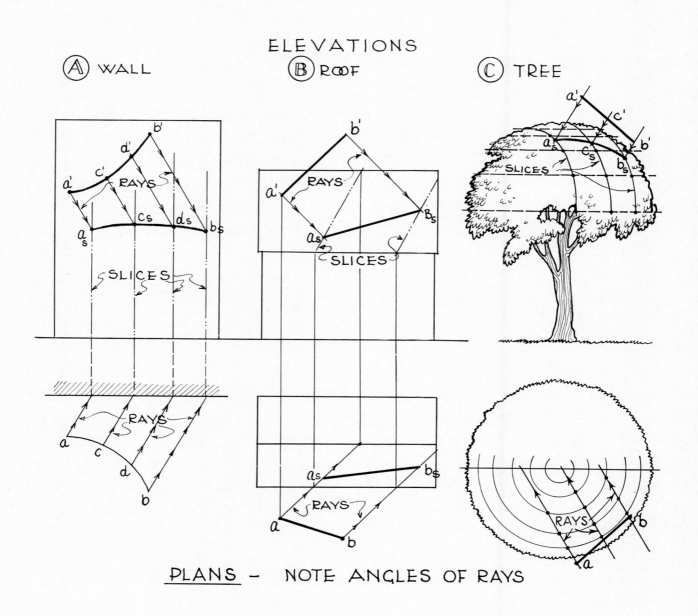

PLANS — NOTE ANGLES OF RAYS

7. THE SLICING METHOD

There are many possible ways of solving the graphical problem of casting shadows. When certain angles are given for the rays, special geometrical relationships can be worked out for particular objects and particular surfaces receiving. Some of these are short and elegant mathematical procedures (such as the shade and shadow of a sphere on a wall). They are interesting exercises in descriptive geometry and valuable training in analysis and presentation. When the occasion for using them presents itself, they have real advantages. However, they offer no general method which will **always** apply to **all** problems, and be universally applicable under all conditions.

As long as architects were content to design within a chosen historic style, the range of forms which they wished to render was limited to those appropriate to the period. It was worth while to learn shorthand methods for casting shadows on the relatively small number of shapes which composed their vocabulary.

Today most designers reject such stylistic restrictions. They wish to be free to use whatever forms their problems indicate, and consequently they need a method of casting shadows so broad as to cover all possible cases. Like Louis Sullivan they want a "rule to which there are no exceptions," not an unending series of individual special procedures.

Fortunately, we have such an all-inclusive solution in the *slicing method*. It is not always the easiest solution, and often involves much careful drafting, but it **always** applies. When in doubt, it is always available as a check on more special solutions, or to carry us on when otherwise we would be stuck. It is easy to apply in a large majority of architectural problems, and can be developed to provide the answer quickly in nearly all cases. While at times it may be tedious to work out, yet when it has been thoroughly mastered, any problem in shadows may be undertaken with confidence—without it, any new situation may find us helpless.

Illustration 11-6 explains the simple theory behind the slicing method, and shows how easily it can be applied when the shadow falls on a wall, a roof, or even a tree. Refer also to this same slicing method as used in perspective and explained on page 117.

In rendering architectural plans, most visible shadows lie on horizontal surfaces, while in elevations a very large percentage of shadows occur on vertical planes like walls, or sloping planes like roofs. For all these situations the slicing method provides a quick and simple solution. When the line casting is curved, the procedure is almost as simple, as long as the shadow falls on a surface which is easy to slice.

In each case, we begin by drawing the plan of the ray through the point whose shadow we wish to determine. We then find the elevation of the slice which is cut from the surface receiving by the vertical plane which contains the ray and is represented by its plan. This slice, being the line of intersection of the surface receiving and a plane containing the ray, must by definition contain the shadow of the point. By definition also the shadow must lie on the elevation of the ray. A point which must be on each of two lines must be at their intersection, so the shadow is found where the elevation of the ray intersects the slice.

Illustration 11-6-A shows the use of sufficient points to fix the shadow of a curved line on a wall. The slices are easy to find, being the vertical lines in which two vertical planes must meet. At B, the shadow of each point requires the construction of a slice through a sloping plane and hence lying at an angle. After the direction of one slice has been established, any additional slices needed can be drawn parallel to it by establishing one point (the eaves) from plan. At C, where the surface receiving is domical, each slice requires the construction by points of a new curve on which to stop the elevation of the ray. With circular objects this is not difficult, though somewhat tedious, as at least three points must be worked out for each line—the two ends and an intermediate which will make certain whether the curve of the shadow is concave up or concave down.

More complex surfaces require further analysis (as explained in Chap. 12).

R° LIGHT

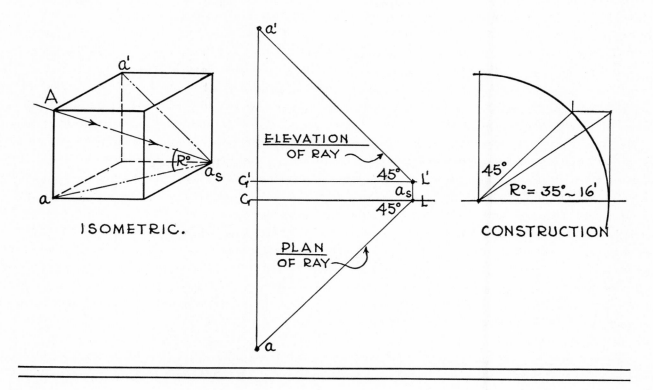

ISOMETRIC.

ELEVATION
OF RAY

PLAN
OF RAY

45°

45°

CONSTRUCTION

R° = 35° ~ 16'

PIER   JAMB & LINTEL   PORTICO

8. $R°$ LIGHT

The slicing method is valid for any direction of light. When the direction of the rays is fixed, further simplifications of the method become possible. Architects have taken advantage of such standardization for well over a century, and today always use a conventional angle of light unless special conditions justify the choice of an unusual angle for the rays.

The standard angle long established for architectural drawings is that of the diagonal of a cube, from the upper left corner nearest the observer to the lower right corner farthest away. The light thus comes over the left shoulder of the person looking at the drawing, at about $35°-16'$ (plus or minus), which agrees approximately with the inclination of sunlight in midmorning, or midafternoon, depending on the latitude and the time of year.

For the Temperate Zones this is as near an average direction for sunlight as could be selected. The sun passes through this angle twice every day at hours when we are apt to be out of doors and looking about us. Of course it will be over our **right** shoulder if we are facing north in the forenoon, but it will shine on three sides of every object (east, west, and south façades) at some time of day throughout a considerable portion of the year. North exposures never receive direct sunlight except in extreme latitudes, and should never be rendered with exact shadows.

One of the great objections to standardized lighting in rendering is that it may be thoughtlessly used in cases (such as north façades) where it could never actually occur. Particularly in studying his buildings, the architect should always consider their geographical situation before making rendered drawings. He deceives only himself (and his client) if he designs in terms of sunlight and shadows where these could never occur. In such cases he should think, compose, and draw in terms of soft gradations of tone and not in the sharp blacks and whites of cast shadows.

$R°$ lighting for rendered drawings has a long history behind it, during which a large number of important works have been published in which it has been used.[1] The most important advantage of the system lies in the commensurate relation of shadow to form under $R°$ lighting. A front view in line only requires the addition of a plan or a side view in order to explain the object. A single rendered elevation, with shadows cast at $R°$, not only shows the general form of the object, but tells exactly **how much** each cornice overhangs or **how deep** is the reveal of each window, etc.

This is because $R°$ rays make the same angle with both the vertical, the horizontal, and the profile planes of projection. Consequently (in elevations), **the shadow of any point is as far below the point as it is to the right.** The shadow of a projecting vertical element on a main wall is thus a vertical strip as wide as the distance by which the element advances from the principal mass. Similarly, the shadow of a lintel ends as much below it as the depth of its soffit; the shadows of columns on a cella wall are as much to the right as the columns are in front of the cella, etc. Thus to the practiced eye $R°$ renderings are exact expressions of form and proportion.

If the use of $R°$ rays gave untypical, misleading, or hard-to-understand results, it would be immaterial that this convention has great practical advantages for the draftsman. Since instead it produces generally desirable lighting conditions, we are fortunate in that it is also the quickest and easiest to use. Our 45° triangles permit us to draw the plans and elevations of the rays easily with our accustomed equipment, and the geometrical symmetry of these lines suggests many short cuts. The graphical problems involved in casting shadows can be solved by simpler constructions under $R°$ lighting than under any other direction that we might select.

However, we must be careful not to become "slaves of the 45°." Buildings are seen under many other angles of light in the course of the sun's journey from dawn to dark. When we choose $R°$ for a drawing, we should do so realizing that it represents a good average direction (except for north façades) but is not the whole story. Buildings should not be designed to look well on 45° renderings (as has unfortunately sometimes been done), but 45° renderings can be made to see how well buildings will look under average conditions. Since in order to render at all we have to choose **some** fixed angle of light, $R°$ is usually a justified decision for a rendering, provided that we do not make the result the criterion of the design, but remember that any drawing is but one means of achieving a good building.

[1] Among many others, see: Fouilles de Delphe, École française d'Athènes, 1925; d'Espouy, Hector, "Fragments antiques," Paris, Schmid, 1905; Les Médailles de Concours d'Architecture, Paris, École Nationale Supérieur des Beaux-Arts.; Magonigle, H. Van Buren, "Architectural Rendering in Wash," New York, Charles Scribner's Sons, 1921.

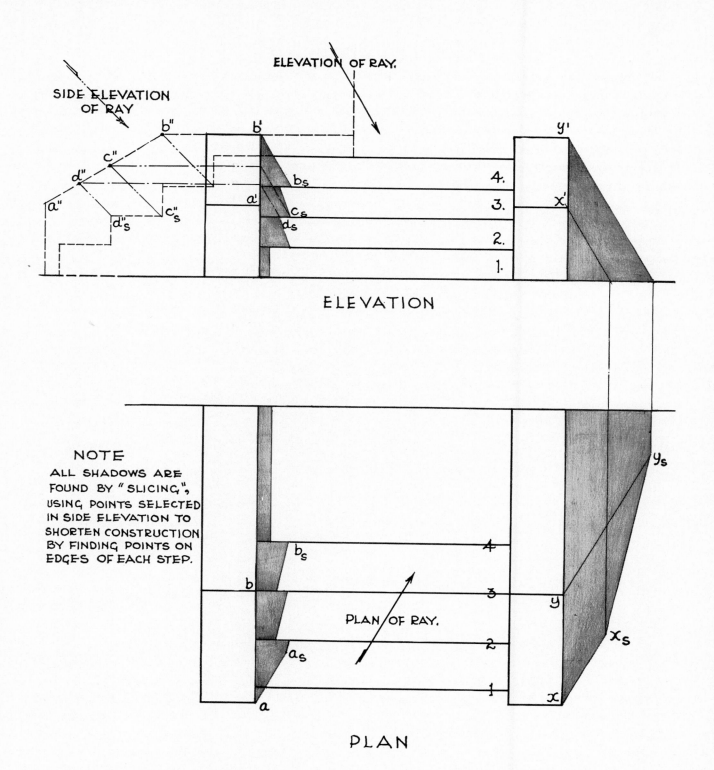

SIDE ELEVATION
OF RAY

ELEVATION OF RAY.

ELEVATION

NOTE
ALL SHADOWS ARE
FOUND BY "SLICING",
USING POINTS SELECTED
IN SIDE ELEVATION TO
SHORTEN CONSTRUCTION
BY FINDING POINTS ON
EDGES OF EACH STEP.

PLAN OF RAY.

PLAN

ILLUSTRATION 11-8

9. RULES FOR SHADOW CASTING

The graphical process of casting shadows will be greatly simplified if certain basic rules are kept in mind. They have all been discussed in previous articles, and are here repeated for convenience of reference. They result from the decisions already made as to direction of light, shade line, etc., and should be followed carefully in Illus. 11-8. Note that the shadow of every point on the shade line is accounted for, either in plan or elevation. It is usually wisest to follow it continuously, and not jump here and there.

1. **The shadow of every point must be on the ray through the point.** This results from the definition of a shadow. The first step in finding any shadow is to draw the ray through the point. In an elevation drawing we can draw only the elevation of the ray (a 45° line downward to the right). The real ray would go through the real point in space, at $R°$, down to the surface on which the shadow falls.

2. **The shadow of a point is a point—of a line is a line.** According to geometric law, a line can pierce a plane in only one point, and this is the condition for producing the shadow of a point. Similarly, since two planes can intersect in only one line, the shadow of any line A-B on any surface Q will be a line, because the shadow is the intersection with Q of the plane composed of the rays through all the points of A-B.

3. **Every point on every shade line must cast a shadow.** In any particular view of any object, some shadows (like some surfaces) will be invisible, but they will exist. We must be able to account for them all in order to be sure that none has been omitted.

4. **Only points on shade lines can cast shadows.** All other points are either in *light* so that the rays striking them illumine directly the surface of which they are a part, or are in shade and hence can never receive a light ray. In either case the basic condition for a shadow cannot be fulfilled—*i.e.*, the ray through the point cannot continue through space until it is intercepted by some other surface.

5. **No shadow can fall on a shade face.** Shadows are by definition parts of *light* faces from which the rays have been excluded by intervening objects. Shade faces, being so turned that rays cannot strike them under the chosen conditions, can thus never receive shadows.

6. **The best reference drawing for casting shadows is the one in which the surface receiving appears as a line.** In order to apply our basic method (slicing) a second projection of the object is necessary. Either a plan, a side elevation or a section may be used. For architectural elevations the first is most commonly employed both because it is usually available, and because it meets our rule whenever most of the visible shadows fall on walls. For roofs, steps, mouldings, etc., a plan is not as useful as a side view or a section (Illus. 11-8).

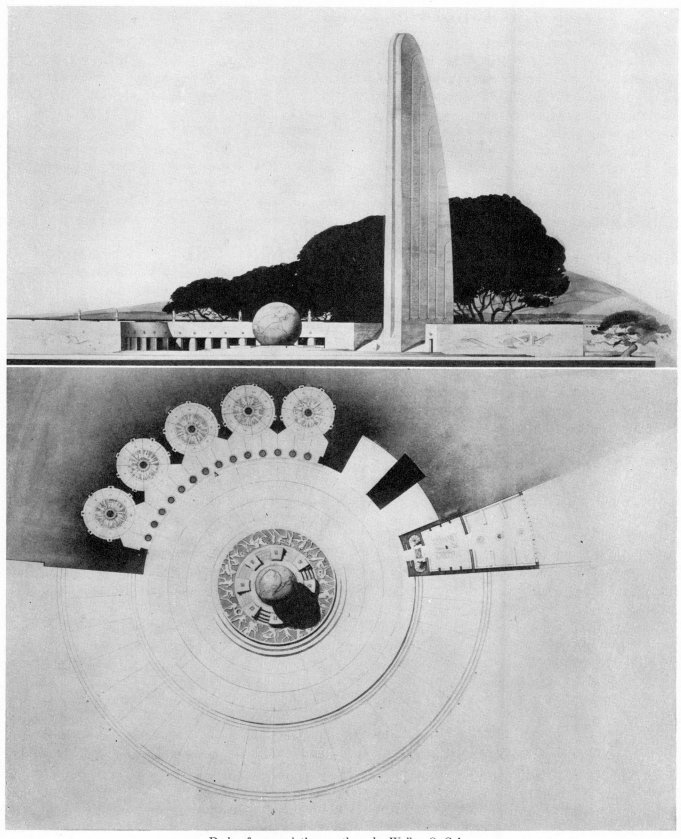

Design for an aviation pantheon by Walker O. Cain.

ILLUSTRATION 11-9

10. RULES OF THUMB FOR RENDERING

In making a rendering, casting shadows is only a step whose purpose is to delimit areas of *light*, shade, and shadow to which we can then apply the proper tones. Once we have established graphically the boundaries of the various areas of each kind, we must decide on relative values for them. For ready reference the rules for rendering, which have been discussed in preceding sections, are summarized below. They are based on the natural process of visual perception—from light, through eye, to mind—and should be checked by continuous observation.[1]

The ability to make effective rendered drawings is best developed, and finally attained, by noting light effects in nature, analyzing them to see which reveal form most clearly, and practicing how to obtain similar results on paper with pencil, pen, and brush (or other media). Each draftsman must have his own reasons for each value that he establishes. In making a drawing he must go beyond any rules and make decisions for expressive purposes that involve more subtle relationships than can be covered by formulas. When asked with what materials he mixed his paints, Whistler is said to have replied, "With brains, Sir."

Under particular conditions, normal values may have to be especially varied. They cannot always be determined as simply as saying "two and two make four." Contrast, juxtaposition, and composition are more important than ordinary visual relationships and transcend any attempt to work by rule alone. In general, however, the following suggestions are valid, and should give an excellent start toward the solution of any problem in rendering. Illustration 11-9 should be carefully studied to see wherein it justifies these rules.

1. The deepest darks and brightest lights are in the foreground. Distance finally reduces all values to a natural gray. Colors are brightest when nearest (even though they are indicated by values only).

2. Shadows are darker than shades; shades than *light*.

3. Solid objects contrast with space—*i.e.*, a light building requires a dark sky (and vice versa).

4. Buildings should grade in value from dark at top to light at bottom (or vice versa); sky the reverse.

5. Voids (windows, etc.) are darker than shadows on surfaces. Shadows on glass are often visible and even darker.

6. Light washes out texture; shadow intensifies it.

7. The shade line (on rounded forms) is blurred. The shade area is darkest near the shade line and lightest near the profile, due to reflected light.

8. Shadows have sharp edges and are darkest at their edges, due to reflected light from the projecting faces which cause them, and to visual contrast with adjoining *light* surfaces. Vertical shadows are darkest at the top due to reflected light from the ground.

9. Back shadows from reflected light often occur within direct shadows, and help give luminosity.

10. All values of objects in *light* are reversed when they are put in shadow.

---

[1] It is reported that in some cases the magnificent renderings published by d'Espouy (*op. cit.*) were not only tested by constant study of the originals *in situ*, but even checked against replicas (or original fragments) under *R*° light. Their authors (holders of the *Prix de Rome*) set up classic capitals, etc., in the garden of their residence (the Villa Medici) and waited until the bright Roman sun made the proper angle. Lights and darks could then be seen as they would appear on the drawings to be made, and actual values could be observed. If more convenient, the exact shadows could be marked on the subject and drawn by measurement rather than worked out on paper by graphic analysis.

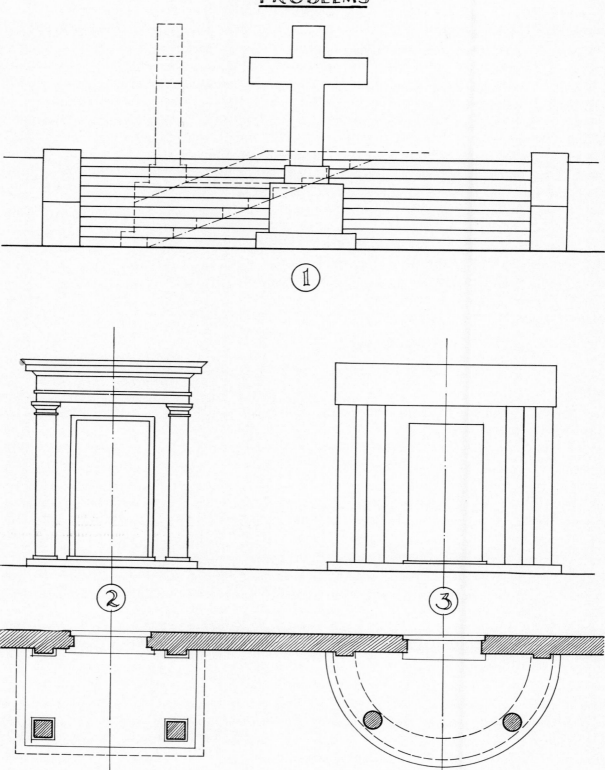

ILLUSTRATION 11-10

QUESTIONS

1. Compare line and rendered drawings, as expressions of exact form.
2. Differentiate between *light*, shade, and shadow by reference to photographs in current magazines.
3. List the steps in casting shadows, and illustrate each.
4. Explain the slicing method in your own words and drawings.
5. Discuss the advantages and disadvantages of $R°$ rays, illustrating by published examples.
6. Explain the procedure in making a rendering.
7. Select in the library a rendering which you like, and point out how it relates to each of the rules of thumb for rendering.
8. Look up a special example which illustrates each of the rules.
9. Draw examples of your own to illustrate any three of the rules.
10. Analyze a published drawing according to our scale of values.

PROBLEMS

1, 2, 3. See Illus. 11-10. Cast shadows with light at $R°$.

4, 5. See Illus. 11-11. Cast shadows using angle of light selected by instructor.

6. See Illus. 11-12. Cast shadows with light at angle to indicate nine o'clock on a summer morning, and then redo for three o'clock on a winter afternoon.

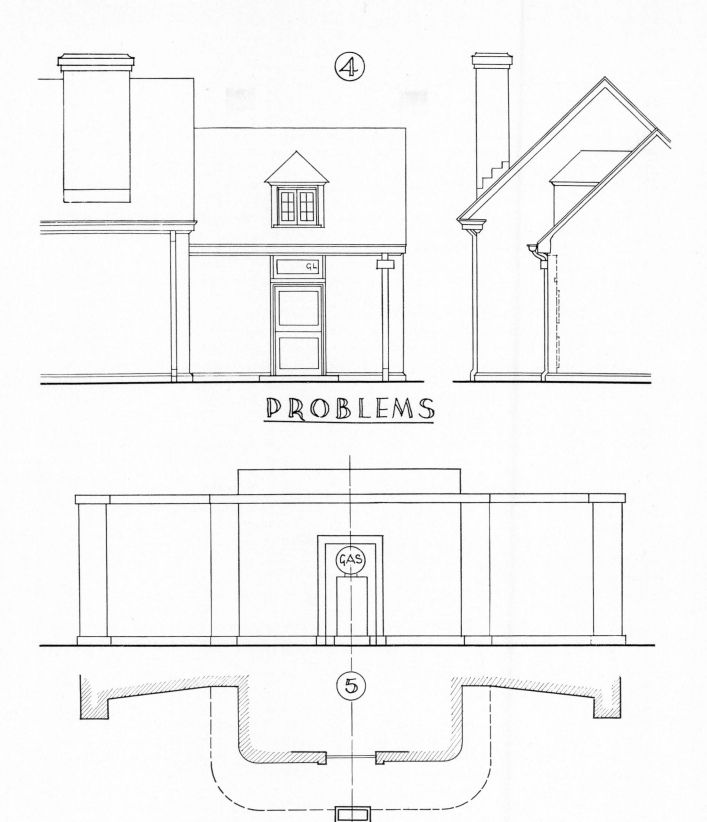

④

PROBLEMS

⑤

ILLUSTRATION 11-11

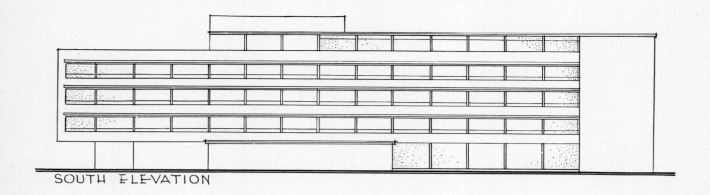

SOUTH ELEVATION

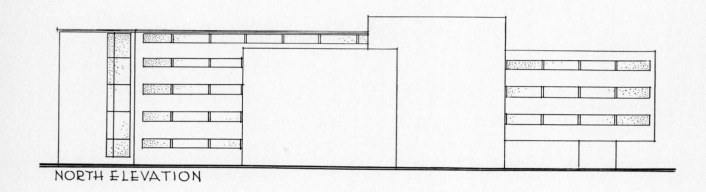

NORTH ELEVATION

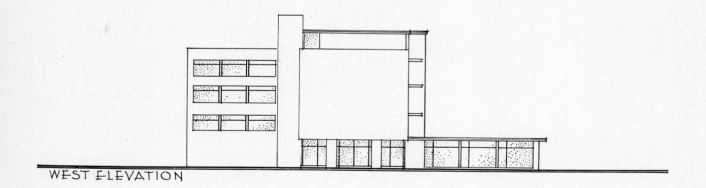

WEST ELEVATION

PROBLEM

ILLUSTRATION 11-12

199

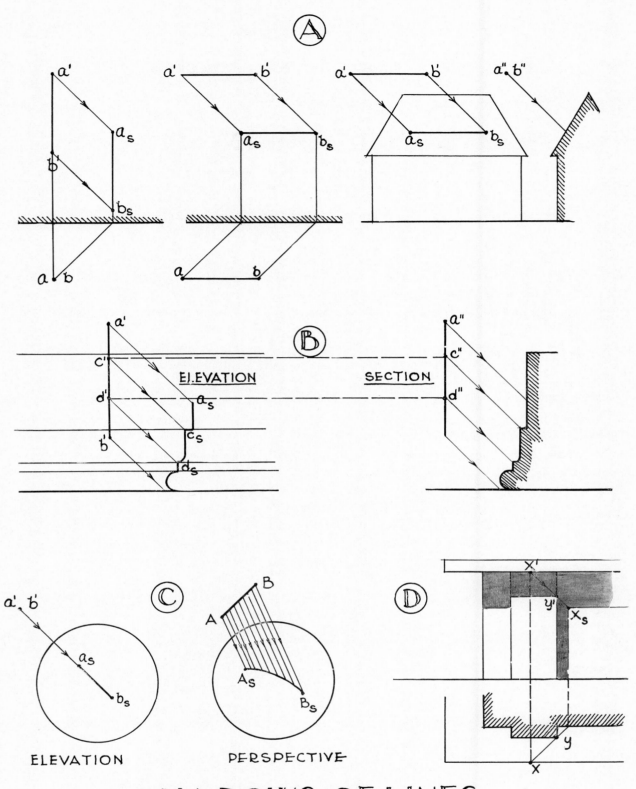

SHADOWS·OF·LINES

Chapter 12

SPECIAL PROBLEMS IN SHADOWS
(ASSUMING R° LIGHT)

1. LINES IN ORTHOGRAPHIC PROJECTION

Much time can be saved in casting shadows by knowing in advance the kind of shadow that certain common lines will cast. In such cases, after the shadow of one end a' of the line casting has been found by the slicing method, the shadow can be drawn through a_s in the proper direction and terminated by a ray through the other end of the line. The following conditions arise so frequently in architectural drawing that they are worth memorizing:

1. **The shadow of a line on a plane parallel to the line is also parallel to the line.** If the line A-B which casts the shadow A_s-B_s is parallel to plane Q which receives the shadow, and the slicing method is used for the shadows of points A and B individually, the shadow of A-B will be the line joining A_s and B_s. But the geometry of this construction makes A_s-B_s parallel to A-B. Thus the shadow of a vertical on a wall is a vertical, and the shadow of a horizontal on a parallel wall or roof is a horizontal (Illus. 12-1-A).

2. **The shadow of a vertical line on a series of planes has the same shape as the profile of the series.** When the slicing method is applied, using the side elevation as a reference drawing, the geometrical necessity for this rule becomes apparent (Illus. 12-1-B).

3. **The shadow of a line perpendicular to the plane of projection is a straight line no matter what surface it falls upon.** In this case we are looking edgewise at the plane of rays that determines the shadow. Consequently we will see the shadow as a single continuous line even though it may actually cut a very broken outline from an elaborate surface. The perspective view at the right of Illus. 12-1-C shows the plane of rays through A-B, cutting a curved shadow A_s-B_s from the surface of a sphere. In the elevation at the left we are looking edgewise at this plane, and therefore any line which lies in it will be seen as part of the straight line which represents the entire plane in this projection.

When $R°$ light is used, this shadow will be a 45° line; downwards to the right in an elevation, upwards to the right in a plan.

4. **By running back from the intersection of two shadows (point Xs) we can find where the shadow of the upper shade line crosses the lower shade line itself** (Illus. 12-1-D). This is one of the most helpful and timesaving procedures at the disposal of the draftsman. In many cases, the shadows of two shade lines are known (or can easily be found) on a wall (or other surface). The point Xs where the shadows cross may be considered to be on a ray through two points X' and Y', one on each shade line. Since a single ray will connect X', Y', and X_s, Y' is itself the shadow of X' on the surface of which Y' is a part. Points to the left of X' will cast their shadows on the projecting surface—those to the right will continue until they strike the wall; as will those through points below Y' on the vertical shade line.

A 45° line through y in plan will locate both x and the slice for X_s. When the former is projected up to X', the ray through it will determine both Y' and X_s. Only two 45° lines and two verticals are needed to find all the shadows.

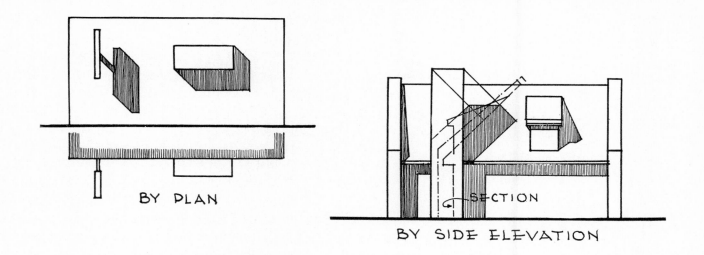

BY PLAN

BY SIDE ELEVATION

SHADOWS OF PLANE SOLIDS

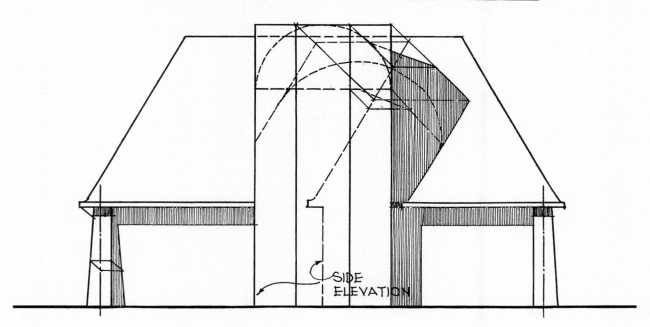

SIDE ELEVATION

ILLUSTRATION 12-2

2. PLANE SOLIDS

The shadows of solids whose surfaces are planes may easily be found, as soon as it has been determined which faces are in shade. The lines separating these latter from the *light* faces together make up the shade line of the object. Once this has been clearly marked, there remains only the work of casting its shadow. Very often some parts of the shade line will not show in the projection, yet their shadows will be visible. The student must accustom himself to "feeling" the shade line as a continuous (though broken) line, which decides the boundaries of the shadow area, and makes a sort of jointed loop around the object.

Since architectural masses are chiefly parallelepipeds bounded by verticals and horizontals (mutually perpendicular), the component parts of their shade lines consist largely of such lines. Consequently their shadows are mostly bounded by edges such as we have learned to find in Sec. 1 of this chapter. With a little practice they can be worked out very rapidly.

Shadows of more complicated forms can be approximated from those of the nearest cubical "envelope," within which they must remain. If the octagonal tower on the building of Illus. 12-2 were changed so as to terminate in a dome (dotted), its shadow on the roof could not exceed that found for the flat top, and a free curve within the boundaries thus established would be sufficiently accurate for a rough study or sketch. More careful drawings demand exact shadows. This problem is an excellent one for the student to work out accurately by himself, point by point, after he has learned how to find the shade line on a hemisphere. Note how the tower is used as its own side elevation in working out the shadows of the points on its upper edge.

SHADOWS OF CIRCLES ON WALLS

(A) LONG METHOD - BY PLAN OR SIDE ELEVATION

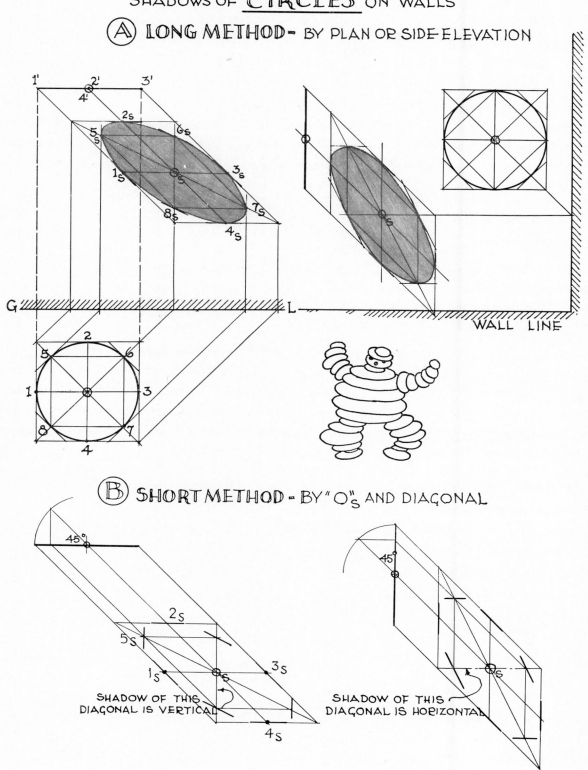

WALL LINE

(B) SHORT METHOD - BY "O's" AND DIAGONAL

SHADOW OF THIS DIAGONAL IS VERTICAL

SHADOW OF THIS DIAGONAL IS HORIZONTAL

ILLUSTRATION 12-3

3. CIRCLES

Next to cubical solids (which make up the vast majority of all architectural forms) the shapes most commonly found are those known as surfaces of revolution. The lathe, the potter's wheel, and other technological means of fabricating the materials of construction, have made it possible to produce easily objects which are revolved around an axis. Hence the cone, the cylinder, and the sphere are found in many architectural monuments, and more complex surfaces, generated in the same manner, are extensively used, especially for ornamental features.

Whether the axis of these surfaces is vertical or horizontal, the section at right angles to it must of course be a circle. If, therefore, we have a quick and easy method of finding the shadows of circles, our problems with surfaces of revolution will be much simplified. We can even consider them to be piles of circles (like the Michelin tire man), and find their shadows as the area bounded by a line containing the shadows of all the circles of which they are made up.

Illustration 12-3-A shows how the shadow of a circle, in either vertical or horizontal position, can be found from that of its circumscribed octagon. Note that the axes of the two ellipses of shadow are not at the same angle. In drawing the ellipses of shadow, pay particular attention to the tangents which govern their curvature. If the latter are well marked, the curves will almost "draw themselves."

It is essential that the student learn to find the shadows of circles as rapidly and surely as he can multiply or divide small numbers. Just as further advance in mathematics is impossible, without mastering such fundamentals, so the shadows of surfaces of revolution cannot be worked out easily unless one is sure of the shadows of circles.

The short method is merely a geometrical simplification of the long method. Begin by locating O_s from plan, or by knowing its distance from the wall. (The shadow of any point is as far to the right and as far down, as the point is from the wall.) Then draw the diagonal of the circumscribed square. It will be **vertical** if the circle is **horizontal,** and **horizontal** if the circle is **vertical.** Complete the shadow of the square and draw the medians through O_s in order to find points 1_s, 2_s, 3_s, and 4_s.

The remaining four points are on the diagonals, at the corners of the inscribed square. These corner points will be useful in other ways and we should learn to find them quickly, or estimate them closely. They lie almost exactly seven-tenths of the distance from the center to the edge of the circle, in elevation.

In order to locate them, turn part of the circle on its elevation, draw the 45° line which represents the diagonal, project down (or across for the vertical circle), and draw the ray to the shadow (5_s) on the diagonal.

CONES

(A) LONG METHOD FOR SHADE & SHADOW

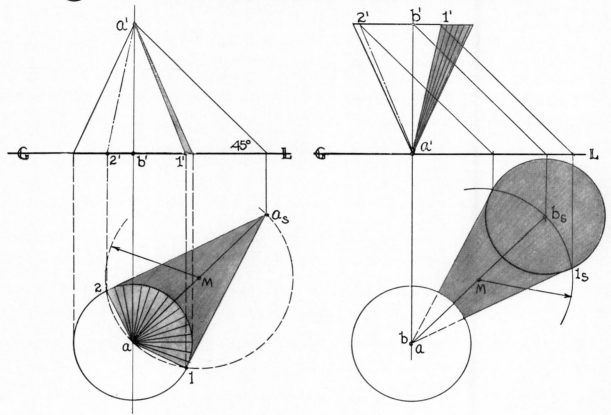

(B) SHORT METHOD FOR SHADE ONLY.

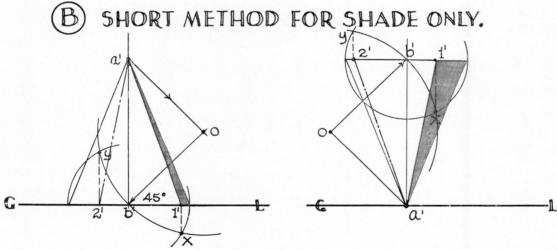

ILLUSTRATION 12-4

4. CONES

Like the circle, the cone is basically important for other surfaces of revolution, as well as for itself. It also must be thoroughly mastered before more complicated forms can be attempted. **Learn,** do not be content with merely **understanding,** how to find its shade and shadow and where the shade area is found on the critical cones. You will have to solve dozens of cones in order to find the shade line on a complex $S.$ of $R.$ (surfaces of revolution will be thus abbreviated hereafter), so you must be able to handle cones rapidly and surely.

The shade on a cone is most easily determined from its shadow. Imagine it to be seated on a level area like a table top. We can then find A_s, the shadow of its apex, by the slicing method. Tangents from A_s to the circle of the base must then bound the shadow, and also fix the points from which the limiting lines of the shade area may be drawn to the apex a. The exact points of tangency are found by the standard geometrical procedure for drawing tangents to a circle from a point outside it. With the midpoint M of a-a_s as a center, a circle is turned, cutting the base at the points required.

The short method for cones is merely a graphical trick, which avoids the necessity of drawing a plan for each cone. If the two figures used in the long method are superimposed, the points of tangency can be found very much more simply.

In Illus. 12-4-B, draw down at 45° from the apex, and up at 45° from the center of the base, intersecting at O. With O as a center turn arc Ob' to intersect the semicircle of the base at X. Project up to $1'$, and draw to a' for the shade line on the front of the cone. Lay off x-$1'$ from b' to find $2'$, or continue the arcs to their second intersection at y, and project. Draw $2'$-a', which is the other boundary of the shade (on the back of the cone).

Note that an inverted cone has exactly an opposite analysis. The arcs locate the shade line first on the left rear, and then on the right front. Whatever is true of an upright cone is true in the reverse sense of the inverted cone of the same angle. Thus the right rear quarter of the 45° upright cone is in shade, and the front left quarter of the inverted 45° cone is in light.

TABLE OF CRITICAL CONES.

ANGLE of CONE	POSITION of SHADE	AMOUNT of SHADE	DETERMINES on S of R
8° UPRIGHT	RIGHT REAR CORNER	ONE LINE ONLY	HIGH-POINT OF SHADE
45° UPRIGHT	RIGHT PROFILE TO REAR AXIS	RIGHT REAR QUARTER OF CONE	POINTS ON RIGHT PROFILE & REAR AXIS
90°(CYLINDER)	RIGHT FRONT CORNER TO LEFT REAR CORNER	ONE-HALF OF CONE	SHADE WHERE PROFILE CHANGES CURVATURE
45° INVERTED	LEFT PROFILE TO FRONT AXIS	THREE-QUARTERS OF CONE	POINTS ON LEFT PROFILE & FRONT AXIS
8°INVERTED	LEFT FRONT CORNER	ALL BUT ONE LINE	LOW-POINT OF SHADE

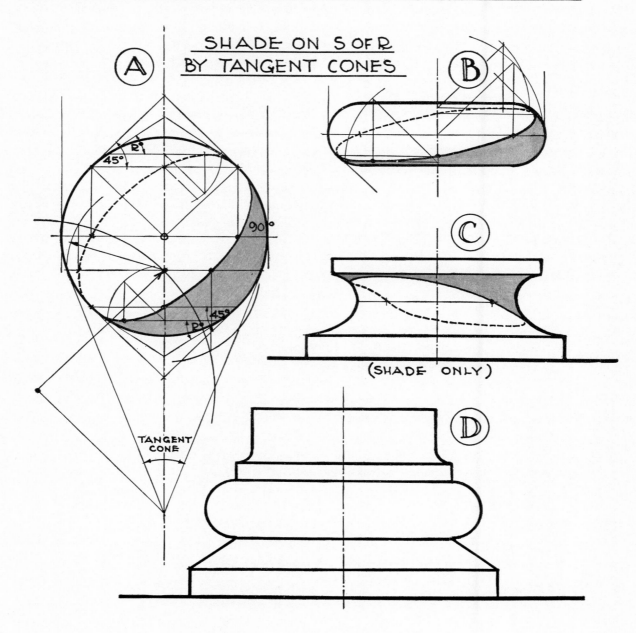

SHADE ON S of R BY TANGENT CONES

(A)

90°

TANGENT CONE

(B)

(C)

(SHADE ONLY)

(D)

ILLUSTRATION 12-5

5. SHADE ON SURFACES OF REVOLUTION

The ability to find the shade quickly on any cone is the key to finding the shade line on any other surface of revolution. If the latter has a vertical axis, any horizontal section through it will be a circle, and hence the tangents to its curved profile **at that level** may be prolonged to define a cone having the same axis, and the circle as its base.

In other words the surface of revolution, and the tangent cone, will be identical along the circle which is the cone's base. Hence the shade on both objects will be the same, **for that level only,** and its limits on the cone will determine two points on the shade line of the *S. of R.* A sufficient number of tangent cones will locate enough points on the shade line of the *S. of R.*, to enable us to draw a freehand curve through them, and thus establish the required shade line.

This method of using tangent cones has the advantage that the most important points found by it require very little graphical construction. Even the short method for cones need only be applied occasionally, because when it is used for certain cones of "critical" angle, the process can be simplified even further. The table of critical cones in Illus. 12-5 shows that the most important angles of slope work out to give us points either on profile, axis, or corner (the point corresponding to the corner of the square inscribed in the circle of the cone's base).

A 45° tangent, found directly by a drafting triangle, will tell us where the shade line on any *S. of R.* meets its right-hand profile, because this is the level of tangency of an upright 45° cone. Projecting horizontally from this point to the axis will tell us where the shade line lies on the surface **behind** the axis at that level, because our horizontal represents the base of that same 45° cone, which has one-quarter in shade, from right profile to rear axis (rear axis meaning of course the point on its base which in elevation projects directly behind the axis).

Many draftsmen find it worth while to cut an $R°$ triangle out of celluloid, in order to find the level of tangency of an $R°$ cone by simply placing their $R°$ triangle against their T square, and judging by eye where it fits the profile of the *S. of R.* Of course, the tangency of the 90° cone (or cylinder) can be determined similarly by using the vertical side of a normal 45° triangle. Do not forget that after finding the points of tangency for both 90° and $R°$ cones, a horizontal must be drawn through it to represent the base of the cone, which is the **circle** of tangency of cone and *S. of R.* Then the corner of this circle will give the point (or points) on the shade line.

The sphere is the perfect *S. of R.*, in that its profile has every conceivable change of curvature. The determination of its shade line, shown in Illus. 12-5-A, should be carefully studied and redrawn several times until the use of tangent cones is perfectly familiar. With practice the method becomes almost automatic in thought and very rapid in execution.

Many *S. of R.* require the use of additional cones in order to locate enough points through which to draw the shade line confidently. Any number needed can be introduced by finding carefully the tangents to the profile at any desired level. The cones thus established can be solved on tracing paper (using the short method), so as to avoid confusion on the drawing. The student should verify by his own tangent cones the construction of the shade lines drawn on the torus and scotia (Illus. 12-5-B and C), and should then work out for himself the shade on *D*.

Note that the shade line of the scotia will be partially included within the **shadow** of the overhanging upper fillet. In this case and wherever overhangs occur the shade line will not **actually** divide *light* from shade, but rather shade from shadow. However, it is valuable to know the theoretical position of such shade lines. They tell us what shadows to cast, and help us to render.

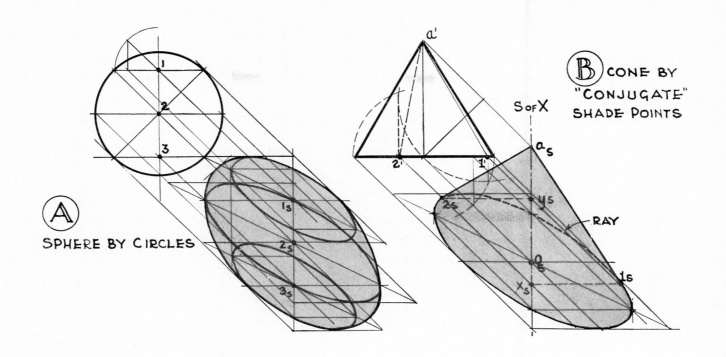

A — SPHERE BY CIRCLES

B — CONE BY "CONJUGATE" SHADE POINTS

SHADOWS of SURFACES of REVOLUTION on VERTICAL WALLS

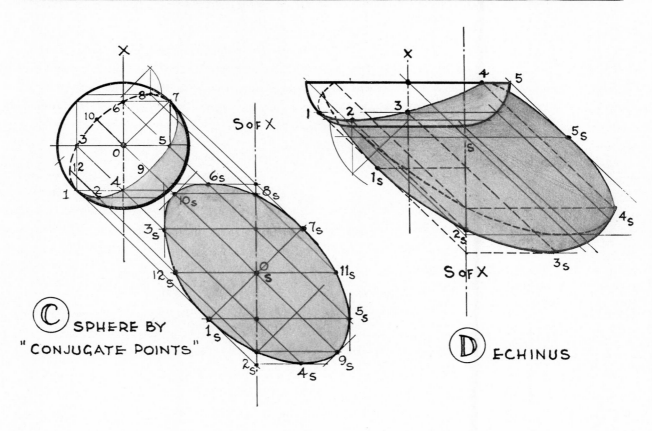

C — SPHERE BY "CONJUGATE POINTS"

D — ECHINUS

ILLUSTRATION 12-6

6. *SHADOWS OF SURFACES OF REVOLUTION*

Having learned how to use tangent cones in order to determine the shade line on an *S. of R.*, we are ready to cast its shadow. The procedure is always the same: (1) decide on the direction of the *light* rays (here $R°$); (2) find the shade line (by tangent cones); (3) cast the shadows.

It has already been pointed out that this last step can be done on a wall or other vertical surface by casting the shadows of the horizontal circles (considered as the bases of tangent cones) on which our shade points lie. These shadows will be ellipses to which we can draw rays through the shade points, and thus locate shadow points through which to draw a freehand curve as our shadow boundary (Illus. 12-6-A). While often a little tedious, this method will always give the answer.

A quicker and simpler procedure is available as a further development of our use of tangent cones. Illustration 12-6-B shows how the shadow of the shade points of any cone may be found on a wall. It can be proven by geometry that they are *conjugate points* with regard to the *shadow of the axis* (hereafter called *S. of X.*). If the shade on a cone is known, the shadows of shade points can be determined reciprocally in pairs which lie at the same level.

The shadow of point 1 will always lie on the ray through it, at a point horizontally opposite that in which the ray through 2 intersects *S. of X.* Conversely, 2_s will be horizontally to the left of the point where the ray through 1 strikes *S. of X.* (Shade points 1 and 2 are located first by the short method, and the shadow of the rest of the base by the usual method for circles.)

Since the shade points which we ordinarily establish on any *S. of R.* all come from tangent cones, the conjugate point theory makes it very simple to determine their shadows. We simply first find *S. of X.* and then locate enough points from it and the rays through the shade points to be able to draw the curve of shadow through them.

Several geometric proofs of the conjugate point method have been developed. Before studying the one given below, the student should test the correctness of the results obtained by casting the shadows of all the critical cones on a wall, using their plans and our basic slicing method. Observation of the resulting figures merely as geometrical diagrams will show clearly that the conjugate relation holds in all cases. The general proof follows.

Using Illus. 12-6-B as the elevation of **any** cone, draw its plan and project points 1' and 2' onto the base at 1 and 2. Draw horizontals through them to intersect the ray through the center a at y and x respectively.

Find the shadows of X-2 and Y-1 by slicing. Points x_s and y_s must lie on *S. of X.*, and their shadows on a wall must be horizontals to the right of x_s and the left of y_s, so that x_s-1_s will equal y-1, and y_s-2_s will equal x-2.

But y_s-2_s must also equal 1'-2' (parallels between parallels) and therefore y' must coincide with 2', and similarly x' with 1'. Thus 1' and 2' are coincident with the elevations of x and y and hence may be used conjugately (Q.E.D.).

Illustration 12-6-C shows the application of the conjugate point theory to casting the shadow of a sphere on a wall. The eight points determined by our critical cones are usually sufficient to control the shadow curve, especially if one draws the tangents through them to help guide his freehand line. Note that in the special case of a sphere the rays through the shade points of the $R°$ cones (points 2 and 8) also determine points 9_s and 10_s (the major diameter of the ellipse of shadow) by a conjugate relation to *S. of X.*, and points 11_s and 12_s by relation to O_s.

In Illus. 12-6-D the position of *S. of X.* shows that this echinus is partially imbedded in the wall. At 4_s the shadow has a distinct "bump" where the outline changes from that of the shade line on the rounded surface to that of the horizontal upper edge (a circle).

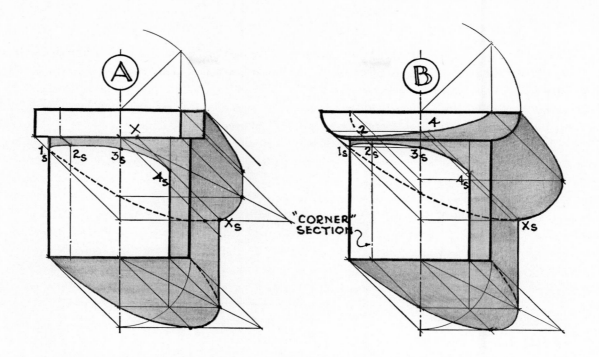

SHADOWS ON SURFACES OF REVOLUTION
BY THE AXIAL WALL METHOD

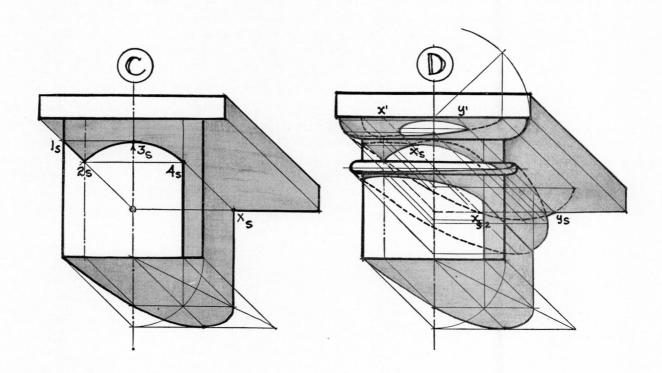

ILLUSTRATION 12-7

7. SHADOWS ON SURFACES OF REVOLUTION

The shadow of any *S. of R.* on a wall is not only often useful in itself, but also helps in finding the shadow of projecting portions of such objects on their own lower surfaces. The subtle visual quality gained by the play of light, shade, and shadow on an *S. of R.*, lies behind the appeal of many traditional architectural motifs, such as capitals, bases, balusters, finials, etc. Even the austere volumes favored in contemporary design often include simple cylinders, cones, etc., made dramatic by the clean geometric forms of their shadows.

If the object alone is being rendered (against a neutral background) a vertical plane can be assumed through the axis of the *S. of R.*, whose profile thus becomes also its line of intersection with this imaginary wall, while *S. of X.*, coincides with the axis. Then the wall can be erased, if not needed, after helping to establish the shadow **on** the object.

Whether we assume such an "axial wall," or use an actual one, we begin by casting shadows on it completely, before working on the *S. of R.* itself (Illus. 12-7-A). It is obvious that the shadow **on** the object will begin on its left profile wherever the wall shadow crosses its outline. This point 1_s will also give us an axis point 3_s horizontally to the right, because of the axial symmetry of both the object and $R°$ light. The profile is simply a 90° view of the "front axis" (and vice versa), hence there must be a point exactly symmetrical to that causing the profile shadow, whose shadow will strike the *S. of R.* on the line marking its nearest surface, *i.e.*, in front of the axis and coinciding with it in an elevation drawing.

Now go to the wall shadow and use our theory of intersecting shadows. By running back at 45° from point X_s, we will find the point where the shadow of the upper shade line crosses the lower shade line itself (Chap. 12, Sec. 1). In this case we thus find 4_s, where the shadow of the lower edge of the upper cylinder "runs off" the lower cylinder's surface.

A fourth important point is that cast by the lowest point of the shade line (2_s on Illus. 12-7-B). Because this point is located from the shade on an inverted $R°$ cone, it is on the corner of its circle, and hence its shadow must fall on the corner of some other one of the many circles of which the object is composed. Since we can find the corners of circles easily, without even drawing a plan, we can construct a corner section through the lower surfaces, and run down the ray from our inverted $R°$ cone's shade point until we find its shadow on the corner section. In the case under discussion, this construction is very simple. It involves only finding the corner of one circle and then drawing a vertical, but the procedure is never difficult, even for complex objects.

Now that its four most important points are established, we can draw our shadow as a smooth curve through them. Start with a "quirk" at the left profile; do not come away from it almost perpendicularly. A full quarter of the visible surface of the object is foreshortened in elevation into the narrow strip between the profile and the corner section. A "hook" at the start gives the visual impression of the existence of this area.

In the block capital (Illus. 12-7-D) note how the principle of intersecting shadows may be used, not only on the wall (X_{s2}) but on the surface of the shaft at X_s in order to "jump" the shadow of the abacus from the cylinder back on to the echinus.

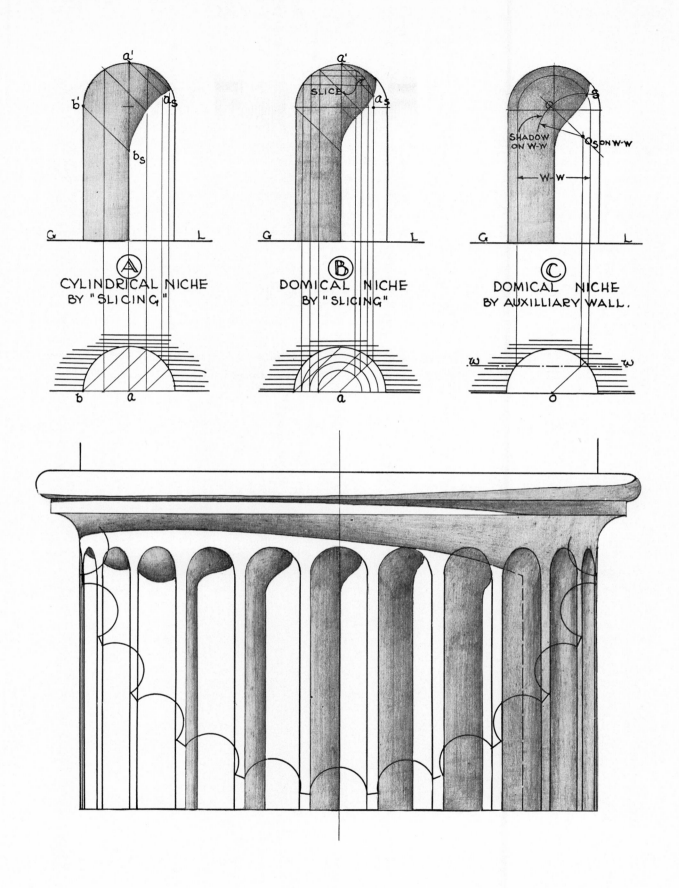

CYLINDRICAL NICHE
BY "SLICING"

DOMICAL NICHE
BY "SLICING"

DOMICAL NICHE
BY AUXILLIARY WALL.

ILLUSTRATION 12-8

8. HOLLOWS

Reentrant forms are less usual in architecture than salient ones, but the hollow vertical semicylinder, whether as an entrance motif, as a niche, or as the fluting on columns, is used so widely that its shade and shadows warrant attention. If it has a cylindrical top (as in Illus. 12-8-A) the slicing method is simple to apply, but if it ends in a half dome (as at B) the process is tedious, though sure.

Illustration 12-8-C explains a quick and easy way of locating points on the shadow in the domical upper portion. No slice curves have to be worked out as was necessary in Illus. 12-8-B. Instead, a compass is all that is needed. The solution involves the assumption of vertical planes (walls). These will cut the niche head in a series of semi-circles. The shadow on any one of these walls is also a semicircle and can be found from the shadow of its center, because the edge of the niche which casts it is parallel to the wall. The intersection of these two circular arcs gives a point (s) on the shadow in the dome.

Only one wall and the resulting point are shown on our figure, in order to make clear the construction. As many more may be used as are necessary to establish the curve of shadow by finding enough points on it.

Fluted columns, drawn at large scale, present us with a series of niches, each increasingly turned in plan, from the front elevation appearing on the axis of the shaft to the side view on the profile. Each has to be worked out separately by slicing if accurate results are required. However, the shadow of the astragal usually cuts across most of the flutes and makes unnecessary the working out of each head. The shade line of the astragal on the surface of the column, drawn as if no flutes existed, can be cast into the hollow cylinders by the slicing method.

ORIENTATION BY "ALL-DAY" SHADOWS

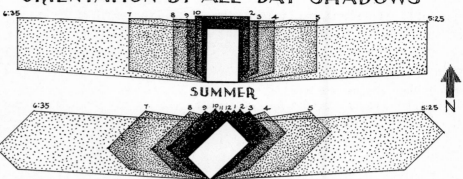

SUMMER

HOUR	SUN BEARING	SUN ANGLE
NOON	180°	57°-30'
1-11	152°	54°-25'
2-10	132°	46°-30'
3-9	117°-30'	36°-15'
4-8	106°-15'	24°-30'
5-7	98°-15'	12°-15'
5:25-6:35	93°-25'	5°-10'
R6:04	90°	0
S6:12	90°	0

WINTER

SPRING - FALL
TABLE OF SUN ANGLES
FOR LATITUDE OF BUILD-
ING SITE.

SPRING·FALL

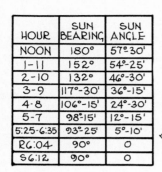

SPRING·FALL SHADOWS OF SHED·ROOF BUILDING

SHADOWS AND URBAN CONGESTION.

ILLUSTRATION 12-9

9. ALL–DAY SHADOWS

In all our previous discussions we have decided on a fixed angle for the light rays, as the first step in determining *light*, shade, and shadow on any object which we are to render. The result of this procedure is a "snapshot". We represent the object as it will look under fixed, but momentary, conditions. Even though our standard $R°$ angle of light gives us a fairly average illumination, such a drawing at best can produce only a fleeting impression of reality. The sun's relation to any site changes steadily as time advances from dawn to dark. If our object does look at any one particular instant exactly as we have depicted it, it will as surely have quite different areas of light and dark after a few hours (or even minutes) have passed.

How can this apparently inherent difficulty be resolved? Only by taking time into consideration in making our drawing, and by representing simultaneously conditions which actually follow one another in a time sequence. Such a representation will not and cannot be a picture in the ordinary sense of the word. Since it will superimpose on one another light and dark relationships which in nature are successive, no one of them can be completely and faithfully reproduced in our rendering without interfering with several others. Consequently we must limit such drawings to a diagrammatic type of simplified and conventionalized representation.

In this form, however, they can be extremely useful for study purposes in developing the basic qualities of a design, and in deciding such fundamental things as the general form of a building, and the relation it will bear to its site. Illustration 12-9 shows such a study, made to determine the orientation and shape most desirable for an airplane hangar. Its location on the earth being known, the angle of the sun's rays for differing times of day and season of year can easily be tabulated. Then the shadows on the ground can be worked out by the slicing method, and the results compared.

If the use and construction of the particular building justifies the decision to cover it by a shed roof, with the higher side at the south, the shadow area can be reduced, and the penetration of light into the interior increased, particularly at the season (winter) when light is most needed.

The study of all-day shadows may well be extended from individual buildings to the planning of communities and cities, both in peace and war. The necessity of protection from aerial bombardment during the Second World War led to a scientific investigation of camouflage (the art of concealing form) so as to make recognition of targets difficult for the bombardier. The lessons learned from this negative "design for confusion" have proved happily to be equally valuable in "design for better living."

The geometric shadow patterns cast by man-built architectural shapes contrast very noticeably with the soft blending of lights and darks in nature. Hence the elimination of sharp shadow outlines became a primary requirement in camouflage. The desired result could only be achieved by minimizing the spatial forms which cause large straight-edged shadows. The desire to avoid identifiable shadows led to keeping buildings low, widely spaced, flooded with sunlight, and interrelated to trees and other natural forms. The observance of these precautions meant the elimination of the conditions which cause congestion, darkness, disease, and even crime in cities. The imposition of unnecessarily geometric street patterns, without regard to the existing site, of gridirons and forced axes, was thus shown to be unsafe as well as unpleasant, because of the shadow patterns.

Shadow studies show the price that others have to pay for skyscrapers located without consideration for their effect on the light needed by their neighbors. The dark slums of most of our cities would never have been built if their owners had thought in terms of letting in sunlight by planning for minimum shadows.

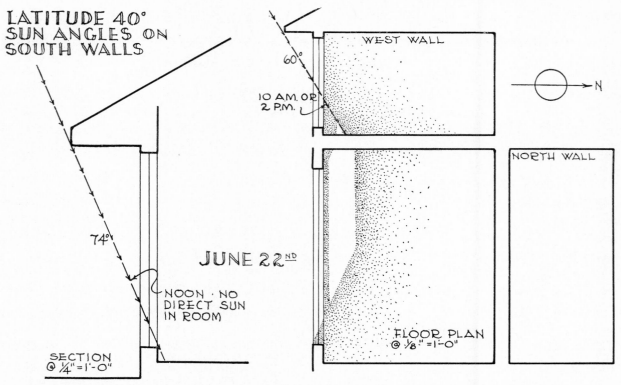

LATITUDE 40°
SUN ANGLES ON
SOUTH WALLS

60°

WEST WALL

10 A.M. OR
2 P.M.

NORTH WALL

N

74°

JUNE 22ND

NOON · NO
DIRECT SUN
IN ROOM

SECTION
@ 1/4" = 1'-0"

FLOOR PLAN
@ 1/8" = 1'-0"

PROFILES THAT CONTROL SHADOWS

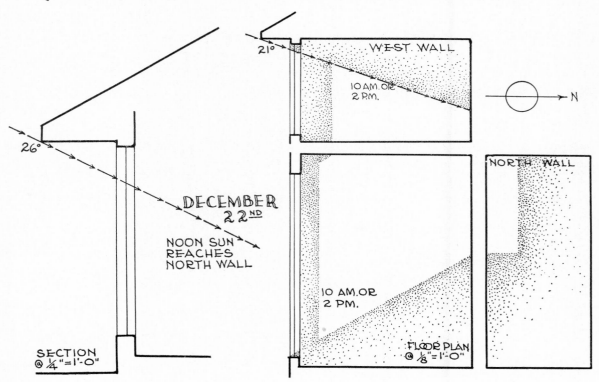

21°

WEST WALL

10 A.M. OR
2 P.M.

N

26°

DECEMBER
22ND

NOON SUN
REACHES
NORTH WALL

SECTION
@ 1/4" = 1'-0"

10 A.M. OR
2 P.M.

NORTH WALL

FLOOR PLAN
@ 1/8" = 1'-0"

ILLUSTRATION 12-10

10. PROFILES AND SHADOWS

Since the shadows caused by sunlight are one of the principal means of giving architecture its visible form, the average angles of light throughout the year should determine to a large degree the character of a building's profile, which is chiefly responsible for the play of light and dark. It has long been observed that the most successful architectural styles show a sensitive response to the normal light of the latitudes where they originated and developed. Classic buildings reflect in their moldings and ornamental detail, as well as in their general outlines, the clarity and brilliance of the Mediterranean climate, while the softer, grayer light of northern Europe leads naturally to the deeper and more broken profiles of the Gothic. Greek forms are apt to look thin and wiry when reproduced in an unsuitable environment, while mediaeval styles seem spotty and restless when used under a southern sun.

This instinctive feeling for the expression of light was not merely an aesthetic reaction. It accorded also with the need for interior illumination. Big windows to catch all of the scanty sunshine are as characteristic of northern architecture as are small openings in the south where solid walls keep out glare. Wide overhangs which protect from the heat of a sun almost overhead become desirable as one enters tropical climates, but are unnecessary (even depressing) in the North Temperate Zone.

The profile of a contemporary building may be studied by determining precise sun-angles and resulting shadows, as carefully and as sensitively as were those outlines which we now think of as being characteristic of the great historic styles of architecture. Thus the casting of accurate shadows may become an important element in design rather than merely a device for rendering a drawing.

The frontispiece of this book illustrates a building designed in this way and accurately rendered to show its appearance both in summer and in winter. The architect, Mr. Joseph D. Murphy of St. Louis, studied carefully how to obtain the maximum winter sun in the patients' rooms, and yet keep out summer heat and glare. The profile of Faith Hospital was the result of this analysis. The perspectives of the building have shadows carefully cast according to calculated sun-angles for January and July.

The proportions of rooms, and the amount and position of the fenestration required to illumine them adequately may likewise be worked out exactly by *casting* the light which will come in through the windows at different critical periods during the year. Projecting members above the windows can be precisely determined so as to keep out the hot sun in summer, and yet let in its cheerful rays in winter. The graphical problem involved is a simple application of our slicing method, as is shown in Illus. 12-10.[1]

PROBLEMS

1. Work out by the short method the shades on the critical cones.
2. Select a Greek vase in the library and find the shade on it, using $R°$ light.
3. Stand your vase on a rectangular plinth in front of a wall, and cast $R°$ shadows.
4. In Illus. 12-7-C the shadow from 2_s to 4_s is the arc of a circle whose center is at point O. Why?
5. Account for the shadows of all points of the shade lines of abacus and echinus in Illus. 12-7-C and D.
6. Hold a model of a Doric capital with light at $R°$, and check shadows against McGoodwin's drawing in his "Architectural Shades and Shadows."
7. Check shade and shadow of an Ionic capital in d'Espouy.
8. Render fully the shadows on the figures of Illus. 12-7.
9. Check the summer and winter shadows cast by the eaves of a building which you have designed.
10. Work out the profile for the south side of a one-story living room in your home town, so as to obtain optimum sun-lighting.

[1] The "Solarmeter," a double-disk protractor designed and sold by R. W. Justice of Belvedere, Calif., is a simple device by which the angle of the sun's rays may be determined quickly for any latitude, any date, and any hour, with any orientation of the building's walls and openings.

Above — Reception lobby and courtyard.

DESIGN FOR ST. BARNABAS HOUSE,
NEW YORK CITY; KETCHUM, GINA,
& SHARP, ARCHITECTS. DRAWN BY
VINCENT FURNO.

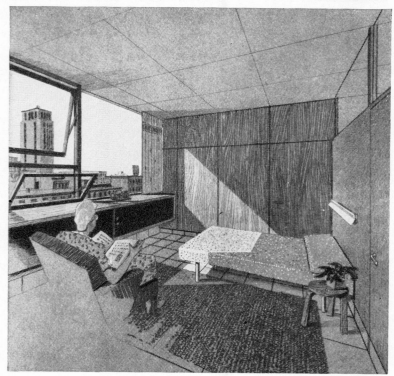

Right — Typical bedroom.

ILLUSTRATION 13-1

Chapter 13

SYMBOLS AND DEFINITIONS

A—Any point in space.

A'—perspective image of A, *i.e.*, its projection on PP by a ray from S.

a—orthographic plan of A.

a'—orthographic front elevation of A.

a''—orthographic side elevation of A.

a_1—intersection of HH and vertical plane containing visual ray from S to A.

Bird's-eye view—A perspective made from an S higher than the object, but with *C.V.R.* horizontal.

C—The center of the picture, *i.e.*, point in which *C.V.R.* pierces PP, and hence the point in which HH intersects the vertical axis.

Cone of correct vision—A cone of which *C.V.R.* is the axis whose trace on PP corresponds to the most sensitive portion of the retina of the eye—rarely exceeds 45° at apex for architectural subjects, better limited to 30°.

C.V.R.—The central visual ray, *i.e.*, the axis of the cone of correct vision. PP must be perpendicular to *C.V.R.*, because the human eye is formed with that relation of retina to pupil.

Diminution—The apparent reduction in the size of an object as its distance from the spectator increases; caused by the decrease in the angle subtended at the eye.

Elevation—The orthographic projection of an object on a vertical plane by lines perpendicular to that plane. Called *front* if plane is parallel to main façade of building and *side* if perpendicular to it.

Foreshortening—Decrease in apparent length of a line or plane because of its angular position in relation to S. When pointed directly at the spectator a line seems to be merely a point.

G. L.—The ground line—line of intersection of PP (or vertical plane of projection) with horizontal plane at level assumed for surface of earth.

HH—The horizon—the line in which a horizontal plane through S meets PP.

H.L.M.—A horizontal line of measure, *i.e.*, any horizontal line lying in PP, and therefore one on which measurements may be laid off at their true (scaled) length.

Horizontal—In space, means perpendicular to the force of gravity; on a drawing means parallel to the line joining the hands of a person holding the picture in front of him by its sides.

Light—The flux of radiant illumination which enables the eye to perceive external objects. In a drawing the parts of the object which receive direct illumination.

M—A measuring point—the vanishing point of a series of parallel lines so drawn as to cut off equal distances on another series of parallels and on *H.L.M.*

M^{Ray}—The M of the rays of the sun (considered to be parallel).

Object—Anything external to the eye, which is made the subject of a drawing.

Office method—A means of making linear perspectives in which any point is found as the intersection of the trace on PP of its visual ray, and the perspective of a horizontal line (actual or assumed) through the point.

One-point perspective—A perspective in which the principal planes of the object are either parallel to, or perpendicular to, PP.

Parallel perspective—Same as one-point perspective.

Study for Cheney House, Princeton, N.J.; Henry A. Jandl, architect; drawn by William F. Shellman, Jr.

ILLUSTRATION 13-2

Perspective—The representation of any object on a plane surface by a process similar to that by which the human eye would perceive it. Technically, the representation of any point (line, plane, etc.) in space by its projection on *PP* by a visual ray from *S*.

Perspective plan—The plan of any object as seen in perspective.

Picture plane—The plane on which a perspective is projected. Normally vertical, it **must** be perpendicular to *C.V.R.*

Plan—The orthographic projection of an object on a horizontal plane, by lines perpendicular to the plane.

Ray—A straight line radiating from a point. Visual rays diverge from the eye of the spectator; light rays from the source of light (those from the sun are considered to be parallel).

R°—The angle between the diagonal of a cube and its base (35°-16' plus or minus).

S—The point of station, *i.e.*, the position of the eye of the spectator whose visual image of an object is duplicated in a perspective.

S. of R.—A surface of revolution—the surface of a volume formed by revolving a line around an axis—*e.g.*, cones, cylinders, spheres, etc.

S. of X.—Shadow of the axis.

Shade—The parts of the surface of an object which are so situated that the light rays from any given source cannot strike them directly.

Shade line—The line that divides those portions of an object which are in *light*, from those which are in shade.

Shadow—The parts (surface areas) of an object from which light is excluded by the interposition of another object between the source of light and the portions originally illumined.

Slicing method—A graphic process for determining shadows. A plane containing the light ray is passed through any point *A*, and the slice which is cut by this plane out of the receiving surface *Q* is found. The shadow lies (by definition) where the ray through *A* hits the slice through *Q*.

Trace—The line in which one plane intersects another—particularly the line cut out of *PP* by a plane containing the visual ray through any point.

Three-point perspective—A perspective in which the *C.V.R.* is not horizontal; hence *PP* is inclined, and vertical lines vanish as well as horizontals, making a third vanishing point necessary in depicting normal architectural forms (parallelepipeds).

V—Any vanishing point, or point of convergence in perspective, of any series of parallel lines.

V^A—the *V* of **any** series of lines.

V^L—the *V* of horizontal lines going to the left when prolonged beyond *PP*.

V^R—the *V* of horizontal lines going to the right when prolonged beyond *PP*.

V_S—the *V* of the boundary (edge) of a shadow.

V^{PR}—the *V* of the plans of the light rays.

V^{Ray}—the *V* of the light rays.

V_3—the *V* of the third (vertical) series in a three-point perspective.

V's—plural of *V*

V.L.M.—A vertical line of measure—*i.e.*, any vertical line lying in *PP*, and hence one on which dimensions may be measured at their true (scaled) length.

Vertical—In space, parallel to the force of gravity; on a drawing, perpendicular to the line joining the hands of a person holding the picture in front of him by its sides.

Vertical axis—In a perspective, the vertical line through *C* (hence perpendicular to *HH*).

Worm's-eye view—A perspective made from an *S* lower than the object, but with *C.V.R.* horizontal.

Study for courtyard of a residence by Bernard F. McMahon.

ILLUSTRATION 13-3

SELECTED BIBLIOGRAPHY

Ames, Adelbert: "Some Demonstrations Concerned with the Origin and Nature of our Sensations," Hanover, N.H., Hanover Institute, 1946.

Beal, George M.: "Perspective, A Practical Development of Basic Principles," (3d.ed.) Ann Arbor, Edwards Bros., Inc., 1947.

Blomfield, Reginald: "Architectural Drawing and Draftsmen," London, Cassell & Co., Ltd., 1912.

Calibron Notebook No. 3, "Perspective and Optical Illusions of Depth," Orange, New Jersey, Calibron Products Inc., May, 1936.

Deneux, Henri Louis: "La Métrophotographie appliquée à l'architecture," Paris, Catin, 1930.

d'Espouy, Hector: "Fragments Antiques," Paris, Schmid, 1905.

de Postels, Theodore: "Fundamentals of Perspective," New York, Reinhold Publishing Corporation, 1942.

Doust, L. A.: "A Manual on Simple Perspective," New York, McGraw-Hill Book Company, Inc., 1943.

Durand, Henri: "Traité de Perspective Linéaire," Paris, A. Vincent, 1912.

Farey & Edwards: "Architectural Drawing, Perspective and Rendering," London, Batsford, 1931.

Field, W. B.: "An Introduction to Architectural Drawing," New York, McGraw-Hill Book Company, Inc., 1943.

Freese, Ernest Irving: "Perspective Projection," New York, Pencil Points Press, Inc., 1930.

Gordon, John William: "Generalized Linear Perspective," London, Constable & Co., Ltd., 1922.

Guadet, Paul: "Cours de Perspective," Paris, A. Vincent, 1929.

Guptill, Arthur Leighton: "Sketching and Rendering in Pencil," New York, Pencil Points Press, 1922.

——— "Color in Sketching and Rendering," New York, Reinhold Publishing Corporation, 1935.

Ivins, William Mills: "On the Rationalization of Sight . . . ," New York, Metropolitan Museum of Art, 1938.

Kautzky, Theodore: "Pencil Broadsides," New York, Reinhold Publishing Corporation, 1940.

Kirby, John Joshua: "The Perspective of Architecture," London, The author, 1761.

Lawson, Philip J.: "Practical Perspective Drawing," New York, McGraw-Hill Book Company, Inc., 1943.

Longfellow, William P. P.: "Applied Perspective for Architects and Painters," Boston, Houghton Mifflin Company, 1901.

Lubschez, Ben Jehudah: "Perspective," 4th ed., New York, D. Van Nostrand Company, Inc., 1926.

Magonigle, H. Van Buren: "Architectural Rendering in Wash," New York, Charles Scribner's Sons, 1921.

McGoodwin, Henry: "Architectural Shades and Shadows," Boston, Bates & Guild Co., 1922.

Medworth, Frank Charles: "Perspective," London, Chapman & Hall, Ltd., 1936.

Monge, Gaspard: "Géometrie Déscriptive," Paris, An. VII, (modern edition) 1922.

Morehead, James C.: "A Handbook of Perspective Drawing," Pittsburgh, The author, 1941.

Norling, Ernest R.: "Perspective Made Easy," New York, The Macmillan Company, 1939.

Parker, Stanley B.: "The Vertical Vanishing Point in Linear Perspective," Cambridge, Harvard University Press, 1947.

Pillet, Jules Jean: "Traité de Perspective Linéaire, etc.," Paris, Blanchard, 1921.

Reile, Adolf: "The New Perspective for the Architect," translated and published by Alfred Metscher, Los Angeles, 1927.

Taylor, Brook: "Linear Perspective," London, printed for R. Knaplock at the Bishop's-Head, 1715 (many later editions).

Ware, William Robert: "Modern Perspective," rev. ed., New York, The Macmillan Company, 1914.

——— "Shades and Shadows," Scranton, International Textbook Company, 1912.

Willson, Frederick Newton: "Practical and Theoretical Graphics," Princeton, The Graphics Press, 1909.

——— "The Perspective of Reflections," New York, The Macmillan Company, 1900.

INDEX

References are to pages unless otherwise stated.
Items marked with an asterisk * are defined in Chapter 13.

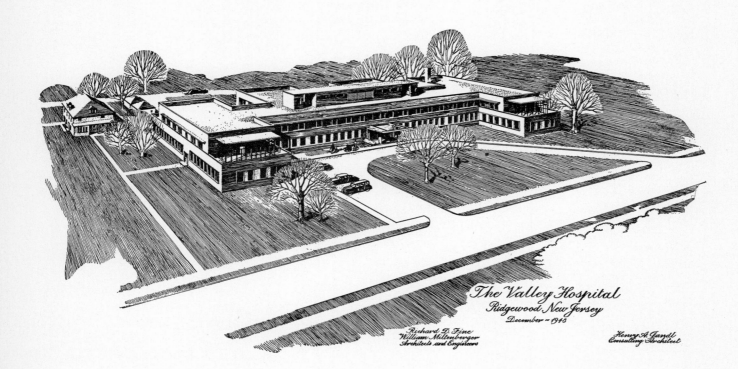

The Valley Hospital
Ridgewood, New Jersey
December – 1948

Richard D. Fine
William Miltenberger
Architects and Engineers

Henry A. Gandl
Consulting Architect